'*The Residential Pathway – APC Essentials* p........... .... guide for APC candidates. The key strengths are the detailed examples of potential case studies; the likely questions that they will generate; and the references to further resources, which are vitally important in the current dynamic residential property environment.'

Dr Jan Wilcox, BSc, MBA, Dip Proj Man, PGCE, PhD, FRICS, SFHEA, *Director of Employability School of Applied Management and Senior Lecturer Real Estate, Westminster Business School, University of Westminster. Examiner, The Property Institute.*

The Residential Pathway

The Residential Pathway – APC Essentials was written to facilitate and encourage candidates preparing for the RICS Assessment of Professional Competence (APC) to become Chartered Surveyors. This book will help candidates, their Counsellors and supervisors to understand:

- The requirements of the Residential pathway;
- The detail of the technical competencies;
- How to select suitable competencies;
- How to demonstrate the required knowledge and experience; and
- How to succeed in the final interview.

It will also be a useful reference for AssocRICS candidates and qualified professionals.

This concise book has clear headings to guide readers, with bullet-point checklists and signposting to key themes and important sources for further reading. It alerts readers to the need to be aware of changes and developments in the residential sector, and to the wider economic, social, and political factors that influence it. This book includes lists of relevant RICS (and other) professional publications, the laws and regulations that frame professional surveying practice, and example written submissions for the technical competencies at each level. It will help to motivate and reassure candidates, giving them confidence to recognise the value and relevance of their knowledge and practical experience, and to understand how to best apply this to demonstrate their professional competence.

Jane Forsyth, BA (Hons), FRICS, FTPI, AFHEA, is a Chartered Surveyor, a fellow of The Property Institute, and a former property solicitor. She has 35 years' experience in the real estate sector, including as a residential and commercial landlord, director of her residential management business, and director of a national property association. Jane has academic experience, including as Associate Tutor at the University College of Estate Management (UCEM), and she is now a Senior Lecturer in Property Law on the BSc (Hons) and MSc Real Estate degrees at Oxford Brookes University. Her RICS assessment experience includes sitting on final APC interview panels, and she has successfully mentored many Residential pathway candidates at Property Elite, in addition to providing training for candidates and qualified professionals. Jane is co-author of *Real Estate: The Basics* (Routledge 2022).

APC Essentials

APC Essentials is a series of books providing guidance to RICS APC and AssocRICS candidates on various mandatory and technical competencies, relevant to each individual pathway.

Whilst this series is structured to cover the full scope of APC competencies, AssocRICS candidates will still find the content and knowledge helpful for the requirements of their assessment.

Mandatory Competencies
APC Essentials
Jennifer Lemen

The Residential Pathway
APC Essentials
Jane Forsyth

The Residential Pathway

APC Essentials

Jane Forsyth

Routledge
Taylor & Francis Group

LONDON AND NEW YORK

Designed cover image: Jane Forsyth

First published 2025
by Routledge
4 Park Square, Milton Park, Abingdon, Oxon OX14 4RN

and by Routledge
605 Third Avenue, New York, NY 10158

Routledge is an imprint of the Taylor & Francis Group, an informa business

British Library Cataloguing-in-Publication Data
A catalogue record for this book is available from the British Library

ISBN: 978-1-032-70508-8 (hbk)
ISBN: 978-1-032-67968-6 (pbk)
ISBN: 978-1-032-70509-5 (ebk)

DOI: 10.1201/9781032705095

Typeset in Times New Roman
by codeMantra

Parts of chapters 1, 15 and 16 are adapted from *Mandatory
Competencies – APC Essentials*, 1st edition by Jen Lemen, Copyright
(©2024), Routledge. Reproduced by permission of Taylor & Francis Group.

This book is dedicated to my dad, Thomas
Paulin Forsyth, 1929 to 2023.

Contents

Acknowledgements

Thanks to Ed Needle for commissioning this book; my family and especially my husband David Schermer for his support, suggestions, and help proofreading the drafts; Jen Lemen for the idea and for kick-starting the *APC Essentials* series; to Jen again, and to Brian Robinson, for their constructive comments on the drafts. I would also like to thank all those people who have helped me along the way. It is difficult to progress without help and many colleagues have been generous with their support: people like Jen Lemen (again!) who has mentored me through some major career stages, Ian Perry who spent hours teaching me new skills, Jan Wilcox who first suggested that I try teaching and invited me to co-author my first book, Rebecca Gee for the teaching opportunities, and Nick Cox for his interest and support for more than 30 years.

Preface

I wanted to write this book because I enjoy sharing my experience. It was written to facilitate and encourage others preparing for the APC, and its foundations are in my interesting and fulfilling role mentoring and supporting candidates. Many candidates' experience will mirror my own, working towards the APC with limited support, perhaps because their firm is not resourced to provide this, or because they are working alone or remotely, with restricted opportunities to learn from colleagues. Even if good support is available, clear, precise, and informative guidance is always helpful for candidates, qualified professionals, Counsellors and supervisors. This book complements the first in the series, *APC Essentials – Mandatory Competencies,* and I wish that I'd had *APC Essentials* when I was working towards becoming chartered.

My career in real estate and surveying has given me opportunities that I could not have envisaged as a new, non-cognate graduate. I have been a director of my own business, and of a national property association, and I have spent time teaching in Saudi Arabia. Lifelong learning, gaining new experience and qualifications, and becoming chartered are all challenges that I recommend, as the process will help you to develop personally and professionally.

I have aimed to keep this book concise, with bullet-point checklists and signposting to key themes and important sources for further reading. I hope that it helps to motivate you and to give you the confidence to recognise the value and relevance of your knowledge and practical experience, to tackle your written submissions, and to prepare for interview. Good luck!

Jane Forsyth Oxford 2024

1 Introduction

Introduction

APC Essentials is a series of books providing guidance to RICS APC and AssocRICS candidates on various mandatory and technical competencies, relevant to each individual pathway.

Whilst this series is structured to cover the full scope of APC competencies, AssocRICS candidates will still find the content and knowledge helpful for the requirements of their assessment.

The series is split into several individual books, starting with an edition on the mandatory competencies, which will be of interest to all candidates.

This book covers the Residential pathway and related technical competencies.

Overview of the APC Assessment

All APC candidates, irrespective of their chosen route, must undergo assessment via a written submission and an online interview.

The online interview is based on the candidate's written submission and lasts for one hour. The final decision as to whether a candidate becomes MRICS is solely based on performance in this interview.

All candidates, including those undertaking the senior professional, specialist, and academic assessments, must choose from one of the 22 sector pathways that most closely reflect their experience, role, and knowledge. These are:

1 Building Control;
2 Building Surveying;
3 Commercial Real Estate;

DOI: 10.1201/9781032705095-1

4 Corporate Real Estate;
5 Environmental Surveying;
6 Facilities Management;
7 Geomatics;
8 Infrastructure;
9 Land and Resources;
10 Management Consultancy;
11 Minerals and Waste Management;
12 Personal Property/Arts and Antiques;
13 Planning and Development;
14 Project Management;
15 Property Finance and Investment;
16 Quantity Surveying and Construction;
17 Research;
18 Residential;
19 Rural;
20 Taxation Allowances;
21 Valuation;
22 Valuation of Businesses and Intangible Assets.

At the time of writing over 2023 and 2024, the competencies and pathways were under review by the RICS, and a new Residential pathway guide was published in February 2024. This book focusses on the requirements of the 2024 guide. It is possible that some competencies will be combined on a date in the future, and new specialisms may be introduced. Although the competencies pathway is under review, the fundamental skills, knowledge, and expertise required of a residential surveyor remain, and this book supports candidates seeking to demonstrate those skills in order to become MRICS professionals.

What Are the APC Competencies?

Competencies are the individual mandatory ('soft') and technical ('hard') areas where you must demonstrate your skills, knowledge, and experience. The competency requirements for each separate pathway are set out in the relevant pathway guides, for example, Residential, which can be downloaded from the RICS website.

The requirements of each specific competency are divided into three levels. The level of competence (either level 1, 2, or 3) required by a candidate will depend on their chosen pathway and competencies.

For example, all candidates must satisfy the mandatory competency, Ethics, Rules of Conduct, and Professionalism to level 3. All Residential candidates must satisfy the core technical competencies Inspection, Measurement, and Valuation, to level 2 or 3. The pathway guide sets out the individual requirements of each level and each competency, e.g., required knowledge for level 1 and required activities or advice at levels 2 and 3, respectively.

This series of books is based on the competency descriptors in each relevant pathway guide. You can use the books to ensure you choose competencies reflecting your knowledge and experience. You can also use the books as a guide to level 1 knowledge and level 2 and 3 examples to write up in your summary of experience and ensure that your case study includes sufficient competency-based knowledge, experience, and advice.

You should continually refer to the competency descriptors and these books to ensure that what you write in your submission is accurate, relevant, and sufficiently detailed. This is because your submission will guide potential areas of questioning in your final assessment interview. The RICS pathways, competencies, and assessment methods were under review at the time of writing. One suggestion in the Interim Report from the Entry and Assessment Steering Group[1] is that some competencies could be combined, where they overlap. There are certainly similarities and overlapping between some competencies, which can make it difficult for candidates to decide upon their technical competencies and select suitable examples.

The 2024 Final Report recommended that all pathways should be retained, except for Infrastructure, Taxation Allowances, and Valuation of Businesses and Intangible Assets. The Residential pathway therefore looks set to continue, with the proposed creation of a new Chartered Residential Surveyor designation. A further recommendation is that all competencies should be reviewed to reflect current practice, with a greater emphasis on sustainability.[2] It is therefore very important that you keep up to date whilst you develop your fundamental technical knowledge and skills that underpin your role as a residential surveyor.

What Are the Three Competency Levels?

The three competency levels are defined as follows:

- Level 1 – Knowledge and understanding. This requires candidates to explain their knowledge and learning relevant to the description included in the competency guide. This could be through academic learning, e.g., degree level courses, CPD, or on-the-job training. However, candidates should avoid too much repetition as their CPD record will be set out separately. Generally, level 1 will be met by including a brief list of knowledge of relevant topics, given the limitations of the overall word count. These books will provide candidates with guidance on the scope, depth, and breadth of each competency.

- Level 2 – Application of knowledge and understanding. Demonstrating level 2 requires a candidate to apply their level 1 knowledge and understanding in practice, i.e., through practical work experience. This relates to 'doing', rather than just knowing the theory and fundamentals, or underpinning theory with practice. Candidates should refer to specific projects, instructions, or examples to clearly demonstrate their practical activities and experience, including their role and relevance to the competency description. These books will provide candidates with guidance on relevant experience to include within each competency.
- Level 3 – Reasoned advice and depth of knowledge, expanding on level 2 work experience or tasks to provide reasoned advice to clients. This involves considering the options available and offering recommendations and advice on solutions. These books will guide candidates on relevant advice to include within each competency.

Assessors are trained to begin questioning at the highest level declared, with supporting level 1 knowledge-based questions potentially being asked to explore the justification for the advice or actions of the candidate. Candidates should ensure they are familiar with any examples included in levels 2 and 3, as these should form the basis of the majority of their answers.

You should not be asked questions on competencies you have not selected or at levels beyond those stated; i.e., you will not be expected to give reasoned advice (level 3) if you have declared a competency only to level 2 (acting or doing).

All pathways have the same mandatory competencies. However, each pathway will have a different set of technical competencies, split into core (primary skills) and optional (additional skills) technical competencies.

What Are the Mandatory Competencies?

Common to all pathways, the 11 mandatory competencies comprise business skills. This means that they need to be demonstrated by all candidates, irrespective of role, sector, or position. They aim to show that you can work with others, manage your workload, and can act ethically and professionally.

The mandatory competencies include:

- Ethics, Rules of Conduct, and Professionalism (level 3);
- Client Care (level 2);
- Communication and Negotiation (level 2);
- Health and Safety (level 2);
- Accounting Principles and Procedures (level 1);
- Business Planning (level 1);
- Conflict Avoidance, Management, and Dispute Resolution Procedures (level 1);
- Data Management (level 1);
- Diversity, Inclusion, and Teamworking (level 1);
- Inclusive Environments (level 1);
- Sustainability (level 1).

You can also pursue some of the mandatory competencies to higher levels as part of your core or optional technical competency choices. On the Residential pathway, Conflict Avoidance, Management and Dispute Resolution Procedures; Data Management; and Sustainability are available to select as technical competencies.

What Are the Technical Competencies?

The technical competencies relate to the candidate's specific area of practice, rather than being more general business skills. They are split into core and optional competencies, depending on the specific requirements of each pathway. You should pay particular attention to the requirements of the core competencies as these must be demonstrated to the required level. This may require you to seek additional work experience or secondment to fill gaps in experience; e.g., Residential pathway candidates in property management roles may need to identify additional Valuation and Measurement experience to fulfil these as core technical competencies to the required levels.

Subsequent books will cover the technical competency requirements of a further range of pathways, focussing on the core technical competencies, but with additional supporting guidance on a variety of optional technical competencies.

The Residential pathway competencies can be broadly divided into categories:

- Investment;
- Landlord and tenant;
- Lettings;
- Planning and development;
- Residential management;
- Purchase and sale of residential property;
- Valuation;
- Survey.[3]

This book provides guidance on the technical competencies most commonly selected in the author's experience mentoring and assessing on the Residential pathway. If you are selecting competencies not covered individually, you can refer to this book to:

- Identify the types of RICS and other publications that you need to be familiar with;
- Identify relevant laws;
- Recognise suitable examples, how to summarise them, and the types of questions that you can expect to encounter in your interview.

Selecting Your Competencies

Residential candidates must select a total of eight technical competencies. Competency selection is complicated, and you must always refer to the Residential pathway guide and the pathway requirements to ensure that you comply fully. Each chapter of this book provides guidance to help you to select your technical competencies and the levels. Competencies can overlap and many can usefully complement each other. You may find it helpful to refer to the chapters and reading lists for competencies that you have rejected. This is because so much of a surveyor's work is interconnected with other roles, and the content and reading in these chapters may still be relevant to your declared competencies, or it may give you ideas for reading around your selection.

Structure of This Book

Each chapter of this book will focus on a separate technical competency on the Residential pathway and should be read in conjunction with the Residential pathway guide.

The structure of each chapter will be as follows:

- Guidance on selecting the competency;
- An outline of key competency skills and requirements;
- Guidance on what candidates need to know at level 1, including legislation, RICS guidance, and hot topics;
- Examples of how candidates can achieve level 2 (doing);
- Examples of how candidates can achieve level 3 (advising);
- Sample APC interview questions on each level;
- Suggested further reading and resources.

As listed above, each chapter includes suggested reading and resources. Some of this is at an introductory level, and some will already be archived, as the RICS updates its publications. Archived publications are indicated in the text. However, they can still provide useful overviews and will help you to revise and address gaps in your knowledge. There are many more resources than those listed, and it is recommended that you read around your area of practice, considering different perspectives to develop depth of understanding and considered opinions on the competency and on relevant 'hot topics'.

The RICS online information service 'isurv' is an extremely useful source of up-to-date information. Some of this information is publicly available, but much of it requires a subscription. Isurv content that requires a subscription has not been included in the lists of further reading and resources. If you have access to isurv, it is well worth spending time exploring it. If you or your firm do not have an isurv subscription, there are plenty of other free sources of information (including the RICS professional publications, Modus and Journals, and some of the accessible information contained in isurv).

What Does This Book Not Do?

This book is to help you to:

- Select your competencies and levels;
- Identify suitable examples to demonstrate your knowledge and practical experience;
- Prepare your written submissions;
- Prepare for interview.

It will not teach you how to do your job; how to, for example, value, or how to measure. Rather, it is intended to support and guide you towards your APC, and to signpost you to key documents and further reading. Suggestions for further reading and resources are not exhaustive and will be subject to review and updates. It is very important to ensure that you are familiar with all RICS publications and laws relating to your area of practice and that you keep up to date with changes and 'hot topics'.

Candidates sometimes ask for the APC syllabus. The answer to this question is that there isn't one as such. This can seem daunting. However, the APC is not an exam, it is an assessment of your professional competence. In other words, are you a safe pair of hands, capable of doing your job in a way that will promote trust in the profession? To do this, you need knowledge, technical skills, and practical experience, but you do not need to know everything. This book provides example submissions and questions at each level, but it does not provide the answers, rather you should think about how you would respond to the questions. Answers need to be concise and precise, in your own words, in the first person "I", and reflecting your own experience of what you actually did/advised etc. Further guidance is contained in Chapter 16 Interview Advice.

Conclusion

When you prepare for your final assessment interview, this series of books will provide an essential source of knowledge to supplement revision, mock interviews, and other preparation. Remember that this book is accurate as of the date of writing. You will need to carry out your own research to fact-check any updates or new hot topics following this date. You should also keep up to date with future changes to the pathway and the competencies. There are a range of excellent resources online, but ensure you use those that are accurate, reliable, and written by a credible source.

Continue reading Chapter 2 onwards to explore the RICS APC Residential pathway technical competencies.

This chapter is based on Lemen J (2024) *Mandatory Competencies: APC Essentials Chapter 1* Abingdon: Routledge.

Reference List

1 RICS (2023) *Review of entry and assessment into the profession* [Online] Available at: https://www.rics.org/profession-standards/standards-of-qualification/review-of-entry-and-assessment-into-the-profession (Accessed 5 July 2023).

2 RICS (2024) *Final report review of entry and assessment for RICS membership – summary of recommendations* [Online] Available at: https://www.rics.org/content/dam/ricsglobal/documents/standards/Executive-summary-and-recommendations-EN.pdf (Accessed 12 August 2024).
3 RICS (2024) *Residential pathway guide* [Online] Available at: https://www.rics.org/join-rics/sector-pathways (Accessed 26 August 2024).

2   Inspection

Introduction

The ability to carry out an inspection suitable for its purpose is a fundamental skill required by all surveyors in practice. This is reflected in the status of Inspection as a core technical competency, required to at least level 2 for Residential candidates. This means that candidates need to write up their summary of experience at both levels 1 and 2, with the option to select the competency to level 3.

The Residential pathway guide sets out the relevant knowledge (level 1), practical application (level 2), and reasoned advice (level 3) for this competency. However, candidates do not need to have encountered everything listed, as this will depend on their experience and role.

This competency should be read in tandem with several other relevant competencies, depending on your role and the purpose of the inspection, e.g., Health and Safety, Leasing and Letting, Landlord and Tenant, Building Pathology, Valuation, Loan Security Valuation, Market Appraisal, and Purchase and Sale.

This chapter will explain what you should know in relation to Inspection, covering the main requirements of level 1, with guidance on levels 2 and 3.

Should You Select This Competency?

As a core technical competency, you must select Inspection as one of your technical competencies. However, you can choose whether to declare it to level 2 or level 3.

Inspection is an inherent part of a residential surveyor's role, regardless of the surveyor's specialist areas of expertise. This means that all candidates must have experience of inspecting properties for

DOI: 10.1201/9781032705095-2

varying purposes and be familiar with inspection methods. Check the pathway guide and think about inspections that you have carried out. In relation to each, think about why you inspected the property, how you carried out your inspection, and the issues you observed during your inspection. This will help you to decide whether to choose level 2 or level 3.

The pathway guide outlines the requirements of each level and the sections later in this chapter will help to identify suitable examples for each level. Surveyors carry out inspections for a very wide range of purposes, depending on their roles. A surveyor doing a level 2 survey will have a different focus to a property manager carrying out a compliance inspection, for example. However, there will be common threads, such as the need for desktop research, risk assessment, a thorough methodical approach, and good record keeping.

For level 2, you must provide examples of inspections carried out, with brief explanations of your observations, such as defects identified or compliance breaches. Level 3 is more in depth, with reasoned advice. For example, did the inspection identify a serious defect that required detailed advice on the cause(s), and on the options for remedying the defect, or recommendations for further or specialist investigations? If you can provide specific examples of reasoned advice to your employer or to a client, consider selecting the competency to level 3.

Inspection Skills

Candidates must demonstrate good observational skills combined with technical knowledge and understanding of the principles of property inspection. Assessors will need to be confident that all candidates have a good knowledge of building construction, location analysis, and defects.[1]

Surveyors cannot usually advise on a property until they have inspected it, although on occasion desktop research may suffice, for example, a desktop valuation. Inspections of residential property are undertaken for many purposes, but examples include valuation, level 1, 2, or 3 surveys, acquisitions, sales, letting, property management, asset management, stock condition surveys, progress checks on works, and preparation of planned preventative maintenance schedules.

Individual surveyors have different approaches to inspecting properties; the key point is to ensure that all required areas are inspected where accessible, and that the inspection is sufficiently thorough for its purpose. Client requirements need to be checked carefully and reflected in the terms of engagement. Any limitations must be notified to the client. Think about how you have approached an inspection; you can explain this in your summary of experience, and you may be questioned on your methods during your interview. You could, for example, be asked about the equipment you take with you on an inspection. This does not just cover technical surveying equipment and personal protective equipment (PPE). It could include the clothes you wear, depending on the time of year and weather conditions, and other items such as a water bottle or a flask with a hot drink, even a shovel if snow is forecast. Think about how you prepare for an inspection, what desktop research do you carry out? On arrival, do you assess the immediate locality first, before inspecting the exterior then the interior? Is your approach to inspect from the top downwards, or from the lowest floor upwards? How do you ensure that you have not omitted any part of the property? How do you deal with areas at height, such as lofts and inaccessible roofs? Do you use drones for surveying purposes? If so, what licensing laws apply and how do you ensure compliance with these laws? This is the type of day-to-day practice that assessors will want to know about, to establish whether you carry out your inspections competently and professionally.

The degree of inspection will depend on the purpose, and it is important to understand and comply with RICS Professional Standards and Practice Information. For instance, the Home Survey Standard requires differing degrees of inspection depending on the level and purpose of the survey. Online guidance is available from the RICS regarding the scope of inspections, together with equipment and health and safety checklists.[2]

There will be times when inspections are limited, perhaps because of access constraints. A garden may be too overgrown to enable you to view an elevation. You may therefore need to use your initiative: can the elevation be viewed from neighbouring properties, with permission, for example?

Awareness of health and safety is vital to this competency and suitable desktop preparation must be undertaken pre-inspection, to include a risk assessment. Risks might include, during the COVID pandemic, risk of infection and legal constraints on inspection and social distancing. Other risks must be assessed; for example, is the property vacant or occupied, are you assessing alone – if so, what is your company's lone worker policy? Consider what is known about the property, are there hazards known to be present, such as an aggressive pet, vermin infestation, or rotten floorboards? Assess whether any PPE is needed. Simple steps such as parking your car in a safe and accessible position are important, as is checking the safe condition of equipment such as ladders. Risk assessment must continue throughout the inspection – this is known as a dynamic risk assessment. When writing up your summary of experience, think about unexpected risks that you have encountered, not flagged up by the desktop risk assessment. The ability to adapt to issues onsite is important. It may have been necessary to cancel or abandon an inspection until a serious hazard was addressed. You will find more information on health and safety on the Health and Safety Executive (HSE) website, in the RICS Requirements and Competencies Guide (2018, updated in 2022) and in *APC Essentials – the Mandatory Competencies*, details of which are included at the end of this chapter.

As mentioned, good observational skills are key to this competency. Think about what you have seen when inspecting. Was anything missing; e.g., were fire action notices missing from communal areas? Inspection is not just visual, so mention use of your other senses in your summary of experience or your case study. Smell and touch can be important too, for example, when identifying damp. Hearing can identify noise pollution, e.g., from occupiers, traffic, trains running on nearby lines, and aircraft overhead.

The ability to identify issues such as building defects and breaches of leasehold covenants is essential for this competency. Building defects need to be investigated as part of the inspection (if this is within the remit of the inspection), to follow the trail of suspicion to identify the cause. For example, in relation to a specific example, did inspection of a building reveal damp and the likely cause? Writing about how you investigated a defect during an inspection demonstrates your observational skills and understanding of the potential cause and remedies. In other words, the assessors want to know whether you understand what to look for, where to look for it, and the significance and implications of what you have seen.

Good, clear note-taking skills are essential. A surveyor must be able to record the inspection and the findings in a clearly worded report to the employer or client. Photographs, annotated site plans, and/or hand-drawn sketch plans may be required, as may specialist software such as inventory apps. These records form the basis of the report to the client, and you may also need to refer to photos, notes, and plans if there are any queries or complaints following issue of the report. Pro-forma documents (i.e., checklists and standard forms) can be helpful and reports should be prepared promptly while the inspection is fresh in your mind.

When drafting your summary of experience, demonstrate knowledge of relevant legal authority. For example, Hart v Large is an important case relevant to this competency:

The key take-aways from this case are relevant to the requirements set out in the new RICS Home Survey Standard, coming into effect on 1st March 2021, namely:

* *Being clear on the report about the scope of inspection including limitations, caveats, and actions available to the client;*
* *Recommending justifiable further investigation;*
* *Taking all reasonable steps to ensure clients understand the differences between the levels of service, including the extent and limitations of each option.*[3]

Ryb v Conway Chartered Surveyors (unreported) emphasises that a surveyor's duty of care may extend to the grounds of the surveyed property as well as to the property itself. A failure to identify Japanese knotweed during a survey was negligent. Surveyors need to ensure that they are trained to identify Japanese knotweed and other issues and defects relevant to their role, and that they have suitable inspection notes and photographs to evidence the inspection and support the findings.[4] If an issue or defect identified during an inspection is outside your area of expertise, you may need to advise on further specialist investigations.

As with each competency, the examples in the RICS pathway guide are not prescriptive, so it is not necessary to have experience of each bullet-point listed; rather, these provide guidance on the nature of the professional knowledge and experience expected of a surveyor at the specified level. Look at the pathway guide and think about examples of when you have recorded the features of a building during a site inspection, for example, the age or era of the property, the type of construction including local types such as mundic, features such as solar panels and septic tanks, and hazardous or deleterious materials such as asbestos-containing materials and aluminium composite material cladding. Reinforced autoclaved aerated concrete (RAAC) has also recently been in the news at the time of writing. These materials are likely to continue to be 'hot topics' for some time in view of the extent of their use and the significant problems they present to building owners, occupiers, managers, surveyors, and other property professionals.

It is important to be specific in your summary of experience. Avoid general statements that you 'understand relevant RICS Professional Standards and Practice Information and your firm's policies'. Instead, state, for example, that you are familiar with Surveying Safely, 2nd edition, 2018, and the 'safe person' concept[5] and that you understand and comply with your firm's lone worker policy.

Consider why you carry out inspections and refer to relevant Professional Standards and Practice Information. For example, if you inspect for valuation purposes, refer to VPS 2 of the 2022 Global Red Book (VPS 4 of the revised Red Book effective 2025) in your summary of experience. Recognise that, for valuations, inspections must be to the extent necessary to produce a professionally adequate valuation, suitable for its purpose.[6] When referring to RICS publications, provide the full title, including the edition. Ensure that you understand the status of the document, i.e., whether it is mandatory or best practice, or supplementary guidance. At the time of writing in 2023, the RICS had recently introduced two new document types: Professional Standards and Practice Information. These are being rolled out on all newly published RICS guidance and in some cases existing guidance is being reissued using the new definitions.[7] You should also be aware of whether a document applies globally or nationally. This will help you to demonstrate precise knowledge. A useful tip is to search for 'inspection' in each publication to ensure that you understand and apply the principles relevant to your role.

Remember that if you state in your summary of experience that you understand a publication or law, make sure that you can answer questions on it!

When preparing this competency, think about the types of issues that you have identified during an inspection – after all, the purpose of an inspection will usually be to inform your report and advice. These include:

- Access, e.g., an easement needed to access the property, or evidence that a neighbour has access over part of the inspected property;
- Breaches of freehold or leasehold covenant;
- Breaches of planning permission or Building Regulations;
- Cladding and fire safety issues;

- Construction types – traditional, non-traditional, designs, and materials typical in your area;
- Contaminated land;
- Deleterious and hazardous materials, such as asbestos;
- Desktop research and due diligence that could identify relevant issues, such as flooding, Conservation Areas and listed building status;
- Environmental issues;
- Radon gas;
- Reinforced autoclaved aerated concrete;
- The age of the houses or apartments that you are inspecting, and how you can date them. This could include, for example, information obtained from the Land Registry title certificate, a date provided on an original electricity meter, or local knowledge.

Other chapters in this book may provide further helpful information and you should refer to Chapter 11 (Building Pathology), Chapter 12 (Housing Maintenance, Repairs and Improvements), Chapter 13 (Legal/Regulatory Compliance), and Chapter 14 (Mandatory Competencies as Technical Competencies [& Other Technical Competencies]).

RICS Professional Standards and Practice Information

This list of RICS Professional Standards and Practice Information relevant to the Inspection competency is not exhaustive, and it will be subject to change as the RICS updates its publications and processes. However, it should be a helpful indication of the relevant documentation. It is important to check for further standards and information relevant to your role, and for updates to those listed below. Examples are:

- Asbestos UK, 4th edition, 2021;
- Health and safety for residential property managers, 1st edition, 2016;
- Home survey standard, 1st edition, 2019;
- Japanese knotweed and residential property, 1st edition, 2022;
- RICS Insight paper, drones: Applications and compliance for surveyors, May 2019;
- Service charge residential management code, 3rd edition, 2016;

- Surveying safely, 2nd edition, 2018;
- UK Residential real estate agency, 6th edition, 2017;
- Valuation of buy-to-let and HMO properties, 2nd edition, 2022;
- VPS 2 of RICS Valuation – Global Standards 2022 (the Red Book), VPS 4 of the updated (2024, effective 31st January 2025) Global Red Book, and UK VPGA 11.3 of the 2023 edition of the UK National Supplement.

How Can You Demonstrate Level 3?

Your assessors will start at the highest level you have declared, which will be either level 2 or level 3. At level 3 the RICS expects you to present specific examples of reasoned advice that you have provided to a client or your employer as a result of an inspection, perhaps considering and explaining the options available, to demonstrate a deeper level of understanding than is needed at level 2.

Check the pathway guide carefully and think about whether you can provide your own examples to reflect the examples given in the guide. The guide is not exhaustive, and, as mentioned, you do not have to provide an example of each bullet-point, but the guide does provide a useful indication of the type of knowledge and experience that you need to demonstrate.

The 2024 Residential pathway guide suggests relevant scenarios that you might encounter in your everyday working practice at level 3:

- Preparing reports for clients, containing detailed information particularly regarding valuation reports and the marketing of residential property;
- Providing detailed reasoned advice to clients;
- Making clients aware (where appropriate) of their statutory responsibilities.[8]

Example level 3 summaries of experience could be:

*At (**example**) I inspected a one-bedroom house for tenancy compliance purposes. My desktop research and risk assessment noted that the tenant was vulnerable and disabled, with limited mobility and impaired vision. I ensured that the tenant was aware of the inspection, by emailing my written notice to his carer as requested on the tenant record system. I followed this up with a phone call to remind the tenant. During the inspection I noticed water stains down the hall* *wall, beneath the bathroom. I checked the walk-in shower and noted that the silicone sealant was damaged. The tenant had not noticed the water stains due to his impaired vision. I recorded the damage in my report and asked the tenant's carer to promptly report property damage in future. I advised that the inspection frequency be increased from annual to bi-annual, to ensure more timely identification of repairs.*

Questions on this example could include:

- Talk me through your desktop research.
- Talk me through your risk assessment.
- What were the findings of your risk assessment?
- How much notice did you give to the tenant?
- How did you follow the trail to identify the source of the water staining?
- How did you resolve the issue?
- Talk me through your advice to increase the frequency of inspections.
- Why did you recommend bi-annual inspections?
- How did you address this with the tenant?
- Has/how has the increased frequency been effective in managing repairs?

*At (**example**) I carried out a level 2 survey of a modern apartment in a block of ten. I carried out my desktop research and risk assessment and arranged access with the agent. I noted that the property had a timber frame, but that the build quality and the quality of repairs were poor. In particular, I noted evidence of water ingress to the timber frame, and an inadequate external repair using silicone sealant. I took detailed notes and reported to the client. I recommended that legal advisers raise enquiries with the management company regarding plans and funds for repairs, before proceeding. The client decided not to proceed with the purchase due to the condition of the building, based on my advice.*

Questions on this example could include:

- Talk me through your desktop research.
- Talk me through your risk assessment.
- Talk me through your inspection.
- What building components did you inspect/not inspect?
- How did you comply with Surveying safely, 2nd edition, 2018?

- What equipment did you take with you on your survey?
- Why did you take detailed notes?
- What building defects did you note?
- Why did you conclude that the build quality and the quality of repairs were poor?
- Talk me through your advice to the client as a result of your inspection.
- Why did you recommend that legal advisers raise enquiries with the management company regarding plans and funds for repairs, before proceeding?

*At (**example**) I inspected a Victorian terraced house following a report by tenants of water ingress to the basement. On inspection, I discovered a saturated basement carpet. There was no evidence of a leak inside the house. I also observed that the adjoining large commercial garage that had formed the end of the terrace had been demolished. I considered it likely that the water ingress had occurred during heavy rain, due to the exposure of the neighbouring site and loss of the rainwater goods and mains drainage. During my inspection I observed builders' vans onsite and established that the commercial garage was to be replaced by three terraced houses. I reported the outcome of my inspection to my client and advised that the affected wall was a party wall and that the Party Wall etc. Act 1996 applied. My client confirmed that they had not been notified of the adjoining owners' intentions. I advised that a party wall specialist surveyor be appointed to advise further and to liaise regarding proposed works.*
Questions on this example could include:

- Talk me through your inspection.
- How did you prepare for your inspection?
- How did you ascertain that there was no leak within the house?
- Were the basement walls damp?
- Was there a basement to the demolished site?
- How did you know that there had been a large commercial garage?
- Were there infilled vehicle pits adjacent to the house?
- Why did you consider the cause to be demolition of the adjoining building?
- How did you establish that the commercial garage was to be replaced by further terraced houses?
- How did you report the outcome of your inspection?

- When did you advise your clients about the party wall actions?
- Did you advise your client to seek legal advice?
- Why did you consider it to be a party wall?
- Tell me about the Party Wall etc. Act 1996.
- Talk me through your advice regarding the party wall.
- What is a party wall?
- Why did you recommend that a party wall specialist be appointed?

How Can You Demonstrate Level 2?

Level 2 Inspection is about practical experience of inspecting a range of properties for various purposes. You will be expected to have carried out inspections and applied the information gained to prepare reports, schedules, and/or registers of equipment, presenting appropriate information gained from the inspection.[9] Examples of activities and knowledge comprised within this level are:

- Accurate recording of building and site characteristics;
- Preparing (or assisting in the preparation of) reports for clients;
- Understanding potential defects in buildings (both structural and environmental) and related implications;
- Assessing quality of location, design, and specification.[10]

Typical level 2 questions will start with, 'How have you...', 'Tell me about an example when you...', or 'How did you ...'. Remember, all the assessors' questions should be based upon the examples that you provide in your write-up for this competency in your summary of experience – rather than being hypothetical or general. However, assessors may also ask for more examples of inspections that you have carried out, especially if they want additional evidence of your practical experience.

Example level 2 summaries of experience could be:

*At (**example**) I inspected a period house following its abandonment by the tenant of 14 years. My desktop research established that the landlord had not inspected the house or undertaken maintenance during the tenancy. I inspected with a colleague as I did not know the condition of the house. The tenant had left personal belongings in the house so I could not inspect fully due to obstructions. The house was also in a dangerous condition, with broken banisters on the landing. I observed vermin droppings throughout and two dead rats in the* *kitchen. I terminated the inspection, and reported to my supervisor that I could not complete the inspection due to the unsafe condition of the property.*

Questions on this example could include:

- Tell me about your desktop research.
- For whom were you inspecting the property?
- How did you establish that the landlord had not inspected the house or undertaken maintenance during the tenancy?
- How did you know that the tenant had abandoned the house?
- What concerns led to your decision not to inspect alone?
- How did you ensure your own personal safety and that of your colleague?
- What was the purpose of your inspection?
- What site notes did you make during your inspection?
- Why did you terminate your inspection?
- At what stage did you terminate your inspection?
- What health risks are associated with rats?

*At (**example**) I inspected a property following the tenant's report that her young son had fallen down the stairs and broken his arm. The tenant alleged that the cause was the poor condition of the carpet. Before inspecting, I checked the most recent annual inspection report, with photographs, which showed the carpet in good condition. I inspected the stair and landing carpet and noted that it was still in good condition, with no evidence of slip or trip hazards. I made detailed notes, with photographs, and reported my findings to my supervisor to forward to my employer's liability insurers.*

Questions on this example could include:

- What allegations did the tenant make about the condition of the carpet?
- Talk me through the annual inspection report.
- What was your employer's role (landlord or agent)?
- Why were your employer's liability insurers notified of the allegation?
- Talk me through your inspection.
- Describe the condition of the carpet.
- What notes and photographs did you take?
- Why did you take detailed notes and photographs?

How Can You Demonstrate Level 1?

Although the assessors will focus on your highest level, you may be asked some level 1 questions, focussing on the knowledge behind your practical level 2 (and potentially level 3) examples. Level 1 requires you to demonstrate your knowledge and understanding of the requirements for inspection, together with the required information and factors affecting the approach to an inspection.[11] This includes thorough technical knowledge, which will depend on your area of practice. In addition to RICS publications, it is important to understand relevant laws. Examples include the Defective Premises Act 1972, the Occupiers Liability Acts 1957 and 1984, and the Landlord and Tenant Act 1985 (depending on your area of work). Be aware of other sources of information, for example, government publications and resources such as the '.gov' and HSE websites.

As mentioned, awareness of 'hot topics' is also required so you must keep up to date with news and developments relevant to the Inspection competency. Assessors may ask questions about current issues during your interview.

One way of enhancing your level 1 knowledge and understanding is to explain how you gained your knowledge. This can be through continuing professional development (CPD; formal or informal), through your studies during a degree, and through work experience such as shadowing a colleague. Think about your CPD; does any of your CPD relate in the Inspection competency? Perhaps, for example, you have spent time reading and making notes on VPS 2 (VPS 4 of the updated 2024 Red Book), which could be logged as informal CPD. Candidates' CPD logs are available to assessors and they can question candidates on this, so logging relevant CPD can support your submission.

A level 1 summary of experience could include, for example:

I carry out inspections for a variety of purposes, including building surveys, planned preventative maintenance schedules, and valuations. I understand the importance of desktop research and risk assessment, and I am familiar with Surveying safely, 2nd edition, 2018. I comply with my firm's lone worker policy. I check the scope of an inspection in advance, and I take necessary access equipment and a tablet with camera, calibrated measuring tools, and a charged mobile phone. I understand the importance of a methodical approach to ensure that all necessary areas and components are inspected, in accordance with the scope and purpose of the survey.

Questions on this example could include:

- Why is desktop research important?
- Tell me about your firm's lone worker policy.
- How do you check the scope of an inspection in advance?
- What access equipment do you take with you on a survey/inspection?
- Why is a methodical approach important?
- Which parts of the Red Book relate to inspection?
- What does the Home Survey Standard say about inspections?

Conclusion

Inspection plays a fundamental role in surveying practice and the RICS considers it important enough to make it a compulsory core competency. Assessors will expect all candidates to demonstrate knowledge and understanding, and practical experience of inspecting a range of properties for a range of purposes. However, it is not enough to just visit a property. It is important to understand the purpose of the inspection, to have suitable knowledge of building construction and defects, and of other important factors, such as location, and relevant leasehold covenants in the case of a leasehold property. It is also very important to understand the level and scope of inspection required.

Surveyors must also take sufficiently detailed notes during an inspection, with photographs, sketch plans, and measurements if appropriate, to support a suitably detailed report to meet the purpose of the inspection. There will be times when inspections are limited, perhaps because of access constraints – for example, a garden is too overgrown to enable the surveyor to view an elevation of the property. Surveyors may therefore need to use initiative; can the elevation be viewed from neighbouring properties, with permission, or can, for example, a drone be used for inaccessible areas?

Continue to read from Chapter 3 to understand how inspection skills are put into practice in a variety of contexts, applicable to further technical competencies.

Reference List

1 RICS (2024) *Residential pathway guide* [Online] Available at: https://www.rics.org/join-rics/sector-pathways (Accessed 26 August 2024).

2 RICS (2023) *Home survey standard* [Online] Available at: https://www.rics.org/profession-standards/rics-standards-and-guidance/sector-standards/building-surveying-standards/home-surveys/home-survey-standards (Accessed 29 September 2023).

3 RICS (2021) *News & opinion Hart v Large case update* [Online] Available at: https://www.rics.org/news-insights/hart-v-large-case-update (Accessed 25 October 2023).

4 Strong F (2020) *Surveyors* [Online] Reynolds Porter Chamberlain LLP [Online] Available at: https://www.rpc.co.uk/thinking/insurance-reviews/annual-insurance-review-2020/surveyors/ (Accessed 13 August 2024).

5 RICS (2018) *Surveying safely* 2nd Edition [Online] Available at: https://www.rics.org/profession-standards/rics-standards-and-guidance/sector-standards/building-surveying-standards/surveying-safely (Accessed 26 August 2024).

6 RICS (2021) *RICS valuation – global standards* [Online] Available at: https://www.rics.org/profession-standards/rics-standards-and-guidance/sector-standards/valuation-standards/red-book/red-book-global (Accessed 26 August 2024).

7 Lemen J (2023) *Hot topic highlight – new RICS guidance types* Property Elite Blog [Online] Available at: https://www.property-elite.co.uk/post/hot-topic-highlight-new-rics-guidance-types (Accessed 21 October 2023).

8 RICS (2024) *Residential pathway guide* [Online] Available at: https://www.rics.org/join-rics/sector-pathways (Accessed 26 August 2024).

9 RICS (2024) *Residential pathway guide* [Online] Available at: https://www.rics.org/join-rics/sector-pathways (Accessed 26 August 2024).

10 RICS (2024) *Residential pathway guide* [Online] Available at: https://www.rics.org/join-rics/sector-pathways (Accessed 26 August 2024).

11 RICS (2024) *Residential pathway guide* [Online] Available at: https://www.rics.org/join-rics/sector-pathways (Accessed 26 August 2024).

Further Reading and Resources

Health and Safety Executive: https://www.hse.gov.uk.

Lemen J (2022) *Hot topic highlight – the impact of Hart v Large* [Online] Property Elite Blog & Podcast Available at: https://www.property-elite.co.uk/post/hot-topic-highlight-impact-of-hart-v-large (Accessed 13 August 2024).

Lemen J (2023) *Hot topic highlight – Hart v Large* [Online] Property Elite Blog & Podcast Available at: https://www.property-elite.co.uk/post/hot-topic-highlight-hart-v-large (Accessed 13 August 2024).

Lemen J (2023) *Hot topic highlight – new RICS guidance types* Property Elite Blog [Online] Available at: https://www.property-elite.co.uk/post/hot-topic-highlight-new-rics-guidance-types (Accessed 21 October 2023).

Lemen J (2023) *Estates gazette APC series – tools of the trade (Inspection)* [Online] Available at: https://www.property-elite.co.uk/post/estates-gazette-apc-series-tools-of-the-trade-inspection (Accessed 13 August 2024).

Lemen J (2024) *APC essentials – mandatory competencies* Abingdon: Routledge.

RICS (2023) *RAAC: advice and FAQs* [Online] Available at: https://www.rics. org/news-insights/current-topics-campaigns/raac-advice-and-faqs#:~:text= What%20is%20Reinforced%20Autoclaved%20Aerated,1950s%20to%20 the%20mid%2D1990s (Accessed 12 October 2023).

Robinson B (2023) *Hot topic highlight – inspection (Parts 1 and 2)* Property Elite Blogs [Online] Available at: https://www.property-elite.co.uk/blog (Accessed 21 October 2023).

3 Measurement

Introduction

Measurement is a core technical APC competency, required to at least level 2 for Residential pathway candidates. This means that you must write up your summary of experience at both levels 1 and 2, with the option to select the competency to level 3. However, level 3 is not generally within the experience of a residential surveyor, so candidates will usually declare level 2. The RICS pathway guide sets out the relevant knowledge (level 1), and the practical application required for level 2.

Evidence of this competency will reflect your experience of other competencies depending on the purpose of the measurement. For instance, you may measure for purposes related to the Landlord and Tenant, Valuation, Market Appraisal, Leasing and Letting, and Purchase and Sale competencies.

This chapter will explain what you should know in relation to Measurement, covering the main requirements of level 1, with guidance on level 2. Level 3 is not covered, as this is usually outside the professional competence of a residential surveyor.

Should You Select This Competency?

As a core technical competency, you must select Measurement. Although you can choose whether to select the competency to level 2 or level 3, as mentioned earlier, for surveyors on the Residential pathway, it is usual to declare Measurement to level 2 because level 3 requires more specialist experience than residential surveyors typically acquire in practice. The RICS advises that *Level 3 is only recommended for candidates with specialist knowledge and experience of sophisticated measurement and data capture practice. Most property*

DOI: 10.1201/9781032705095-3

candidates will only attain Level 2. For guidance on Level 3 please refer to the RICS Geomatics pathway guide.[1] For this reason, this chapter focuses on levels 1 and 2. For level 3, the RICS advice applies, and you should download and check the Geomatics pathway guide.

At the time of writing over 2023 to 2024, Residential candidates were required to select their core technical competencies as follows:

Two to Level 3 and two to Level 2 of which candidates must select Inspection, Measurement, and Valuation to at least Level 2.[2] It is therefore important to consider the core technical competencies together and to decide which to select to level 2 and which to select to level 3. Candidates intending to become MRICS Registered Valuers will need to select Valuation to level 3. When considering core competencies, if Measurement is declared to level 2, either or both Valuation and Inspection will need to be selected to level 3 depending on the candidate's experience and ambition to become a Registered Valuer.

For those surveyors who do not routinely measure properties, it is important to become familiar with the professional standards and to gain experience of measuring properties using a range of bases. For example, if you are a property manager, try shadowing a surveyor measuring, e.g., for sales or letting purposes, for service charge apportionment, or to calculate building reinstatement costs. This will help you to understand the requirements and to put them into practice yourself so that you can obtain the necessary examples for your summary of experience.

Measurement Skills

It is not the purpose of this book to explain how to measure, as that will be learnt through careful study of the relevant RICS standards and experience of their application in practice. However, this chapter will outline some key points as guidance for revision topics, and for writing your summary of experience. In brief, for level 2, candidates must provide examples of measurements carried out, indicating the purpose of the measurement, the selected basis of measurement, and the tools used.

Measurement purposes include:

- Service charge apportionment – a leasehold block manager may not typically measure their managed properties. However, they may need to calculate service charges based on floor area, and they

may need measurements in the event of disputes or re-calculation of service charge apportionment.
- Comparable evidence – a valuer's measurements will assist in the identification and analysis of comparable properties.
- Sales and lettings – adverts are likely to include room dimensions and floor areas.

The process of measurement is important. Think about how you prepare to measure a property; what desktop research do you carry out? Do you obtain floor plans in advance? How do you decide what measurement tools to take with you? What are the limitations of those tools? How do you ensure accuracy? Client requirements need to be checked carefully and reflected in the terms of engagement. Any limitations must be notified to the client.

International Property Measurement Standards

The International Property Measurement Standards (IPMS) are developed by the International Property Measurement Standards Coalition (IPMSC). This is a group of organisations collaborating to develop standards to ensure consistency, and transparency – important in global markets.

RICS Property Measurement

At the time of writing this book in 2023 and 2024, RICS Property measurement, 2nd edition, 2018, had been reissued as a global professional standard. The publication incorporates and outlines the requirements of IPMS, including for residential properties.

Also, at the time of writing, the RICS was preparing a new edition of RICS Property measurement incorporating the concepts and principles of 'IPMS: All Buildings', which will be outlined later in this chapter. Candidates will need to check for updates to RICS Property measurement and ensure that they are familiar with the contents of the current and future versions.

Remember, because RICS Property measurement is a global professional standard, compliance is mandatory where the word 'must' is used in the statement. Use of the word 'should' in the statement indicates best practice. It is important to follow best practice guidance, as this maintains professional standards and can be a defence to a negligence claim or disciplinary proceedings. However, the RICS accepts that there may be exceptional circumstances in which surveyors may not adopt this good practice; in which case it is important to explain, and document, the reason for doing so.

RICS Property measurement contains a helpful glossary and definitions of core terms. It is useful to refer to this when preparing your summary of experience, and when preparing for your assessment.

The definitions are not replicated here, and you should check them in the document itself. However, important definitions in the glossary include:

- Component;
- External wall;
- Finished surface;
- Floor area;
- Gross External Area (GEA);
- Gross Internal Area (GIA);
- Internal Dominant Face (IDF);
- Internal Dominant Face (IDF) Wall Section;
- Net Internal Area (NIA).

The IPMS measurement bases as incorporated in RICS Property Measurement are:

- IPMS 1, which equates closely to GEA under the Code of measuring practice, 6th edition;
- IPMS 2 – Residential, which equates closely to GIA and Net Sales Area;
- IPMS 3 – Residential, which is the floor area available on an exclusive basis to an occupier. IPMS 3 is sub-divided into three categories:

    - IPMS 3A describes 'an external measurement of the area in exclusive occupation – equates somewhat to GEA (gross external area)';
    - IPMS 3B, which is 'an internal measurement including internal walls, etc. – equates somewhat to GIA (gross internal area)';
    - IPMS 3C described as 'an internal measurement excluding internal walls, etc. – equates somewhat to EFA (Effective Floor Area)'.[3]

Section 4 of RICS Property measurement provides more detail on the measurement of residential buildings, including useful comparisons, with diagrams, between IPMS and the Code of measuring practice.

Demonstrating an understanding of the differences between the Code and IPMS is important, and this is a common line of questioning in the APC interview.

There is further guidance on the application of each measurement basis, in a useful table in RICS Property measurement. It is worth familiarising yourself with this, particularly the applications relevant to your role. This will help you to explain why you have selected a particular measurement basis in relation to an example.

If a client or your employer has stipulated the use of the Code of measuring practice, 6th edition, instead of IPMS, RICS Property measurement requires surveyors to advise their client or employer on the benefits of using IPMS. They must also clearly document the reason for departure from IPMS. One option is to dual report, i.e., to measure in accordance with both IPMS, followed by the Code of measuring practice, 6th edition, 2015. This ensures compliance with IPMS and RICS Property measurement, whilst also enabling analysis of comparable evidence that follows the Code of measuring practice (if the measurements are for valuation purposes). For this reason, you should also be familiar with this document, including the bases of measurement, e.g., GEA, GIA, and NIA, and their application. Remember that the Code of measuring practice is a guidance note, embodying best practice at the time. RICS Property measurement is a professional standard, and compliance is mandatory for RICS members and regulated firms.

IPMS: All Buildings

The most recent IPMS version is 'The International Property Measurement Standards: All Buildings'. This was published in 2023 and supersedes the previously published IPMSC standards for individual asset classes (i.e., residential, office, retail, and industrial). The standards apply to all types of buildings, improving consistency across global markets. RICS Property measurement was being updated to reflect these changes, at the time of writing this book. Some of the IPMS: All Buildings numbering may differ from that listed in RICS Property measurement (pre-update).

The IPMS 'All Buildings' is as follows:

- IPMS 1 relates to external measurements;
- IPMS 2 relates to internal measurements;
- IPMS 1 and 2 can apply to the whole or part of a building;

- IPMS 3.1 relates to the external measurement of areas of exclusive occupation;
- IPMS 3.2 relates to the internal measurement of areas of exclusive occupation;
- IPMS 4.1 and IPMS 4.2 relate to the internal measurement of selected areas only.[4]

The 'All Buildings' document provides guidance on selection of the measurement basis, measurement practice, calculation, reporting, and essential definitions, with detailed explanations and diagrams. Candidates need to be able to answer questions on these. It is important to be aware of the 'All Buildings' standards and it is best to read the document itself. This can be daunting but focus on the main aspects that are relevant to your role.

Units of Measurement

The RICS does not specify whether units of measurement should be metric or imperial, so surveyors can adopt the most appropriate in the circumstances. However, it is essential to be clear about whether a measurement is imperial or metric. Some surveyors may choose to use both, in which case it is useful to know the conversion factor if converting between the two units of measurement. To convert floor areas measured in square metres to square feet, multiply the square metres by 10.7639. To convert an area from square feet to square metres, divide the square footage by 10.7639. To convert linear measurements from feet to metres, multiply the length in feet by 0.3048. To convert from metres to feet, multiply the length in metres by 3.28084.

It is also useful to know how to convert a measurement from one basis to another, e.g., from one of the measurement bases in the Code of measuring practice to IPMS. Knowledge of the different component areas helps here, as they can be used for conversion between bases.

Accuracy

Accuracy is critical, but the degree of accuracy will vary according to the purpose of the measurement. Candidates should consider how they ensure that a measurement is suitably accurate for its purpose to meet the client's needs. You may be asked how you ensure that a measurement is accurate. For example, is a laser measure checked against a known distance before going out onsite? Are measurements repeated to check them? These are common areas for questioning, and you should familiarise yourself with RICS requirements regarding accuracy and tolerances, as outlined in RICS Property measurement.

Good, clear note-taking skills are essential. You must be able to record measurements and observations (for example, of limited height areas) clearly and accurately so that they can be relied upon for their intended purpose. Annotated site plans or hand-drawn sketch plans may be required, as may specialist digital drawing and measurement tools. These records form the basis of the report to the client, and you may also need to refer to notes and plans if there are any queries or complaints following issue of the report.

Pro-forma documents can be helpful, and reports should be prepared promptly while the measurement is fresh in your mind.

Practise using measuring equipment so that you are confident using it, and ensure that you are aware of appropriate uses, advantages, and disadvantages of each. For example, a laser measure is a very useful tool when measuring indoors but can be difficult to use outside in bright sunlight. A fabric tape measure may stretch, compromising its accuracy, but can be useful for measuring small areas. A laser measure needs to be recalibrated periodically, and batteries may run low, so keep a replacement set of batteries with you.

As with each competency, the examples in the RICS pathway guide are not prescriptive, so it is not necessary to have experience of each of the bullet-points listed; rather, these provide guidance on the expectations of the specified level. Look at the pathway guide and think about examples from your own experience. In the summary of experience, it is important to be specific. Avoid making general statements that you understand RICS Property measurement without giving some brief examples of something that you understand from the standard.

When writing your summary of experience, you can also indicate your understanding of the wider context of the measurement, and other relevant documentation. For example, if a measurement is for valuation purposes, you could mention that under the Red Book you understand that you must have regard to IPMS wherever applicable.

RICS Professional Standards and Practice Information

This list of RICS Professional Standards and Practice Information relevant to the Measurement competency is not exhaustive, and it will be subject to change as the RICS updates its publications and processes, particularly as the IPMS evolve. However, it should be a helpful indication of the relevant documentation. It is important to check for updates to those listed here. Measurement takes place during inspections, so health and safety is also important.

Examples of relevant publications are:

- Code of measuring practice, 6th edition, 2015;
- Home survey standard, 1st edition, 2019;
- International Property Measurement Standards: All Buildings, 2023;
- RICS Property measurement, 2nd edition, 2018;
- RICS Valuation – Global Standards (the Red Book, effective 2022) (note that this is being updated at the time of writing, with a new version expected to take effect in January 2025);
- UK Residential real estate agency, 6th edition, 2017 (the Blue Book).

PS1 (compliance with standards where a written valuation is provided) and PS2 (ethics, competency, objectivity, and disclosures) of the 2022 Red Book (both of which are mandatory) recognise the IPMS. The Red Book requires members undertaking valuations to have regard to IPMS wherever applicable.[5] At the time of writing in 2024 the Red Book was being updated, so you should ensure that you are familiar with the revised version, which takes effect from 31st January 2025, and refer to the version current at the dates of your examples used.

How Can You Demonstrate the Levels?

Level 3

At level 3, the pathway guide requires candidates to evaluate, present, manage, analyse data, and/or apply spatial data and information. Candidates also need to show an advanced understanding of accuracy, precision, and error sources. Because the RICS only recommends level 3 for candidates *with specialist knowledge and experience of sophisticated measurement and data capture practice*[6], the pathway guide does not provide level 3 examples. Level 3 is therefore outside the scope of most Residential candidates and the author has not encountered any candidates who have selected Measurement to level 3. For this reason, level 3 questions are not provided in this book. As advised by the RICS, candidates considering level 3 will need to refer to the Geomatics pathway guide.

Level 2

Level 2 Measurement is about practical experience of measuring a range of properties for various purposes. You will be expected to have carried out measurements and presented the appropriate information gained from the measurement.[7]

Check the pathway guide and think about properties that you have measured. The guide is not exhaustive, and you do not have to provide an example of each bullet-point, but the guide does provide a useful indication of the expectations of the competency. In relation to each of your proposed examples think about 'what/why/how':

- What did you measure?
- Why did you measure the property?
- What measurement basis did you use?
- Why did you select the measurement basis?
- What instrumentation/tools did you use?
- Why did you use them?
- How did you measure the property?
- How did you ensure accuracy?
- How did you apply/report your measurements?
- What issues and limitations did you encounter when measuring?

Examples of the type of level 2 experience that could be included in a summary of experience are:

*At (**example**) I used a calibrated laser measurer to measure a modern detached house for valuation purposes. I selected IPMS 2 – Residential and measured to the internal dominant face. The property had an external balcony, which I included but stated separately in accordance with RICS Property measurement. My measurement supported my comparable evidence analysis and valuation.*

Questions on this example could include:

- Why did you use IPMS 2 – Residential?
- Define IDF.
- How does RICS Property measurement treat external balconies?
- Talk me through how you measured.
- How did you ensure the accuracy of your measurements?

*At (**example**) I measured an apartment for loan security valuation purposes. The lender client required measurement on a gross internal area* basis. In accordance with my firm's policy, I dual-reported using IPMS 2 – Residential, and Gross Internal Area to meet the client lender's requirements, and the requirements of RICS Property measurement. Measuring using GIA also helped me to identify suitable comparable evidence, as GIA is widely used in my local area.

Questions on this example could include:

- Why did the lender require measurement of the GIA?
- What is your duty under RICS Property measurement if the client instructs you not to use IPMS?
- Why did you dual report?
- What were the differences between IPMS 2 – Residential and GIA in this example?
- Talk me through how you measured the property.
- How did you ensure the accuracy of your measurements?

As can be seen above, typical level 2 questions will start with, 'How did you...' or 'Tell me about/talk me through ...'. Remember, all the assessors' questions should be based upon the examples that you provide in your write-up for this competency in your summary of experience – rather than being hypothetical or general. However, assessors may also ask for more examples of measurements that you have carried out, especially if they want additional evidence of your practical experience.

Some further example level 2 questions could include (depending on the example provided):

- How did you ensure that you presented your measurements clearly?
- What did you do when you were unable to use your laser measurer in the direct sunlight?
- How did you calibrate your laser measurer?
- How did you measure the unevenly shaped room?
- Talk me through how you measured the property.

Level 1

Although the assessors will focus on your highest level, you may be asked some level 1 questions, focussing on the knowledge behind your practical level 2 examples. This will focus primarily on IPMS and RICS Property measurement, but it is important to be aware of any changes and updates.

As with all competencies and levels, check the pathway guide carefully. Level 1 requires knowledge and understanding of measurement principles and the limitations that can be encountered. Your knowledge will relate to your area of practice, but the examples provided in the 2024 pathway guide cover:

- Accuracy;
- Appropriate standards and guidance;
- Data capture techniques (e.g., lasers and tape measures);
- Measurement bases: definitions and application;
- Potential sources of error;
- The limitations of different methods of measurement, and of plans and drawings;
- Using plans and drawings.[8]

This is an example of the type of knowledge that could be included in a level 1 submission:

I understand the importance of IPMS in creating consistency and transparency when measuring. I am familiar with RICS Property measurement professional standard, 2nd edition, 2018 e.g., I know that IPMS 2 – Residential, measures to the Internal Dominant Face for external features and otherwise to the finished surface. If instructed to use the Code of Measuring Practice, I understand that RICS Property measurement expects RICS members to advise their client or employer of the benefits of using IPMS, and to document the reason for departure.

Some example level 1 measurement questions include:

- Explain your understanding of IPMS: All Buildings to me.
- How can you ensure your measurements are accurate?
- Why do you calibrate a laser measurer?
- Tell me about a strength and weakness of a measuring technique you have used.
- Tell me about your understanding of RICS Property measurement.
- What are limited-use areas and how do you report these?
- What IPMS bases are you aware of and when would each of these used?
- What is a potential source of error when measuring?
- What is dual reporting and when would you use it?
- What is IPMS?

- When would you use a tape measure?
- Why would you take check measurements?
- Why has IPMS been introduced?
- Why is accuracy important when you measure buildings?

Conclusion

Measurement is a useful skill to master and for residential surveyors it is essential for many roles; hence, it is a core technical competency. It is important to understand the correct basis of measurement, depending on the property and the purpose of the measurement. Accurate measurement underpins, for example, valuations, and service charge calculations. Assessors will therefore expect all candidates to demonstrate knowledge and understanding, and practical experience of taking accurate measurements.

Reference List

1 RICS (2024) *Residential pathway guide* [Online] Available at: https://www.rics.org/join-rics/sector-pathways (Accessed 26 August 2024).

2 RICS (2024) *Residential pathway guide* [Online] Available at: https://www.rics.org/join-rics/sector-pathways (Accessed 26 August 2024).

3 RICS (2018) *RICS property measurement* 2nd Edition [Online] Available at: https://www.rics.org/profession-standards/rics-standards-and-guidance/sector-standards/real-estate-standards/rics-property-measurement-2nd-edition (Accessed 26 August 2024).

4 IPMSC (2023) *International property measurement standards: all buildings* [Online] Available at: www.ipmsc.org (Accessed 26 August 2024).

5 RICS (2021) *RICS valuation – global standards* [Online] Available at: https://www.rics.org/profession-standards/rics-standards-and-guidance/sector-standards/valuation-standards/red-book/red-book-global (Accessed 26 August 2024).

6 RICS (2018) *RICS property measurement* 2nd Edition [Online] Available at: https://www.rics.org/profession-standards/rics-standards-and-guidance/sector-standards/real-estate-standards/rics-property-measurement-2nd-edition (Accessed 26 August 2024).

7 RICS (2024) *Residential pathway guide* [Online] Available at: https://www.rics.org/join-rics/sector-pathways (Accessed 26 August 2024).

8 RICS (2024) *Residential pathway guide* [Online] Available at: https://www.rics.org/join-rics/sector-pathways (Accessed 26 August 2024).

Further Reading and Resources

IPMSC (2023) *International property measurement standards: all buildings* [Online] Available at: www.ipmsc.org (Accessed 15 August 2024).

Lemen J (2022) *Hot topic highlight – IPMS update* Property Elite Blog [Online] Available at: https://www.property-elite.co.uk/post/hot-topic-highlight-ipms-update (Accessed 11 November 2023).

Lemen J (2023) *Hot topic highlight – measurement tools* Property Elite Blog [Online] Available at: https://www.property-elite.co.uk/post/hot-topic-highlight-measurement-tools (Accessed 26 July 2024).

Pugh T (2023) Ensuring best practice in property measurement *RICS Property Journal* [Online] Available at: https://ww3.rics.org/uk/en/journals/property-journal/ipms-best-practice-property-measurement.html (Accessed 11 November 2023).

Pugh T (2023) New IPMS aims to enable consistent measurement *RICS Property Journal* [Online] Available at: https://ww3.rics.org/uk/en/journals/property-journal/ipms-enables-consistent-measurement.html (Accessed 11 November 2023).

Pugh T (2023) *What you need to know about IPMS all buildings* Hollis Global Ltd [Online] Available at: https://www.hollisglobal.com/our-perspective/insights/what-you-need-to-know-about-ipms-all-buildings/ (Accessed 26 July 2024).

Pugh T (2024) How IPMS 3 and 4 refine standards to ensure consistency *RICS Property Journal* [Online] Available at: https://ww3.rics.org/uk/en/journals/property-journal/ipms-refines-measurement-standards.html (Accessed 26 July 2024).

RICS (2024) *Property measurement* 2nd Edition [Online] Available at: https://www.rics.org/profession-standards/rics-standards-and-guidance/sector-standards/real-estate-standards/rics-property-measurement-2nd-edition#:~:text=RICS%20IPMS%20data%20standard,use%2C%20as%20they%20are%20published. (Accessed 15 August 2024). This webpage contains a link to RICS Property Measurement 2018, and information on the update.

4 Valuation

Introduction

Valuation is a core technical competency, required to at least level 2 for Residential pathway candidates. This means that all candidates need to write up their summary of experience at both levels 1 and 2, with the option to select the competency to level 3.

The RICS pathway guide sets out the relevant knowledge (level 1), practical application (level 2), and reasoned advice (level 3) for this competency. However, as with all competencies, candidates do not need to have encountered everything listed, as this will depend on their experience and role. The Valuation competency relates to both capital and rental valuations. This competency should be read in tandem with several other competencies, such as Health and Safety, Inspection, Measurement, Loan Security Valuation, Landlord and Tenant, Building Pathology, Market Appraisal, Leasing and Letting, and Purchase and Sale.

This chapter will explain what candidates should know in relation to Valuation, covering the main requirements of level 1, with guidance on levels 2 and 3.

Should You Select This Competency?

As a core technical competency, you must select Valuation as one of your competencies. However, you can choose whether to select the competency either to level 2 or level 3. All candidates must therefore have experience of valuing properties for varying purposes and be familiar with valuation standards and methods. Check the pathway guide and think about valuations that you have carried out. In relation to each, think about why you valued the property, how you carried out your valuation, the issues you observed during your valuation, and

DOI: 10.1201/9781032705095-4

whether you provided reasoned advice in relation to your valuation. This will help you to decide whether to choose level 2 or level 3.

The pathway guide outlines the requirements of each level and the sections later in this chapter will help to identify suitable examples for each level. However, in brief, for level 2, candidates must provide examples of capital and rental valuations, including the purpose of the valuation and the method used, why this method was used, and an outline of the process, for instance, the analysis of comparable evidence. Level 3 is more in depth, with reasoned advice. For example, did the valuation result in reasoned advice or recommendations for further investigation by legal advisers or other specialists?

RICS Registered Valuers

Candidates who wish to become Registered Valuers **must** select Valuation to level 3. This means that candidates are effectively seeking a second qualification alongside MRICS, and the assessors will expect thorough knowledge of valuation principles and relevant publications, and suitable and varied valuation experience. It is not generally recommended that candidates without extensive valuation experience select this competency to level 3, if the main motivation is to become MRICS, without a need to achieve Registered Valuer status. If you will struggle to provide specific examples of reasoned advice to your employer or to a client, and are not confident with valuations, consider selecting the competency to level 2. If you are selecting the competency to level 3, check the pathway guide carefully, review your valuation experience honestly and carefully, and consider whether you can gain the necessary experience before submitting.

Valuation Skills

Valuation covers both capital and rental valuations. Valuations of residential property are undertaken for many purposes, but examples include levels 1, 2, and 3 home surveys, loan security valuations, acquisitions, sales, lettings, and asset and portfolio management purposes. Specific valuation skills will depend on the surveyor's role, although some of the expertise needed will be common to many tasks. For example:

- A pre-purchase valuation will focus on market value and factors that affect this;

- A loan security valuation will consider market value and reflect lender guidelines;
- A valuation for Inheritance Tax purposes will need to comply with the requirements of the Inheritance Tax Act 1984;
- A landlord will require a valuation of the market rent;
- A landlord of long residential leasehold flats, or leaseholders of those flats, may require valuations for lease extension and enfranchisement purposes.

A valuer requires good inspection and note-taking skills; they must be able to carry out desktop research, record onsite observations, analyse the comparable evidence (if the comparative method is used), and communicate their opinion of value in a clearly worded report to the client. The valuer may need to refer to these notes and research in the event of post-valuation queries or complaints.

As with each competency, the examples in the RICS pathway guide are not prescriptive, so it is not necessary to have experience of each of the bullet-points listed in the guide; rather, these provide guidance on the nature of the professional knowledge and experience expected of a valuer at the specified level. Look at the pathway guide and think about relevant knowledge and suitable examples of when you have assisted or carried out valuations for inclusion in your summary of experience.

Despite Valuation being a core technical competency, the reality is that some candidates will not have extensive valuation experience because it is not part of their day-to-day role. Block managers for example do not typically carry out valuations. If this is the case, try to shadow a colleague or gain work experience at another firm or in another department. This can be difficult to arrange, so allow plenty of time to find someone who can help. This experience could be for a period of full-time secondment, or if this is not possible, regular involvement over a longer period can suffice. Perhaps you could accompany a colleague for a half-day at a time when a valuation is planned. Remember that you need experience of carrying out valuations yourself, though it is fine to do so under supervision.

A good way to gain experience is to take a step-by-step approach, shadowing a valuer at first, then inspecting together but doing your own research and valuation, which you can compare to the valuer's report, then carrying out the valuation, to be reviewed and approved by the valuer. Another approach is to start by taking responsibility for a particular aspect, such as the comparable evidence research, then to build up your areas of responsibility so that you gain experience of the process of valuation, from start to finish. These are just suggested approaches; the main point is to make good use of work experience or secondments if the time available is limited.

Key Valuation-Related Themes

While it is obviously important to have knowledge and experience of valuations in practice, candidates must also understand the themes and issues that relate to this competency. These include:

Automated Valuation Models

Automated Valuation Models (AVMs) use computer databases and statistical models to provide valuations of real estate. They require sufficient relevant and accurate data to be effective and are used for a range of purposes, as they can provide quick and cost-effective valuations. Candidates should be aware of AVMs and be able to express an opinion on their advantages and disadvantages. The RICS has published a 2021 AVM Roadmap and a 2022 Insight Paper 'Automated valuation models (AVMs): information for the profession and their clients' both of which are useful reading. Further details of these, and of other sources of information, are at the end of this chapter.

Fire Safety

The Lakanal House and Grenfell Tower fires brought the tragic consequences of fire safety breaches to public, political, professional, and media attention and changed risk management for residential blocks of flats. Candidates should be familiar with requirements for External Wall System (EWS) 1 forms and with RICS professional standard 'Valuation approach for properties in multi-storey, multi-occupancy residential buildings with cladding' England and Wales, 2nd edition, December 2023, effective 1 January 2024. This is particularly relevant for valuers carrying out loan security valuations, but it will assist with valuations carried out for other purposes. The standard is intended to support valuers in providing risk-based, proportionate valuation advice. Valuers should also follow the guidance issued by their lender client and have regard to the Red Book and UK National Supplement.[1]

This practice standard is detailed, and it is not replicated here as you should familiarise yourself with the detail of the document directly, particularly if you carry out valuations of flats in high-rise blocks. If you do not value properties in affected blocks, it is still useful to be aware of RICS publications in case of level 1 questions on the topic.

Another useful publication is RICS professional standard 'Valuation of properties in multi-storey, multi-occupancy residential buildings with cladding' UK, 1st edition, 2021. This contains information on EWS1 forms. EWS1 forms are not a legal obligation, but they may be requested by lenders. They are valid for five years and provide information on remedial works, to support valuers and lenders in their advice and decision-making. EWS1 forms are not required in all circumstances and valuers should be able to justify requests for EWS1 forms.[2]

EWS1 forms can specify five possible results:

- Category A: A1 applies if materials are non-combustible. A2 materials have limited combustibility. Category A1 and A2 materials are not likely to lead to further action. A3 means that remedial work may be needed on attachments, e.g., balconies.
- Category B applies where combustible materials are present. B1 means that the risk is low, and no remedial action is needed. B2 means that fire safety is inadequate, and remediation is needed.[3] Of these, B2 is most likely to impact on value and availability of mortgage finance.

Guidance on fire risk appraisal for external walls and cladding is provided by Publicly Available Specification (PAS) 9980: 2022.

Liability for remediation costs is important. The Building Safety Act 2022 protects qualifying leaseholders from remediation costs for historical safety defects. Protection is evidenced by a Leaseholder Deed of Certificate. Non-qualifying leaseholders may be liable for a share of remediation costs, which may impact on the value of the property, the willingness of lenders to lend, and the market for the property, even if just in the short-term pending remediation of defects. Other potential sources of funding for remedial works could include the Building Safety Fund, the Cladding Safety Scheme, building warranties, and a building's original developers. These could potentially be taken into account when valuing.

Remember that if you are providing examples of valuations of affected properties, you need to be aware of the guidance and fire safety requirements applicable at the date of the valuation.

There are two useful links in the resources section at the end of this chapter:

- One to the RICS Cladding EWS FAQs;
- Another to the RICS Fire Safety web page, which contains links to news and industry guidance, including regarding valuation.

International Valuation Standards

These standards are the foundations of global consistency and transparency regarding valuations. The International Valuation Standards Council's Standards Board sets, reviews, and updates the International Valuation Standards (IVS), which have been incorporated into the Red Book.

Margins of Error

The accuracy of a valuation is a key aspect of establishing its reliability, and, therefore, a valuer's potential liability. Valuation is an art as well as a science and there can be an element of subjectivity when valuing. It is therefore generally accepted that there may be a margin of error, so in a valuation there may be a minimum and maximum figure that may be reached by a reasonable valuer. The permitted margin of error may vary according to the type of property and the purpose of the valuation. For residential valuations this tolerance is usually up to 15%.[4] Candidates should ensure that they are familiar with VPGA 10 of the Red Book and matters that may give rise to uncertainty, such as limited comparable evidence, and the effects of the COVID pandemic on the market.

Risk and Liability

Valuation is generally acknowledged to be a relatively high-risk area of work for surveyors. This risk stems from potential breach of contract, and from allegations of negligence. Risk management is therefore important, and candidates must understand their duty of care and to whom they owe this duty. If a claimant can establish that the valuer has failed to comply with the terms of engagement, or that there is a duty of care, that has been breached, causing loss to the claimant, the valuer may find that they are liable for damages to cover those losses.

Valuers are expected to use the skill and care of a reasonable body of the valuer's peers.[5] Valuers have a contractual obligation towards their client, whether the client is, for instance, a borrower, purchaser, landlord, or lender. A valuer may also owe a duty of care in tort. Tort is an area of law that includes negligence. This duty of care in the tort of negligence will be owed to the client. However, it may also be owed to third parties (who are not parties to the contract) if the third party may be expected to rely upon the valuer's report. For example, a borrower might decide to rely upon a valuation carried out for the lender instead of instructing the borrower's own valuer. Therefore, a valuer who breaches this duty of care could be liable to their client for both breach of contract and negligence, and to third parties in negligence.

The time limit for a breach of contract claim regarding a negligent valuation is six years from the date the service (valuation) was provided (the limitation period is 12 years for a service provided under a deed). There is a 'long-stop' limitation period of 15 years for claims in the tort of negligence. You will find a detailed explanation of limitation periods and the Limitation Act 1980 in the RICS guidance note 'Risk, liability and insurance' UK, 1st edition, 2021.

In view of the potential scope of a negligence claim, valuers must understand the issues surrounding third party reliance on a valuation and other related areas such as liability caps and professional indemnity insurance. Candidates should therefore ensure that they are familiar with relevant RICS guidance, including 'Risk, liability and insurance', 1st edition, 2021, mentioned above.

Case law establishes the general rule that (in addition to the client) a valuer may owe a duty of care to a borrower unless the valuation is for commercial or buy-to-let purposes or is at the higher end of the residential market. This is because borrowers in these circumstances can reasonably be expected to afford and to obtain their own valuation. Candidates should familiarise themselves with valuation case law, including:

- Freemont (Denbigh) Ltd v Knight Frank LLP [2014] EWHC 3347 (Ch);
- Hubbard v Bank of Scotland PLC [2014] EWCA Civ 648;
- Scullion v Bank of Scotland PLC [2011] EWCA Civ 693;

- Smith v Eric S Bush and Harris v Wyre Forest [1990] 1 AC 831;
- South Australia Asset Management Corp v York Montague Ltd [1996] UKHL 10;
- Yianni v Edwin Evans & Sons [1981] 2 EGLR 118; [1982] QB 438.

Sustainability

As awareness of environmental issues continues to grow, so the value of a property can be affected by the sustainability of its design and construction. For example, a buy-to-let property with an A or B Energy Performance Certificate rating might be more desirable and potentially command a higher market rent. The same may apply to market value, reflecting demand for energy-efficient homes, lower, more stable energy bills, and a reduced carbon footprint. In the UK, relatively few homes are built or retrofitted to a high level of energy efficiency, perhaps creating a scarcity value. A 2022 Santander bank survey of over 2,300 homebuyers, owners, estate agents, and mortgage brokers found that retrofitting energy efficiency upgrades created an average 9.4% premium on homes.[6]

For valuers, this translates to a green premium, the opposite of which is a brown discount[7]; i.e., a poorly performing home that does not meet market expectations may be less desirable, resulting in a discounted market rent or market value.

When you are writing your summary of experience, think about examples when sustainability has impacted on your valuation. These could be suitable for either the Valuation or Sustainability competencies.

Valuer Registration Scheme

We have mentioned the Valuer Registration Scheme above and candidates selecting valuation to level 3 need to be familiar with its requirements. Valuers carrying out valuations to which the Red Book applies must become RICS Registered Valuers. A candidate who is an AssocRICS Registered Valuer must still pass Valuation level 3 to become an MRICS Registered Valuer.

RICS Professional Standards and Practice Information

This list of RICS Professional Standards and Practice Information relevant to the Valuation competency is not exhaustive, and it will be subject to change as the RICS updates its publications and processes. However, it should be a helpful indication of the relevant documentation. It is important to check for further standards and information relevant to your role, and for new guidance and for updates to those listed below. Examples include:

- Comparable evidence in real estate valuation, 1st edition, 2019 (reissued as a professional standard in 2023);
- Conflicts of interest Global, 1st edition, 2017;
- Home survey standard, 1st edition, 2019;
- Japanese knotweed and residential property, 1st edition, 2022;
- Reinstatement cost assessment of buildings, 3rd edition, 2018 (reissued in 2024);
- RICS Valuation – Global Standards 2022 (the Red Book) and the 2024 updated version due to take effect from 31st January 2025;
- RICS Valuation – Global Standards: UK National Supplement, 2017, and updated version 2023;
- Risk, liability and insurance UK, 1st edition, 2021;
- UK residential real estate agency, 6th edition, 2017;
- Valuation approach for properties in multi-storey, multi-occupancy residential buildings with cladding – valuation flowchart Version 2, December 2023;
- Valuation of buy-to-let and HMO properties, 2nd edition, 2022;
- Valuation approach for properties in multi-storey, multi-occupancy residential buildings with cladding – valuation flowchart Version 2 (Wales), December 2023;
- Valuation approach for properties in multi-storey, multi-occupancy residential buildings with cladding England & Wales, 2nd edition, December 2023. Effective from 1 January 2024;
- Valuation of properties in multi-storey, multi-occupancy residential buildings with cladding UK, 1st edition, March 2021. Effective from 5 April 2021;
- Valuation of individual new-build homes, 3rd edition, 2019;
- Valuation of residential leasehold properties for secured lending purposes, 1st edition, 2021;
- Valuing residential property purpose built for renting England, Scotland and Wales, 1st edition, 2018.

There are also links to further useful reading at the end of this chapter.

'RICS Valuation – Global Standards' (the Red Book) is a particularly important document. The Red Book incorporates the IVS and should be read in conjunction with the relevant national supplement. It is important to refer to the correct edition current at the time a valuation was carried out, when writing the summary of experience and case study.

The Red Book can be an intimidating document, being almost 300 pages long, but there are ways to make it more manageable. This chapter focuses on the 2022 version, current at the time of writing, but you should also review the updated version when it takes effect. A good starting point is to look at its application and at the basic structure of the Red Book:

Part 1: Introduction. This provides a very useful summary of key points and explains that sections of the Red Book with a 'PS' number or the 'VPS' reference are mandatory (unless otherwise stated) for members supplying written valuations, whereas those with a 'VPGA' reference number are for guidance, embodying best practice.[8]

Part 2: Glossary. This provides some very helpful definitions, such as market value and market rent. Candidates should ensure that they are familiar with these, particularly those definitions that are relevant to the candidate's role.

Part 3: Professional Standards. This section is divided into two parts – PS1 and PS2 – both of which are outlined briefly below.

PS1: Compliance with standards where a written valuation is provided (mandatory). This states that *All members, whether practising individually or within an RICS-regulated or non-regulated firm, who provide a written valuation are required to comply with the international standards and RICS global standards set out below. Members must also comply with the requirements of RICS Valuer Registration (VR).*[9]

PS1 also confirms that members and regulated firms must comply with both PS1 and PS2, and VPS 1–5 (subject to some exceptions to VPS 1–5, listed below). The duty to comply includes the provision of written valuations using an AVM. Although PS1 focusses on written valuations, it also advises that verbal valuations should comply as fully as possible with the principles of the Red Book.

There are no exceptions to compliance with PS1 and PS2, but, as mentioned above, there are exceptions to the duty to comply with VPS 1–5. Section 5 of PS1 outlines these:

- Agency and brokerage services for an acquisition or disposal to which 'Real estate agency and brokerage guidance', 3rd edition (2016), applies;
- Acting as an expert witness;

- Performing statutory functions;
- Valuations for internal purposes;
- Valuations relating to litigation or negotiations.

It is important to understand the detail of these exceptions and their application, particularly if providing examples in the summary of experience or case study.

The Red Book Global Standards do not apply to estimated replacement cost figures for insurance purposes as these are not valuations as defined by the Red Book.

PS2: Ethics, competency, objectivity, and disclosures (mandatory). This protects the integrity of a valuation and requires valuers to have the necessary experience, skill, and judgement and to act professionally and ethically.[10] Competence is important here; candidates may be supervised by a more experienced valuer who may review and sign-off valuations. It is acceptable to state that this is the case in the summary of experience.

PS2 addresses other key concepts, such as objectivity, confidentiality, conflicts of interest, disclosures, and terms of engagement. These are detailed provisions, which are not replicated here. Candidates should ensure that they are familiar with PS2 and adhere to it when carrying out valuations. Examples of compliance with PS1 and PS2 can help candidates to demonstrate their professionalism in the summary of experience.

Part 4: Valuation technical and performance standards (mandatory but subject to exceptions – see above). These are abbreviated to VPS 1–5 and are:

- VPS 1 – Terms of engagement (scope of works);
- VPS 2 – Inspections, investigations, and records (relevant also to Chapter 2 'Inspection');
- VPS 3 – Valuation reports;
- VPS 4 – Bases of value, assumptions, and special assumptions;
- VPS 5 – Valuation approaches and methods.

Again, these are very detailed provisions, which are not replicated here. Candidates should ensure that they are familiar with VPS 1–5, and how each is applied in the candidate's firm. For example, check your firm's terms of engagement and cross-reference them with VPS 1. Similarly, when inspecting, have regard to compliance with VPS 2.

Part 5: Valuation applications (advisory). These are abbreviated to 'VPGA' and are advisory rather than mandatory. They generally relate to valuations for specific purposes and so it is not necessary to be familiar with each one. The VPGAs are:

- VPGA 1 – Valuation for inclusion in financial statements;
- VPGA 2 – Valuation of interests for secured lending;
- VPGA 3 – Valuation of businesses and business interests;
- VPGA 4 – Valuation of individual trade-related properties;
- VPGA 5 – Valuation of plant and equipment;
- VPGA 6 – Valuation of intangible assets;
- VPGA 7 – Valuation of personal property, including arts and antiques;
- VPGA 8 – Valuation of real property interests;
- VPGA 9 – Identification of portfolios, collections, and groups of properties;
- VPGA 10 – Matters that may give rise to material valuation uncertainty.

Residential candidates are most likely to need to be familiar with VPGA 2, VPGA 8, VPGA 9, and VPGA 10. However, all candidates should consider their role and the VPGAs relevant to that role.

Part 6: IVS. These are both reprinted in, and incorporated into, the Red Book, so compliance with the Red Book standards will also ensure compliance with IVS.

RICS Valuation – Global Standards 2017: UK National Supplement. This supplements the Global Red Book and the two should be read in conjunction with one another, for valuations carried out subject to UK jurisdiction. Candidates operating in other jurisdictions should check their relevant national supplement.

The UK National Supplement should be approached in the same way as the Global Red Book: check the structure and note the relevant aspects of each section. Focus on mandatory sections, but also have regard to the relevant best practice guidance. The 2017 supplement includes a useful glossary, and the main body comprises:

- UK PS1 (mandatory): Compliance with valuation standards in the UK;
- UK VPS 1 (mandatory): Terms of engagement and reporting;
- UK VPS 2 (mandatory): Terms of engagement (supplementary provisions in Scotland);

- UK VPS 3 (mandatory): Regulated purpose valuations;
- UK VPGAs 1–18 (advisory): For residential valuers the most relevant are likely to be UK VPGA 11, 12, and 13, which relate to a variety of common valuation purposes, and UK VPGA 15 (Valuations for Capital Gains Tax [CGT], Inheritance Tax, Stamp Duty Land Tax [SDLT], and the Annual Tax on Enveloped Dwellings). Others may possibly apply, for example, UK VPGA 7 (Valuation of registered social housing providers' assets for financial statements), and UK VPGA 14 (Valuation of registered social housing for loan security purposes), but as mentioned, it is very important that candidates review all the UK VPGAs and ensure that they are familiar with any that may apply to their role.

At the time of writing, the 2023 edition had been published, taking effect from 1 May 2024. The 2017, or earlier, versions of the UK national supplement will apply to your pre–1st May 2024 valuation examples, and it is very important to refer to the version(s) current at the date of your valuation example(s).

2024 RICS Red Book Global Standards and 2023 UK National Supplement Updates. At the time of writing in 2024 the RICS was reviewing the Global Red Book and the updated version takes effect from 31st January 2025. As of July 2024, the proposals were:

- Alignment with the new 2024 IVS;
- Adaption to evolving practices and processes for issues including ESG and technological advancements;
- VPS 1 will remain as VPS 1 (Terms of engagement);
- VPS 2 will become VPS 4 (Inspections, investigations, and records);
- VPS 3 will become VPS 6 (Valuation reports);
- VPS 4 will become VPS 2 (Bases of value, assumptions, and special assumptions);
- VPS 5 will become VPS 3 (Valuation approaches and methods); and finally, revised VPS 5 (Valuation models).[11]

As mentioned, the UK National Supplement was updated in 2023, effective from 1st May 2024. Ensure that you refer to the version current at the date of your examples. In the updated UK edition:

- UK VPGAs 12 (Valuation of residential property for miscellaneous purposes) and 13 (Residential secured lending guidance for other

related purposes including RICS Homebuyer Service) have been merged into UK VPGA 11;
- UK VPGA 15 remains very important if you carry out valuations for taxation purposes.

Relevant Laws

Refer to the case law mentioned above when preparing for your interview. The Limitation Act 1980 stipulates the limitation periods for claims for negligence and breach of contract (again see above).

Some valuations will be carried out for taxation purposes, so it is necessary to be aware of the relevant legislation:

- The Taxation of Chargeable Gains Act 1992 – this relates to the CGT payable on the disposal of a property, including residential properties in certain situations. You should understand the purpose of a CGT valuation, and that the Act (section 272) defines market value.
- The Inheritance Tax Act 1984 – this applies to Inheritance Tax valuations (sometimes referred to as probate valuations). Section 160 defines market value for the purposes of the Act.
- The Finance Act 2003 – this relates to SDLT. Section 118 provides that market value is determined in accordance with the Taxation of Chargeable Gains Act 1992.

The Fire Safety Act 2021 and the Building Safety Act 2022: fire safety, historic building defects, and remediation requirements and cost can all affect value.

How Can You Demonstrate Level 3?

Your assessors will start at the highest level you have declared, which will be either level 2 or level 3. At level 3 the assessors will expect you to present specific examples of reasoned advice that you have provided to a client or your employer as a result of a valuation. Level 3 examples should enable you to demonstrate a deeper level of understanding than is needed at level 2, with experience of valuing a range of properties, for varied purposes using a range of valuation methods.[12]

Some key points from the pathway guide are mentioned below, but it is important to regularly refer to the guide when writing your summary of experience and to be aware of any changes or updates. As mentioned in earlier chapters, the guide is not exhaustive, and candidates do not have to provide an example of each bullet-point, but the guide does provide a useful indication of the type of knowledge and experience that you need to demonstrate.

Examples of the type of level 3 experience that would typically be included in a summary of experience are given below. Level 3 examples will require level 3 answers (for example, explanations of the reasoned advice provided), but they may also incorporate level 1 (knowledge) and level 2 (the process of valuation). The following illustrate the type of level 3 examples expected of a candidate:

*At (**example**) I carried out a pre-purchase valuation. My opinion of Market Value was (£) below the purchase price due to (e.g., locational factors, building defects, analysis of the comparable evidence, non-compliance with Building Regulations). I advised my client to renegotiate the purchase price.*

Questions relating to this example could include:

- Why did you advise your client to renegotiate the purchase price?
- Talk me through your advice to renegotiate the purchase price.
- What advice did you give regarding the breach of Building Regulations?
- What options did you consider regarding the building defects?

*At (**example**) I was instructed to value for buy-to-let purposes. I identified evidence of dry rot to the rear elevation and recommended that further investigations should be carried out by a specialist before I could provide my opinion of Market Value.*

Questions relating to this example could include:

- Why did you suspect dry rot?
- Why did you advise the client to appoint a specialist?
- What advice did you provide regarding appointment of a specialist?

*At (**example**) I carried out a valuation for Inheritance Tax purposes. I identified a restrictive covenant that prevented further building on the property. I obtained comparable evidence and made adjustments to reflect the covenant. I advised the client that the covenant had a negative effect on value and that it could also restrict the market for the property.*

Questions relating to this example could include:

- How did you identify the covenant?
- Talk me through your advice on the effect of the covenant.

- What adjustments did you make to reflect the covenant?
- Why did the covenant impact on value?

*At (**example**) I was instructed by the tenant to value a flat for lease extension purposes. I identified that the lease had 60 years left unexpired. I advised that this would affect the cost of the lease extension as marriage value would be payable. I also advised that there were government proposals to abolish marriage value, but that these had not yet been implemented, and that failure to extend the lease could restrict the market for the flat and the likelihood of the flat being mortgageable.*

Questions relating to this example could include:

- What is marriage value?
- How is marriage value calculated?
- How did you verify the unexpired term of the lease?
- Talk me through your advice regarding the unexpired lease term.
- Why did you advise that the short unexpired lease term would restrict the market for the flat?
- Tell me about proposals to abolish marriage value.

Occasionally a level 3 question may be general, if, for example, the assessors want more evidence of your reasoned advice, hence, for instance:

- Give me an example of when you have provided reasoned advice in relation to a valuation (for a specified purpose).

How Can You Demonstrate Level 2?

Level 2 Valuation is about practical experience of applying the valuation standards and guidance. Candidates are expected to have carried out valuations from start to finish, with supervision. Again, the pathway guide provides a non-exhaustive list of the experience and knowledge expected at level 2.

Examples of the type of level 2 experience that would typically be included in a summary of experience are:

*At (**example**) I valued a modern two-bedroom house for a purchaser. The interior of the property was in average condition. I researched comparable evidence on my firm's internal database and on external* *databases and identified three comparable properties on the same road, which had sold within the past six months. I created a hierarchy of evidence and adjusted to reflect condition, before reaching my opinion of the market value.*

Questions on this example could include:

- What do you mean by 'average condition'?
- How did you research your comparable evidence?
- How did you comply with 'Comparable evidence in real estate valuation', 1st edition, 2019?
- How did you create your hierarchy of evidence?
- Talk me through your analysis of the comparable evidence.
- How did you adjust to reflect condition?

*At (**example**) I valued a one-bedroom apartment for buy-to-let purposes. I complied with RICS The valuation of buy-to-let and HMO properties, 2nd edition, 2022. I ascertained that there were no onerous ground rent increases. I used the comparable method to value the Market Rent and Market Value.*

Questions on this example could include:

- How did you comply with RICS The valuation of buy-to-let and HMO properties, 1st edition, 2016?
- How did you ascertain that there were no onerous ground rent increases?
- Why did you ascertain that there were no onerous ground rent increases?
- Why did you use the comparable method?
- What alternative method could be used to value a buy-to-let property?
- Talk me through your analysis of the comparable evidence in relation to market value/market rent.

Typical level 2 questions will start with, 'How have you…', 'Tell me about an example when you…', or 'How did you …'. Remember, all the assessors' questions should be based upon the examples that you provide in your level 2 write-up for this competency in your summary of experience, rather than being hypothetical or general. However, assessors may also ask for more examples of valuations that you have carried out, especially if they want additional evidence of your practical experience.

How Can You Demonstrate Level 1?

Although the assessors will focus on your highest level, as is apparent from the examples above, candidates may be asked some level 1 questions, focussing on the knowledge behind the practical level 2 (and potentially level 3) examples. The Residential pathway guide states that valuation at level 1 requires candidates to demonstrate their knowledge and understanding of valuation purposes, methods and techniques, standards, and guidance; and any relevant statutory or mandatory requirements for valuation work in the candidate's area of practice. A full list of examples of knowledge comprised within level 1 Valuation is contained in the 2024 Residential pathway guide, and includes:

- Relevant professional standards and guidance;
- Valuation purposes;
- Factors impacting on value;
- The main principles of property law, and planning and other regulations that may affect value.[13]

An example submission at level 1 could include:

I understand that valuations are carried out for a range of purposes, e.g., loan security, purchase, lease extension, and taxation. I am familiar with RICS Valuation – Global Standards 2022 and the UK National Supplement. For example, I understand that PS1 and PS2 and VPS 1–5 are mandatory, with exceptions to VPS, such as internal purpose valuations. I am familiar with the five valuation methods, particularly the comparative method, through my practical experience and CPD.

The following are examples of level 1 questions:

- How is marriage value calculated?
- What is an assumption?
- How does a special assumption differ from an assumption?
- Tell me about PS1/PS2 of the Red Book.
- Give me an example of an exception to VPS 1–5.
- How can yield be used to calculate value?
- What should a valuer do in cases of material valuation uncertainty?
- Which part of the Red Book relates to material valuation uncertainty?
- Give me an example of valuation case law.

Awareness of 'hot topics' and factors affecting the market and value are also required so it is important to keep up to date with news and developments relevant to the Valuation competency. One way of enhancing your level 1 knowledge and understanding is to explain how you gained your knowledge. As with other competencies, this can be through continuing professional development (CPD), through your studies during a degree, and through work experience such as secondments or shadowing a colleague. Think about your CPD; does any of your CPD relate to the Valuation competency? Perhaps, for example, you have spent time reading and making notes on the Red Book that could be logged as informal CPD. Candidates' CPD logs are available to assessors and they can question candidates on this, so logging relevant CPD can support your submission.

Conclusion

It is important that candidates (especially at level 3) understand and have experience of a range of valuation purposes and, ideally, methods, combined with suitable knowledge of building construction and defects, and of other factors that affect value. Valuation is a key part of many surveyors' roles but for some candidates it may be a challenging competency, so it is one to prioritise when preparing for the APC. This is especially the case if Valuation is selected to level 3. Candidates must select the level that they can achieve and demonstrate with confidence, having regard to their role and ambitions.

Reference List

1 RICS (2024) *Valuation approach for properties in residential buildings with cladding* [Online] Available at: https://www.rics.org/profession-standards/rics-standards-and-guidance/sector-standards/valuation-standards/valuation-approach-for-properties-in-residential-builings-with-cladding (Accessed 19 August 2024).

2 RICS (2021) *Valuation of properties in multi-storey, multi-occupancy residential buildings with cladding UK 1st Edition* [Online] Available at: https://www.rics.org/profession-standards/rics-standards-and-guidance/sector-standards/valuation-standards/valuation-of-properties-in-multi-storey-multi-occupancy-residential-buildings-with-cladding (Accessed 19 August 2024).

3 Wilson W (2023) *The cladding external wall system (EWS)* House of Commons Library [Online] Available at: https://commonslibrary.parliament.uk/the-external-wall-fire-review-process-ews/ Contains Parliamentary information licensed under the Open Parliament Licence v3.0 Available

at: https://www.parliment.uk/site-information/copyright-parliament/open-parliament-licence/ (Accessed 19 August 2024).

4 RICS (2022) Appendix A: concerns about valuations version 1 [Online] Available at: https://www.rics.org/content/dam/ricsglobal/documents/standards/2022_Februry_Appendix_A_Concerns_About_Valuations_Version_1.pdf (Accessed 12 March 2025).

5 RICS (2021) *Risk, liability and insurance UK* 1st Edition [Online] Available at: https://www.rics.org/profession-standards/rics-standards-and-guidance/conduct-competence/risk-liability-and-insurance (Accessed 26 August 2024).

6 Cousins S (2022) *Valuation: green premium vs brown discount* RICS Modus [Online] Available at: https://ww3.rics.org/uk/en/modus/built-environment/homes-and-communities/home-valuation-green-initiatives-residential.html (Accessed 19 August 2024).

7 Cousins S (2022) *Valuation: green premium vs brown discount* RICS Modus [Online] Available at: https://ww3.rics.org/uk/en/modus/built-environment/homes-and-communities/home-valuation-green-initiatives-residential.html (Accessed 19 August 2024).

8 RICS (2021) *RICS valuation – global standards* [Online] Available at: https://www.rics.org/profession-standards/rics-standards-and-guidance/sector-standards/valuation-standards/red-book/red-book-global (Accessed 26 August 2024).

9 RICS (2021) *RICS valuation – global standards* [Online] Available at: https://www.rics.org/profession-standards/rics-standards-and-guidance/sector-standards/valuation-standards/red-book/red-book-global (Accessed 26 August 2024).

10 RICS (2021) *RICS valuation – global standards* [Online] Available at: https://www.rics.org/profession-standards/rics-standards-and-guidance/sector-standards/valuation-standards/red-book/red-book-global (Accessed 26 August 2024).

11 RICS (2024) *Red book global standards* Available at: https://www.rics.org/profession-standards/rics-standards-and-guidance/sector-standards/valuation-standards/red-book/red-book-global (Accessed 22 July 2024).

12 RICS (2024) *Residential pathway guide* [Online] Available at: https://www.rics.org/join-rics/sector-pathways (Accessed 26 August 2024).

13 RICS (2024) *Residential pathway guide* [Online] Available at: https://www.rics.org/join-rics/sector-pathways (Accessed 26 August 2024).

Further Reading and Resources

Cousins S (2022) *Valuation: green premium vs brown discount* RICS Modus [Online] Available at: https://ww3.rics.org/uk/en/modus/built-environment/homes-and-communities/home-valuation-green-initiatives-residential.html (Accessed 19 August 2024).

Home Office (2023) *Fire Safety Act 2021 factsheet: information for lenders* Policy Paper [Online] Available at: https://www.gov.uk/government/publications/fire-safety-act-2021/fire-safety-act-2021-factsheet-information-for-lenders (Accessed 17 August 2024).

Homes England (2024) *Cladding safety scheme overview* [Online] Available at: https://www.gov.uk/government/publications/cladding-safety-scheme/cladding-safety-scheme-overview (Accessed 19 August 2024).

International Valuation Standards Council (2021) *International valuation standards effective 31 January 2022* London: International Valuation Standards Council [Online] Available at: https://www.rics.org/profession-standards/rics-standards-and-guidance/sector-standards/valuation-standards/red-book/international-valuation-standards (Accessed 20 December 2023).

Leasehold Advisory Service (no date) *Do I qualify for protection from paying to fix my building's safety defects?* [Online] Available at: https://www.lease-advice.org/faq/what-is-a-qualifying-leaseholder-for-leaseholder-protections/ (Accessed 19 August 2024).

Lemen J (2021) *Hot topic highlight – valuation duty of care case law* Property Elite Blog & Podcast [Online] Available at: https://www.property-elite.co.uk/post/hot-topic-highlight-valuation-duty-of-care-caselaw (Accessed 16 December 2023).

Lemen J (2021) *Hot topic highlight – RICS automated valuation models roadmap* Property Elite Blog & Podcast [Online] Available at: https://www.property-elite.co.uk/post/hot-topic-highlight-rics-automated-valuation-models-roadmap (Accessed 21 December 2023).

Lemen J (2022) An A-Z of red book for APC *Property Journal RICS* [Online] Available at: https://ww3.rics.org/uk/en/journals/property-journal/red-book-valuation-apc-requirements.html (Accessed 17 December 2023).

Lemen J (2023) *Hot topic highlight – RICS guidance note risk, liability and insurance* 1st Edition Property Elite Blog & Podcast [Online] Available at: https://www.property-elite.co.uk/post/hot-topic-highlight-rics-guidance-note-risk-liability-and-insurance-1st-edition (Accessed 16 August 2024).

Lemen J (2023) *Hot topic highlight – 2023 UK national supplement to the Red Book Global* Property Elite Blog & Podcast [Online] Available at: https://www.property-elite.co.uk/post/uk-national-supplement (Accessed 22 December 2023).

Lemen J (2023) *Hot topic highlight – Valuation approach for multi-storey residential buildings with cladding* Property Elite Blog & Podcast [Online] Available at: https://www.property-elite.co.uk/post/hot-topic-highlight-valuation-approach-for-multi-storey-residential-buildings-with-cladding (Accessed 17 January 2024).

Lemen J (2023) *Hot topic highlight – UK VPGA 11 valuation of UK residential property* Property Elite Blog & Podcast [Online] Available at: https://www.property-elite.co.uk/post/uk-vpga-11 (Accessed 17 January 2024).

Property Elite Blogs: https://www.property-elite.co.uk/blog.

RICS (no date) *Best practice for registered valuers* [Online] Available at: https://www.rics.org/regulation/regulatory-schemes/valuer-registration/best-practice-for-registered-valuers (Accessed 20 August 2024).

RICS (no date) *Valuation standards* [Online] Available at: https://www.rics.org/profession-standards/rics-standards-and-guidance/sector-standards/valuation-standards (Accessed 20 August 2024).

RICS (no date) *Valuer registration* [Online] Available at: https://www.rics.org/regulation/regulatory-schemes/valuer-registration (Accessed 20 August 2024).

RICS (2021) *Automated valuation models roadmap for RICS members and stakeholders* [Online] Available at: https://www.rics.org/profession-standards/rics-standards-and-guidance/sector-standards/valuation-standards/automated-valuation-models (Accessed 21 December 2023).

RICS (2022) *Automated valuation models (AVMs): implications for the profession and their clients* Insight Paper [Online] Available at: https://www.rics.org/profession-standards/rics-standards-and-guidance/sector-standards/valuation-standards/automated-valuation-models-avms-implications-for-the-profession-and-their-clients (Accessed 21 December 2023).

RICS (2022) *Appendix A: concerns about valuations version 1* [Online] Available at: https://www.rics.org/content/dam/ricsglobal/documents/standards/2022_Februry_Appendix_A_Concerns_About_Valuations_Version_1.pdf (Accessed 16 August 2024).

RICS (2024) *Fire safety cladding external wall system (EWS) FAQs* [Online] Available at: https://www.rics.org/news-insights/current-topics-campaigns/fire-safety/cladding-external-wall-system-ews-faqs (Accessed 17 August 2024).

RICS (2024) *Fire safety* [Online] Available at: https://www.rics.org/news-insights/current-topics-campaigns/fire-safety (Accessed 17 August 2024).

RICS (2024) *Red book global standards* [Online] Available at: https://www.rics.org/profession-standards/rics-standards-and-guidance/sector-standards/valuation-standards/red-book/red-book-global (Accessed 22 July 2024).

RICS (2024) *Red book UK national supplement* [Online] Available at: https://www.rics.org/profession-standards/rics-standards-and-guidance/sector-standards/valuation-standards/red-book/red-book-uk (Accessed 22 July 2024).

RICS (2024) *Valuation approach for properties in residential buildings with cladding* [Online] Available at: https://www.rics.org/profession-standards/rics-standards-and-guidance/sector-standards/valuation-standards/valuation-approach-for-properties-in-residential-buildings-with- (Accessed 19 August 2024).

RICS (2024) *Valuation of properties in multi-storey, multi-occupancy residential buildings with cladding* [Online] Available at: https://www.rics.org/profession-standards/rics-standards-and-guidance/sector-standards/valuation-standards/valuation-of-properties-in-multi-storey-multi-occupancy-residential-buildings-with-cladding (Accessed 19 August 2024). This link includes useful case studies on EWS1 forms.

Thakrar P, Lewis J (2023) Five considerations for valuers to reduce claims risk *Property Journal RICS* [Online] Available at: https://ww3.rics.org/uk/en/journals/property-journal/considerations-valuers-claims-risk.html (Accessed 17 December 2023).

Wilcox J, Forsyth J (2022) Chapter 11 Real estate valuation concepts and Chapter 12 Real estate valuation methods. In *Real estate – the basics* Abingdon: Routledge.

5 Loan Security Valuation

Introduction

Loan Security Valuation is an optional technical RICS APC competency, which can be selected to either level 2 or level 3 for Residential pathway candidates. However, as an optional competency, candidates do not have to select it if they do not wish to do so.

The RICS pathway guide sets out the relevant knowledge (level 1), practical application (level 2), and reasoned advice (level 3) for this competency. However, as with all competencies, candidates do not need to have encountered everything listed, as this will depend on their experience and role. Candidates who regularly carry out valuations for lenders are likely to find that this competency complements the Valuation competency. As with the Valuation competency, Loan Security Valuation should be read in tandem with other competencies, such as Health and Safety, Data Management, Landlord and Tenant, Building Pathology, and Purchase and Sale (depending on the candidate's experience and role).

This chapter will explain what candidates should know in relation to Loan Security Valuation, covering the main requirements of level 1, with guidance on levels 2 and 3. You should also refer to Chapter 4 'Valuation', as much of the advice, knowledge, experience, and professional standards and guidance outlined in Chapter 4 will also apply to this chapter.

Should You Select This Competency?

As an optional technical competency, candidates can select Loan Security Valuation as one of their competencies, either to level 2 or level 3 if they wish to do so. Candidates with experience of valuing for loan

DOI: 10.1201/9781032705095-5

security purposes are likely to find that this competency supports and enhances the Valuation competency, particularly helpful if selecting Valuation to level 3 to obtain Registered Valuer status.

As with all competencies, check the pathway guide carefully and think about loan security valuations that you have carried out. In relation to each, think about the instruction: how did you carry out your loan security valuation and what issues did you observe? What were the lender guidelines, how did you ensure compliance with them, did you encounter any potential breaches of the lender's guidelines, have you encountered any instances of potential fraud? This will help you to decide whether to choose level 2 or level 3.

The pathway guide outlines the requirements of each level and the sections later in this chapter will help to identify suitable examples for each level. However, in brief, for level 2, candidates must provide examples of loan security valuations carried out, with brief explanations of how they were carried out.

Level 3 is more in depth, with reasoned advice. For example, did the loan security valuation identify potential breach of the lender's requirements? If you can provide specific examples of reasoned advice to a client, consider selecting the competency to level 3 particularly if you have also selected Valuation to level 3 as the two competencies are complementary.

Loan Security Valuation Skills

Loan security valuations are carried out to help a lender to decide whether to lend money to a borrower. The lender needs to manage their risk, so they need to know the value of the property to decide how much money the lender can safely secure against it. If the borrower defaults in their repayments, the lender needs to be confident that they could repossess and sell the property and that its value would cover the amount of the loan. RICS members carrying out loan security valuations need to comply with both the Red Book (Global and UK National Supplement) and lender guidelines.

It is useful to understand some basic terminology and concepts. Despite the common usage of the word 'mortgage' to refer to the money lent to a borrower, the legal position differs:

- **Mortgage**: This is the interest in a property given by an owner (the borrower) to a lender in return for a loan. The mortgage must usually be created in a type of document called a deed and it must be registered at HM Land Registry. Strictly, the mortgage is not, therefore, the loan but the interest in the land.

- **Mortgagor**: The borrower ('mortgag**or**' denotes the 'giver' of the interest).
- **Mortgagee**: The lender ('mortgag**ee**' denotes the recipient of the interest in the land).
- **Mortgage fraud**: This can take various forms, for example:

  - Forged signatures;
  - Locks on bedroom doors in a family home (this could indicate a multi-occupancy rental property);
  - Unexpected occupants (again, this could indicate a rental property rather than an owner-occupied home).

- **Instalment mortgage**: The loan is repaid by instalments over a period of time.
- **Standing mortgage**: The capital loan is repaid in one single payment at the end of the term, with regular interest payments.
- A '**charge**' is another word for a mortgage.
- **Security**: The mortgagee (the lender) usually has the right to take possession of the property and to sell it at the market value at the time of sale if the mortgagor (the borrower) defaults. This right provides the lender with security in return for the loan.
- **Equity**: The difference between the amount of the loan and the value of the property is known as the equity. Usually, as a borrower repays their loan and/or the value of the property increases over time, the amount of equity in the property will increase. This is because the proportion of the loan in relation to the value of the property will decrease. For example, if a property is valued at £200,000, the borrower pays a 10% deposit of £20,000 and borrows the remaining £180,000, the equity at that date will be £20,000. If, in two years' time, the borrower repays £10,000 of the loan capital, and the property value increases to £220,000, the equity will be £50,000 (£20,000 deposit plus £10,000 loan reduction, plus £20,000 increase in value).
- **Negative equity**: Property prices can fall as well as increase, so negative equity can be a very real concern. If a property value drops, the sale proceeds may be insufficient to repay the loan should the mortgagor decide to sell (the mortgagor – borrower – would usually

repay the loan from the sale proceeds), or if the mortgagee needs to repossess and sell to cover arrears. For this reason, it is extremely important that the loan security valuation is accurate; essentially, the client lender will need to know that the value of the property will cover the value of the loan.

- **Loan to Value (LTV)**: The ratio of the loan to the value of the property, expressed as a percentage. For example, if a mortgagor borrows £375,000 and the value of the property offered as security is £500,000, the LTV will be 75%. In this example, the mortgagee (lender) lends the mortgagor (borrower) 75% of the value of the property. The remaining 25% of the purchase price will be funded by the borrower, as a deposit. The higher the percentage LTV, the higher the risk to the lender, because, for example, if values drop, it is more likely that this will result in negative equity and the value of the property if sold will be insufficient to repay the mortgage. The risk arising from a high LTV ratio of 90% or 95% is also likely to be reflected in a reduced choice of mortgage products and higher interest rates.
- **Remortgage**: The purpose of many residential loans will be to fund the purchase of a home, or a buy-to-let investment. However, some candidates may have experience of valuing for remortgage purposes. If a borrower is remortgaging, the borrower already owns the property and has decided to release funds by offering the property as security once again. The borrower can do this by, for example, using increased equity in the property as security for further borrowing (perhaps because the value has increased), or by taking out a new loan on different terms; the new loan is used to repay the original loan at a lower interest rate.
- **Nil value**: This does not mean that the property is worthless. A valuer may value a property at nil to comply with a lender's criteria; e.g., structural problems can result in a nil value for lending purposes.

As mentioned, loan security valuation is closely linked to the Valuation competency and this chapter does not repeat the contents of Chapter 4. It is very important to refer to both chapters and to the suggested sources and reading if selecting Loan Security Valuation as an optional competency. This is particularly the case with the duty of care, risk, and liability aspects outlined in Chapter 4, as loan security valuations can carry a relatively high risk of a negligence claim, especially in an uncertain property market. A key distinction between the two competencies is that Valuation is a general competency, covering valuations for different purposes (which can include loan security valuations), whereas Loan Security Valuation is specialised, and needs to consider lender guidelines and requirements, the financial risk to the lender, and the risk of mortgage fraud.

Mortgages are a financial product so candidates should be aware of economic and other factors affecting the market for secured loans. For example, unemployment rates, inflation, interest rates, and local, regional, and global events can all affect the availability of, and market for, loans. Current lender policies reflect a more cautious approach to secured lending since 2008 when defaulting higher-risk borrowers destabilised lender institutions (with some collapsing altogether) resulting in a global financial crisis.

Candidates should review and ensure that they are familiar with RICS standards and guidance, their firm's procedures, and lender requirements regarding key issues including:

- Conflicts of interest;
- Client due diligence;
- Risk analysis and management, e.g., credit scoring;
- Mortgage fraud.

VPGA 2 of the 2022 Global Red Book provides advice on the valuation of interests for secured lending and all candidates selecting this competency should be familiar with it. The guidance in VPGA 2 covers some key points such as independence and conflicts of interest, terms of engagement, basis of value, and special assumptions, reporting, and disclosures. These are not set out in detail here as it is important to read the original document and to check the 2024, and future, updates.

Candidates selecting Loan Security Valuation should also understand UK VPGAs 11, 12, and 13 of the 2017 Red Book UK National Supplement, which will apply to examples during the currency of this version of the National Supplement. UK VPGA 11 includes a useful list of supporting RICS valuation guidance. Candidates who value registered social housing should also be familiar with UK VPGA 14. Valuations carried out following the date the 2023 UK National Supplement becomes effective will need to comply with this. In the 2023 Supplement UK VPGAs 12 and 13 have been merged into UK VPGA 11. UK

VPGA 14 relates to the valuation of registered social housing for loan security purposes, so as with the 2017 edition, it is important that you are aware of this if you undertake this type of valuation.

RICS Professional Standards and Practice Information

This list of RICS Professional Standards and Practice Information relevant to the Loan Security Valuation competency is not exhaustive, and it will be subject to change as the RICS updates its publications and processes. However, it should be a helpful indication of the relevant documentation. It is important to check for further standards and information relevant to your role, and for updates to those listed below. Remember that your examples in your summary of experience will need to reflect and apply the standards and guidance at the time the example valuation was carried out. UK VPGA 11 of the Red Book UK National Supplement also contains a useful list of supporting RICS guidance.

Publications include:

- Bank lending valuations and mortgage lending value Europe, 1st edition, 2018;
- Comparable evidence in real estate valuation, 1st edition, 2019 (reissued as a professional standard in 2023);
- Conflicts of interest Global, 1st edition, 2017;
- RICS Valuation – Global Standards 2022 (the Red Book) and the updated version expected to take effect on 31st January 2025;
- RICS Valuation – Global Standards: UK National Supplement, 2023 (see also 2017 UK National Supplement);
- Risk, liability and insurance UK, 1st edition, 2021;
- Valuation of individual new-build homes, 3rd edition 2019;
- Valuation of residential leasehold properties for secured lending purposes England and Wales, 1st edition, 2021;
- Valuing residential property purpose built for renting England, Scotland and Wales, 1st edition, 2018.

How Can You Demonstrate Level 3?

Your assessors will start at the highest level you have declared, which will be either level 2 or level 3. Check the pathway guide carefully and think about whether you can provide your own examples to reflect the examples given in the guide. The guide is not exhaustive, and you do not have to provide an example of each bullet-point, but the guide does provide a useful indication of the type of knowledge and experience that you need to demonstrate. Level 3 requires the provision of complex reasoned quantitative valuation advice to a client. The complex reasoning necessary for this level can include, for example, SWOT analysis, comments on the market and on performance of the investment, with recommendations on mitigating risk.[1] Level 3 therefore requires a deeper level of understanding than is needed at level 2.

Examples of the type of level 3 experience that would typically be included in a summary of experience are:

*At **(example)** I was instructed by the lender to value for a home-owner mortgage. The borrower was present during the valuation and mentioned their plans to let the property. I checked lender guidelines and submitted a suspicious activity report to the lender regarding the potentially fraudulent activity.*

Sample questions on this example include:

- Talk me through your advice to the lender.
- Why were you concerned that the borrower was not intending to occupy the property?
- How did you identify the suspicious activity?
- What information did you provide in the suspicious activity report?
- Why was the borrower's intended use of the property relevant?
- How did you ensure that you met lender guidelines?

*At **(example)** I valued a flat above a town centre 'take-away' shop for secured lending purposes. I identified that the ground floor commercial use included late-evening and weekend opening hours. I checked lender guidelines, which stipulated that properties above commercial premises could be acceptable provided there was a suitable market for resale. I advised that due to the location and resulting noise and nuisance, and the lack of evidence of demand on resale, the property was not suitable security.*

Sample questions on this example include:

- Describe the property to me.
- How did you identify the potential noise and nuisance?
- Talk me through the relevant lender guidelines.

- How did you research the potential demand for the property?
- Talk me through your advice to the lender.

*At (**example**) my lender client requested market value and market rent valuations of a two-bedroom terraced house for buy-to-let purposes. The property was unoccupied on the valuation date and had a very dated interior. I used the comparable method for both valuations and extended my search area due to a shortage of sales comparable evidence. I provided a SWOT analysis to assist my client in managing its risk. I advised that updating the interior would improve the marketability, the market value, and the market rent. This would help to reduce the risk posed from competing properties in the local rental market. I provided my opinions of value and recommended that the property provided suitable loan security.*

Sample questions on this example include:

- Talk me through your advice to the client.
- Why did you advise that the property was suitable loan security?
- How did you comply with your client's instructions/guidance?
- How did you address the shortage of sales comparable evidence?
- Describe the rental market conditions.
- What is a SWOT analysis?
- Talk me through your SWOT analysis.
- What were the strengths/weaknesses/opportunities/threats?
- What advice did you give to the client to mitigate risk?
- Talk me through your sales/rental comparable evidence analysis.

How Can You Demonstrate Level 2?

Level 2 Loan Security Valuation is about evidencing the ability to value for loan security purposes, including the application of the Red Book and lender requirements, incorporating research into factors affecting lender risk. Candidates also need to be able to identify factors affecting borrowers' ability to obtain finance.[2]

Examples of the type of level 2 experience that would typically be included in a summary of experience are:

*At (**example**) I valued a flat for loan security purposes. Information on the lease term was unavailable so I assumed an unexpired lease term of 85 years, with no action being taken to acquire the freehold or extend the lease term. In doing so, I complied with the Red Book UK*

National Supplement 2017 UK VPGA 11 and Valuation of residential leasehold properties for secured lending purposes, 1st edition, 2021.
Sample questions on this example include:

- Why did you assume an unexpired lease term of 85 years?
- What is the significance of there being no attempt to extend the lease or acquire the freehold?
- What is marriage value?
- When is marriage value payable?
- What enquiries did you make regarding the actual unexpired lease term?
- What was the lender's requirement regarding unexpired lease terms?

*At (**example**) I valued a large four-bedroom house in a rural location. The comparable evidence within the vicinity was very limited. I considered lender guidelines and extended the search area to include local villages and identified three suitable comparable properties. I analysed the comparable properties using a comparable matrix and adjusted to reflect size, location, and condition. I reported on my opinion of market value and confirmed that the subject property was suitable loan security.*
Sample questions on this example include:

- Talk me through your comparable evidence search parameters.
- How did you comply with Comparable evidence in real estate valuation, 1st edition, 2019?
- How did you identify suitable comparable evidence?
- What search radius did you use?
- How did you adjust to reflect size/location/condition?
- Briefly talk me through the relevant lender guidelines.

*At (**example**) I valued a semi-detached house for loan security purposes. At the valuation date the property was let to a tenant. The borrower was intending to occupy the property as their family home. I made enquiries of the agent and was advised that the tenant intended to vacate, and the sale was with vacant possession. I applied a special assumption of vacant possession, having agreed this with my lender client. I researched comparable evidence and analysed this in a comparable evidence matrix to reach my opinion of value with and without the special assumption.*

Sample questions on this example include:

- To whom did you owe a duty of care?
- What is a special assumption?
- Why did you apply the special assumption?
- Was there a material difference between the value with and without the special assumption?
- What was the difference between the value with and without the special assumption?
- Which parts of the Red Book applied to this instruction?
- Talk me through your report to your client.
- How did you ascertain that the tenant intended to vacate?

*At (**example**) the borrower asked me to increase my opinion of market value so that they could potentially borrow more money from my lender client. I politely declined and advised that I could only provide my objective, independent opinion of value in accordance with RICS requirements. I also notified my client lender and submitted a suspicious activity report.*

Sample questions on this example include (note: this example could also be used in the mandatory Ethics, Rules of Conduct, and Professionalism competency):

- Talk me through your report to the client.
- How did you respond to the borrower's request?
- Talk me through your valuation.
- Explain the ethical issues the borrower's request presented.

Remember, all the assessors' questions should be based upon the examples that you provide in your write-up for this competency in your summary of experience – rather than being hypothetical or general. However, assessors may also ask for more examples of loan security valuations that you have carried out, especially if they want additional evidence of your practical experience.

How Can You Demonstrate Level 1?

Although the assessors will focus on your highest level, you may be asked some level 1 questions, focussing on the knowledge behind your practical level 2 (and potentially level 3) examples. Level 1 requires you to demonstrate your knowledge and understanding of the financial market and debt finance, and how this relates to valuation advice.[3] In addition to RICS publications, it is important to have a thorough knowledge of relevant law, for example, duty of care case law. Be aware of other sources of information and updates; suggested resources are listed at the end of this chapter. It is, of course, also important to monitor updates to RICS publications.

One way of enhancing your level 1 knowledge and understanding is to explain how you gained your knowledge. This can be through continuing professional development (CPD; formal or informal), through your studies during a degree, and through work experience such as shadowing a colleague. Think about your CPD; does any of your CPD relate in the Loan Security Valuation competency? Perhaps, for example, you have spent time reading and making notes on loan security valuations that could be logged as informal CPD. Candidates' CPD logs are available to assessors and they can question candidates on this, so logging relevant CPD can support your submission.

A full list of examples of knowledge comprised within level 1 Loan Security Valuation is contained in the Residential Pathway Guide, and includes:

- Relevant financial products;
- Negligence and duty of care case law;
- Conflict of interest procedures;
- Sources of risk and lenders' risk analysis techniques;
- Sources and reporting of potential fraud or criminal activity.[4]

The following illustrates the type of level 1 knowledge that would typically be included in a summary of experience:

I am aware of the risks of mortgage fraud and the need to report suspected fraud to lender clients. I understand that loan security valuations must comply with lender guidelines, RICS Valuation – Global Standards (the Red Book), and the UK National Supplement. I am familiar with VPGA 2 of the Red Book and UK VPGA 11, and I understand valuers' duty of care case law, e.g., Smith v Bush.

Sample questions on this example include:

- Give me some examples of mortgage fraud.
- What should you do if you identify potential mortgage fraud?
- What is a valuer's role in managing risk to lenders?
- Which parts of the Red Book relate to Loan Security Valuation?

- What types of property might be unsuitable for loan security purposes?
- What is your duty of care when acting for a lender in a valuation for buy-to-let/owner-occupier purposes?
- What types of mortgage products are you aware of?
- How do lenders manage risk?

Conclusion

Loan Security Valuation is one of the competencies most closely associated with risk management. In addition to valuation skills, it requires awareness of the property and financial markets, and the ability to comply with practice and lender guidelines. Candidates with experience of loan security valuation should find that it complements the Valuation competency, potentially enabling them to demonstrate further knowledge and experience to support level 3 Valuation to become RICS Registered Valuers.

Reference List

1 RICS (2024) *Residential pathway guide* [Online] Available at: https://www.rics.org/join-rics/sector-pathways (Accessed 26 August 2024).
2 RICS (2024) *Residential pathway guide* [Online] Available at: https://www.rics.org/join-rics/sector-pathways (Accessed 26 August 2024).
3 RICS (2024) *Residential pathway guide* London: RICS.
   RICS (2024) *Residential pathway guide* [Online] Available at: https://www.rics.org/join-rics/sector-pathways (Accessed 26 August 2024).
4 RICS (2024) *Residential pathway guide* [Online] Available at: https://www.rics.org/join-rics/sector-pathways (Accessed 26 August 2024).

Further Reading and Resources

Heming T (2023) *Mortgage loan-to-value ratios* Online Money Supermarket [Online] Available at: https://www.moneysupermarket.com/mortgages/loan-to-value-ratio-explained/#:~:text=As%20a%20general%20rule%20of,paying%20much%20more%20on%20interest (Accessed 12 January 2024).
National Crime Agency (no date) *Suspicious activity reports* [Online] Available at: https://www.nationalcrimeagency.gov.uk/what-we-do/crime-threats/money-laundering-and-illicit-finance/suspicious-activity-reports (Accessed 20 August 2024).
RICS (no date) *Best practice for registered valuers* [Online] Available at: https://www.rics.org/regulation/regulatory-schemes/valuer-registration/best-practice-for-registered-valuers (Accessed 20 August 2024).

RICS (no date) *Residential valuations* [Online] Available at: https://www.rics.org/profession-standards/rics-standards-and-guidance/sector-standards/valuation-standards/residential-valuations [Accessed 20 August 2024).

RICS (no date) *Valuer registration* [Online] Available at: https://www.rics.org/regulation/regulatory-schemes/valuer-registration (Accessed 20 August 2024).

RICS (no date) *Valuation standards* [Online] Available at: https://www.rics.org/profession-standards/rics-standards-and-guidance/sector-standards/valuation-standards (Accessed 20 August 2024).

Todd S (2021) Getting secured lending valuations right *Property Journal* [Online] RICS Available at: https://ww3.rics.org/uk/en/journals/property-journal/getting-secured-lending-valuations-right.html (Accessed 17 January 2024).

StudySmarter (no date) *Understanding credit risk management* [Online] Available at: https://www.studysmarter.co.uk/explanations/macroeconomics/economics-of-money/credit-risk-management/ (Accessed 17 January 2024).

Taylor K (2018) *APC: loan security valuation loan working* isurv [Online] RICS Available at: https://www.isurv.com/info/390/features_archive/11780/apc_loan_security_valuation (Accessed 3 January 2024).

Thakrar, Lewis J (2023) Five considerations for valuers to reduce claims risk *Property Journal* [Online] RICS Available at: https://ww3.rics.org/uk/en/journals/property-journal/considerations-valuers-claims-risk.html (Accessed 3 January 2024).

UK Finance (a range of mortgage-related content) Available at: https://www.ukfinance.org.uk/area-of-expertise/mortgages (Accessed 19 January 2024).

Which? (2024) *Mortgage advice guides* [Online] Available at: https://www.which.co.uk/money/mortgages-and-property/mortgages (Accessed 12 January 2024).

Wilcox J, Forsyth J (2022) *Real estate – the basics chapter 9 interests in real estate* (pp. 177–179) Abingdon: Routledge.

6 Purchase and Sale

Introduction

Purchase and Sale is a core technical RICS APC competency. It is not compulsory to pick Purchase and Sale, but if you do opt for Purchase and Sale, the competency can be declared to level 2 or level 3.

The RICS pathway guide sets out the relevant knowledge (level 1), practical application (level 2), and reasoned advice (level 3) for this competency. However, as with all competencies, you do not need to have encountered everything listed, as this will depend on your experience and role. The competency should be read in tandem with several other relevant competencies, such as Ethics, Rules of Conduct and Professionalism, Health and Safety, Communication and Negotiation, Data Management, Inspection, Measurement, Building Pathology, Market Appraisal, Valuation, and Loan Security Valuation.

Other competencies such as Landlord and Tenant and Sustainability may also be relevant. For example, a buyer may require vacant possession of a let property. Alternatively, an investor may purchase subject to a tenancy agreement. In another example, a high energy efficiency rating may enhance the value and market appeal of a property.

This chapter will explain what candidates should know in relation to Purchase and Sale, covering key requirements of level 1, with guidance on levels 2 and 3.

Should You Select This Competency?

As mentioned, candidates who opt for Purchase and Sale can choose whether to select the competency to level 2 or level 3.

Purchase and Sale is an important area of work for many surveyors in the agency sector, dealing with sales and acquisitions on behalf of clients,

DOI: 10.1201/9781032705095-6

or perhaps directly for their employers. Candidates considering this competency should check the pathway guide and think about transactions that they have been involved in, how they have marketed properties and negotiated sales, or why they have considered an acquisition if acting for a purchaser. Consider transactions that did not proceed smoothly; were negotiation or reasoned advice required? This will help decide whether to choose level 2 or level 3. For level 2, candidates must demonstrate the application of their knowledge and experience of a range of transactions. Level 3 is more in depth; if you can provide specific examples of reasoned advice in more complex or unusual transactions (for example, in relation to leasehold enfranchisement, or in the event of disputes between the parties), consider selecting the competency to level 3.

Purchase and Sale Skills

Candidates should be able to demonstrate knowledge, understanding, and experience of the fundamental aspects of estate agency and property transactions. A useful approach is to consider transactions from start to finish: what was your role; who were the stakeholders (in other words, who was involved in the transaction); what steps were required; and what compliance matters had to be addressed? Areas to cover include the following, but you may be able to think of more, for example, in relation to a particularly complex transaction:

Ethics

There is more information on ethics in the *Mandatory Competencies* book in this series, and in RICS Real estate agency and brokerage, 3rd edition, 2016 ('REAB 2016') and UK residential real estate agency, 6th edition, 2017 (the Blue Book). REAB 2016 is now archived but it is still useful, and referred to extensively in the Blue Book.

Duty of Care

General duties that apply to all competencies do, of course, apply to Purchase and Sale. The standard required is that of a reasonably competent and experienced real estate agency professional and the overarching duty is to act with reasonable care and skill in the best interests of the client. An agent's duty of care should also be considered specifically in relation to the Purchase and Sale competency and, for example, REAB 2016 provides specific instances, such as in relation to sub-agency.[1]

Conflicts of Interest

Conflicts of interest are again a general duty, but its application must be considered in relation to Purchase and Sale. Specific issues could include multiple agency, in which case the agent must pay equal respect to the client's interests.[2]

Discrimination

Agents have a duty not to discriminate unfairly against parties to a property transaction and it is useful to consider this in conjunction with vulnerable customers. For example, agents may need to set out necessary information without making assumptions about the degree of knowledge possessed by that person.[3] The Equality Act 2010 sets out protected characteristics and prohibits direct and indirect discrimination. However, the Equality Act does not prohibit age discrimination in relation to housing, so age restricted retirement housing is common, being a legitimate and proportionate measure.

Client Due Diligence

Before confirming instructions with a client, agents must understand for whom they are acting. This helps to avoid conflicts of interest, but – importantly – confirming a client's identity is also key to countering money laundering. This is a particular concern with the Purchase and Sale competency because real estate transactions and investment are recognised methods of laundering the proceeds of criminal activity so as to appear legitimate. Therefore, it is also important to check a purchaser's source of funds. There is specific RICS guidance on money laundering, with which candidates must be familiar (see 'Further Reading and Resources' at the end of this chapter).

Terms of Engagement

Candidates should familiarise themselves with their firm's agency terms of engagement, including complaints handling procedures and redress schemes, in addition to the terms of engagement sections of REAB 2016 and the Blue Book.

Terms of engagement ensure that both the agent and the client understand the scope and detail of the instruction from the outset. The terms should be considered in tandem with consumer protection legislation, and, under the Consumer Rights Act 2015, terms must be fair. Other relevant legislation includes the Consumer Contracts (Information, Cancellation and Additional Charges) Regulations 2013, which enable consumer clients to cancel agency agreements in certain circumstances.

A key matter for agreement between the agent and a seller client is the type of agency arrangement. This will depend on several factors, such as the type of property, the current market, and client objectives. Candidates need to understand the different types of agency agreement, their suitability, advantages, and disadvantages:

- Sole agency – one agent markets the property, and the agent is only paid if it introduces or negotiates with a purchaser;
- Sole selling rights – the agent is entitled to their fees during the period of the contract, whoever the property is sold to;
- Joint sole agency – two, or more, agents are appointed and share the fee regardless of which agent finds the buyer;
- Joint or multiple agency – two or more agents are appointed, with the fee paid to the one that finds the purchaser;
- Sub-agency – the agent, with the client's agreement, appoints a sub-agent to assist with the transaction. The sub-agent's contractual relationship is with the agent;
- Introductory fee arrangement – an agent who is aware of the property and of an interested purchaser may approach the seller to agree an introductory fee.[4]

The Glossary in the Blue Book provides clear definitions of types of agency agreement and all candidates should familiarise themselves with these.

Redress Schemes

Residential estate agents must join a redress scheme for dealing with complaints. This is otherwise known as an ombudsman scheme, offering independent investigation and determination of complaints. There are two authorised schemes:

- The Property Ombudsman;
- The Property Redress Scheme.

Sections 23A, 23B, and 23C of the Estate Agents Act 1979 apply here.

Marketing

Once again REAB 2016 and the Blue Book set out estate agents' legal obligations and best practice, and candidates selecting Purchase and Sale need to understand the key points, which include:

- Under the Estate Agents Act 1979, agents must explain the difference between a realistic selling price and the asking price and must not misrepresent a property's price.
- Agents must also make it clear that a market appraisal is advice on asking price, not a formal valuation.
- Before advising on asking price, agents must inspect the property and, if measuring, ensure that measurements are accurate and based on an appropriate measurement basis. Agents must also consider the property's condition, and any issues that may impact on the marketing strategy. Suitable comparable data should be obtained, and agents should take into account the current market. Market reports are available from the RICS and from some larger firms of surveyors (see the list of resources at the end of this chapter) and candidates should monitor these. Tenure and boundaries should also be checked,[5] for example, by checking HM Land Registry Title Plans.
- The Consumer Protection from Unfair Trading Regulations 2008 requires agents to disclose material information and to ensure property particulars are accurate. This includes, for example:

  - Physical characteristics of the property;
  - Council Tax;
  - Tenure;
  - Utilities;
  - Parking;
  - Broadband;
  - Other information, depending on the property and location, such as flood risk, easements, and estate rent charges.[6]

The National Trading Standards Estate and Letting Agency Team is a good source of information and has published guidance for estate agents – see the link at the end of this chapter. If you have access to isurv, there is also useful content on disclosure, misdescriptions, and misleading information:

- The Business Protection from Misleading Marketing Regulations 2008 prevent misleading marketing material aimed at business clients;

- The Misrepresentation Act 1967 – this short Act of Parliament covers, e.g., damages for misrepresentation, including for misrepresentation that is not fraudulent, i.e., innocent or negligent misrepresentation.

The Blue Book covers marketing strategy in detail, and it is essential that candidates check this properly and familiarise themselves with the contents. Some key matters to include are the recommended selling price, market analysis, advice on the likely timescale, viewing arrangements, and the method of sale. The latter is outlined further in the next section.

Other considerations include:

- Advertising boards – these are restricted to certain dimensions and positions specified in Schedule 3 of the Town & Country Planning (Control of Advertisements) (England) Regulations 2007.
- An Energy Performance Certificate (EPC) will need to be commissioned if one is not already available. There is no minimum EPC rating for a sale, but the rating needs to be displayed on the property advertisement. UK EPCs can be downloaded from the GOV.UK website and there is a link at the end of this chapter.

Methods of Sale

Candidates should be familiar with the nature, application, advantages, and disadvantages of each of the following methods of sale:

- Private treaty;
- Informal tender;
- Formal tender;
- Auction.

The methods are not considered in detail here, as there is ample material available – see 'Further Reading and Resources' at the end of this chapter. Surveyors must consider the circumstances and advise on the most appropriate method of sale. Factors to consider include the client's objectives (for example, does the client want a quick sale or is a long marketing period acceptable?), public accountability (for example, a charity or public body may need to demonstrate that the best price was obtained), and market conditions. Methods of sale may be combined in a transaction; for instance, a property is marketed for sale by private treaty, generating interest from potential buyers who are then invited to submit their informal tenders.

The Legal Conveyancing Process

The legal conveyancing process comprises the following main stages and features:

1 Pre-contract searches and enquiries – this can be a complex and protracted stage as detailed information is obtained from HM Land Registry, from the seller, and via searches and enquiries. Matters to investigate include ownership and rights, the extent of the property (boundaries, fixtures, and contents), planning permission and Building Regulation consents, access and mains services, lease details and leasehold management arrangements, and other matters such as Conservation Areas, Smoke Control Areas, and Tree Preservation Orders.

2 Exchange of contracts – this is the point at which the parties are committed to the transaction and the buyer acquires an interest in the property. Legal advisers will only proceed to exchange of contracts if they are instructed to do so and the buyer is satisfied with the outcome of the necessary investigations. The buyer pays their deposit, and the completion date will be agreed and inserted in the contract. If one party subsequently withdraws from the transaction, they are likely to be in breach of contract, with the associated legal implications.

3 Completion – the solicitors will date the signed transfer deed (usually an HM Land Registry form TR1) to complete the transaction. At this point the buyer will obtain keys and be able to either move in or receive rents. This is the stage at which the buyer will consider themselves to be the new owner, although the process of transferring ownership requires the fourth and final stage – registration.

4 Registration at HM Land Registry – the buyer's legal advisers will apply for registration of the buyer as the new registered proprietor, which finalises the transfer of ownership.

5 A basic awareness of the taxes payable on a sale or purchase can help candidates to demonstrate their understanding of the implications of a transaction for the parties involved. For example, executors may need to sell to pay Inheritance Tax, a seller may need to pay Capital Gains Tax, and purchases are usually subject to Stamp Duty Land Tax (SDLT). Legal advisers will usually pay the SDLT from funds received from the purchaser, and accountants and/or legal advisers may also be involved if Inheritance Tax or Capital Gains Tax is payable.

6 If the buyer or seller fails to complete the transaction in accordance with the contract, there will usually be remedies in the contract to

protect the other party. These can include damages, interest, forfeiture of the deposit (or return of the deposit if the seller is in breach), and rescission of the contract. You should check the Law Society's Standard Conditions of Sale; there is a link at the end of this chapter. In particular, be aware of:

- Section 6 of the '5th Edition – 2018 Revision' regarding notices to complete;
- Section 7, which provides for remedies for misleading or inaccurate information arising from errors or omissions, and for late completion.

Sales Progression

Candidates should consider the role of the surveyor during sales progression. An agent can help a transaction to proceed by liaising between the buyer and seller and their advisers. This can involve, for example, ensuring that memorandum of sale details are correct, providing access for surveys and further viewings, answering queries, and negotiating issues that arise during the conveyancing process. Surveyors in leasehold management roles may need to provide detailed information in a LPE1 form and provide ground rent and service charge details for apportionment between the buyer and the seller in the completion statement. Post completion, leasehold management surveyors may need to provide certificates of compliance with the alienation clauses in the lease before the buyer can be registered as the new proprietor at HM Land Registry.

Stakeholders

Candidates declaring Purchase and Sale as a technical competency will usually have experience of transactions relating to homeownership and buy-to-let investment. However, the residential sector is large, and you should be aware of the broad scope of the competency and the potential range of stakeholders and examples encountered in practice, e.g.:

- Buy-to-let investors may acquire just one asset, or they may seek advice on the larger-scale acquisition or disposal of a portfolio of assets.
- Housing can include:
  - Owner-occupation;

- Houses in multiple occupation (HMOs);
- Multi-generational homes, e.g., with annex(es);
- Homes with income-generating assets onsite such as a short-term/ holiday let;
- Live/work units (designed to combine residential space with workspace for residents);
- Retirement and sheltered housing;
- Cohousing units (for example, Postlip Hall in Gloucestershire – see the link at the end of the chapter).

You may be able to think of more examples of the different types of homes encountered by surveyors in practice.

- Buyers and sellers could include:
  - Individuals;
  - Limited companies;
  - Charities;
  - Developers (including build-to-rent developers);
  - Social housing providers;
  - Large institutions (e.g., pension funds);
  - Special purpose vehicles;
  - Trusts;
  - Real estate investment trusts (REITs).

Again, you may be able to think of more.

Some Important Concepts

From time-to-time agents may encounter legal terms, some of which are briefly explained in this section:

- An option is an agreement that a prospective purchaser can buy the property if they decide to do so, for example, within a specified period. If the buyer decides to buy, the seller must sell to that buyer.
- A pre-emption agreement is an agreement that a prospective purchaser will have a right of first refusal if the seller decides to sell.
- A conditional contract is a contract to buy and sell the property if a specific event occurs. A common example is the grant of planning permission; if planning permission is granted to meet the condition in the contract, the buyer and seller must proceed with the transaction.

- A lock-out agreement creates exclusivity for the buyer during a specified period; typically, the seller cannot market the property or negotiate with any other buyers during that time.
- An overage agreement is an agreement by a buyer to make an additional payment to the seller if a certain event occurs during a specified timescale. For example, if planning permission for development is obtained after the sale, the overage payment by the buyer to the seller will reflect the resulting uplift in the value of the property.
- Mortgages: many transactions are dependent on mortgage finance. Chapter 5 on the Loan Security Valuation competency contains further information.

It is also useful for candidates to be aware of some leaseholder rights, when acquiring or selling leaseholds or the freehold of blocks of flats. Some issues and rights directly affect the sale and purchase of leasehold properties, for example:

- The leaseholder's right to extend the lease under the Leasehold Reform, Housing and Urban Development Act 1993 (flats) and the Leasehold Reform Act 1967 (houses). Properties with short unexpired lease terms can be difficult to mortgage and sell and this can be reflected in a property's value. A buyer's offer is likely to reflect the unexpired lease term and may need to consider the cost of extending the lease. The buyer may also require the seller to start the lease extension process and assign their rights to the buyer.
- Leaseholders have a collective right to enfranchise (to buy the freehold of their building), under the Leasehold Reform, Housing and Urban Development Act 1993.
- Leaseholders in a block of flats also have a collective right of first refusal under the Landlord and Tenant Act 1987. This means that a landlord who wishes to sell a building containing flats may have to first offer the building to the leaseholders.
- These leaseholder rights are a complex and specialist area, but Purchase and Sale candidates should have a basic understanding of the main principles. At the time of writing in early 2024, an individual leaseholder's rights to extend the lease, and the collective right for leaseholders in a block to enfranchise were under review by the UK government and the Leasehold and Freehold Reform Act was passed in May 2024 (you should note that at the time of writing, much of this Act had not yet taken effect). The Act aims to make it easier and

cheaper for leaseholders to buy their freehold and extend their leases. It is also intended to encourage the adoption of commonhold as an alternative to leasehold. Candidates dealing with the purchase and sale of leasehold properties should keep up to date with political and legal developments, and with the commencement of this Act. The Leasehold Advisory Service is an excellent source of information on this topic and details are provided at the end of this chapter.

RICS Professional Standards and Practice Information

This list of RICS Professional Standards and Practice Information relevant to the Purchase and Sale competency is not exhaustive, and it will be subject to change as the RICS updates its publications and processes. However, it should be a helpful indication of the relevant documentation. It is important to check for further standards and information relevant to your role, and for updates to those listed below. Examples are:

- Auctioneers selling real estate (incorporating common auction conditions), 7th edition, 2018 (reissued 2023);
- Comparable evidence in real estate valuation, 1st edition, 2019;
- Conflicts of interest (Global), 1st edition, 2017;
- Countering bribery and corruption, money laundering and terrorist financing, 1st edition, 2019;
- Property agency and management principles, Global, 1st edition, 2024;
- RICS Real estate agency and brokerage (archived), 3rd edition, 2016;
- UK residential real estate agency, 6th edition, 2017 (the Blue Book).

At the time of writing in 2024, the RICS was consolidating its lettings, sales, and management agency standards and guidance. It is expected that Real estate agency and brokerage, 3rd edition, 2016 and UK residential real estate agency, 6th edition, 2017 and Real estate management 3rd edition 2016, will be superseded by new professional standards. There is a link to the relevant RICS page in the Further Reading and Resources section at the end of this chapter. It is very important that you keep up to date with changes to RICS publications. However, any publications superseded by the new professional standards will still be relevant if they applied at the date of your examples in your summary of experience, so you will need to be familiar with both the archived (e.g., REAB 2016), and new, consolidated documents.

Relevant Laws

This list is not exhaustive, but it indicates the laws that you should be aware of. It is important that you check the law relating to your specific location and area of practice and keep up to date with changes:

- Bribery Act 2010;
- Business Protection from Misleading Marketing Regulations 2008;
- Consumer Contracts (Information, Cancellation and Additional Charges) Regulations 2013;
- Consumer Protection from Unfair Trading Regulations 2008;
- Consumer Rights Act 2015;
- Consumers, Estate Agents and Redress Act 2007;
- Equality Act 2010;
- Estate Agents Act 1979;
- Estate Agents (Redress Scheme) Order 2008;
- Misrepresentation Act 1967;
- Unfair Contract Terms Act 1977;
- Town & Country Planning (Control of Advertisements) (England) Regulations 2007.

Other laws that underpin the legal process are:

- Law of Property Act 1925 – there are two legal tenures: freehold (including commonhold) and leasehold;
- Law of Property (Miscellaneous Provisions) Act 1989 – contracts for the sale of land need to be in writing, contain all the terms agreed between the parties, and be signed by all parties;
- Land Registration Act 2002 – this regulates the registration of land in England and Wales and provides that legal ownership transfers on registration of the buyer as the new registered proprietor.

The Estate Agents Act 1979 is particularly important and a good understanding of the Act is essential for all candidates selecting Purchase and Sale. This is not covered in detail here, as the key sections are referenced in the Blue Book and candidates should revise these thoroughly. Candidates should also be aware of the enforcement role provided by the National Trading Standards Estate and Letting Agency Team – the link is at the end of this chapter.

How Can You Demonstrate Level 3?

As with each competency, the examples in the RICS pathway guide are not prescriptive, so it is not necessary to have experience of each of the bullet-points listed in the guide; rather, these provide guidance on the nature of the professional knowledge and experience expected of a surveyor at the specified level. Your assessors will start at the highest level you have declared, which will be either level 2 or level 3. At level 3 RICS expects you to present specific examples of reasoned advice that you have provided to a client or your employer because of a purchase or sale, considering and explaining the options available, to demonstrate a deeper level of understanding than is needed at level 2. Check the pathway guide carefully and think about whether you can provide your own examples to reflect the examples given in the guide, remembering that you do not have to provide an example of each bullet-point.

Examples of the type of level 3 experience that would typically be included in a summary of experience are:

*At (**example**) I was instructed to sell a leasehold apartment with a short unexpired lease term of 50 years. I advised that this would affect the value and marketability of the apartment but that the seller would have the right to extend the lease under the Leasehold Reform, Housing and Urban Development Act 1993 as they had owned the property for more than two years. I recommended that the seller seek specialist advice on this. After receiving legal advice, the seller instructed my firm to value the property for lease extension purposes and duly served notice on the landlord. I then marketed the property and successfully negotiated a sale subject to assignment of the seller's notice under the Act.*

Questions relating to this example could include:

- Why did you recommend that the seller obtain specialist advice?
- Talk me through your advice to the seller.
- How would the short unexpired lease term potentially impact on value/marketability/saleability?
- Explain the seller's rights to extend the lease.
- What was the significance of the two-year period?

*At (**example**) I was approached by a seller who needed a quick sale of a period property affected by dry rot as they could not afford the remediation work. The property was in an area with strong rental demand and rising rents, although it was vacant at the time due to its condition. I considered the methods of sale and advised that auction would be the most suitable method, as the property would appeal to investors who may be less risk-adverse than the owner-occupier market, and auction would offer the certainty of a binding contract. The client accepted this advice, and the property was sold at auction to a buy-to-let cash buyer.*

Questions relating to this example could include:

- Talk me through your advice to sell at auction.
- Why did you recommend sale by auction?
- What were the risks/advantages/disadvantages associated with this method of sale?
- Talk me through your advice on buyer risk-aversion.
- What information was provided to prospective buyers?
- Why did you discount alternative methods of sale?

*At (**example**) I was instructed by executors regarding the probate sale of a luxury apartment in a desirable block. The executors wanted to maximise value for the beneficiaries but also needed a reasonably quick sale to enable them to wind-up the estate and minimise the running costs whilst vacant. Having reviewed the available comparable evidence in the block and the immediate vicinity, I advised the executors that there was a shortage of reliable comparable evidence due to the nature of the property. I therefore provided a best- and worst-case market appraisal having expanded the search area. I advised the executors that my firm had a database of potential buyers whom I could approach to ascertain the level of interest at £750,000, being the upper end of the price range. I advised that if there was no interest from the database at this price, I could advise further on marketing the property for the upper asking price, or on reducing the asking price to £695,000 to generate more interest on the open market in a different price bracket. Following my negotiations with buyers on my firm's database I ascertained that £750,000 was a realistic asking price but none of them wished to proceed. I advised that the property be marketed with an asking price of £750,000. The executors agreed a sale for £735,000 within a month of marketing, meeting the seller's objectives to achieve a suitable price for the property, within the desired timeframe.*

Questions relating to this example could include:

- Talk me through your advice to the client.
- How did you meet your client's objectives?
- Why did none of the buyers on your database wish to proceed?
- How did you research/analyse your comparable evidence?
- Why did you extend the search area?
- Why did you recommend approaching your firm's database of potential buyers first?
- What do you mean by a 'luxury' apartment?
- Why did you advise on best-case and worst-case asking prices?
- What were the benefits to the client of approaching your firm's database of potential buyers?

*At (**example**) the conveyancing chain collapsed pre-exchange of contracts, so my client's buyer was unable to proceed. I advised my client that the buyer was still interested in proceeding, but that she needed to find a new buyer for her property first. I recommended that I remain in contact with the buyer in case her circumstances changed, but that in the meantime, the property should be re-marketed. The market was slow and over the subsequent two-month marketing period no offers were received. The buyer then advised me that she had found a new buyer for her property, and she was now able to proceed again, but at a reduced price to reflect the reduced price she had received for her property. Having considered the very slow market and a drop in property prices, I advised my seller client that the reduced offer was the best price achievable, and I recommended that they should accept it. My client accepted the offer, and the transaction proceeded to completion.*

Questions relating to this example could include:

- Explain what happened when the chain collapsed.
- What do you mean by the chain collapsing?
- What is the significance of the purchaser withdrawing before exchange of contracts?
- Why did you advise that the property be remarketed?
- Why did you recommend that the seller accept the reduced offer?
- Talk me through the market conditions that informed your advice.
- How did you research the market?

*At (**example**) my firm acted on the sale of a terraced Victorian cottage. I recommended sale by private treaty as the market was strong* *and this would help to generate interest in the property. The property did generate a lot of enquiries, so I recommended changing to informal tender to encourage interested parties' best offers to conclude the transaction. I advised the seller on the offers received and on the preferred tender. The client accepted my advice and exchanged contracts with the buyer.*

Questions relating to this example could include:

- Why did you recommend private treaty initially?
- Why did you advise on changing to informal tender?
- What were the advantages of informal tender?
- Talk me through your advice on the tenders received.
- Tell me about the preferred offer.
- Why was this offer preferred to the others?

*At (**example**) the seller accepted the highest offer received by informal tender. However, this buyer subsequently withdrew their offer. I advised the clients to consider the other offers received to avoid extending the marketing period unnecessarily and I successfully negotiated the sale for the same value to another buyer.*

Questions on this example could include:

- Talk me through your advice to the client.
- Why did you advise the client to consider the other offers received?
- Why did you try to avoid an extended marketing period?
- Why did the first buyer withdraw?
- What due diligence did you carry out on the buyers?
- How did you successfully negotiate the sale to another buyer?

How Can You Demonstrate Level 2?

Typical level 2 questions will start with, 'How have you…', 'Tell me about an example when you…', or 'How did you provide … when…'. Remember, all the assessors' questions should be based upon the examples that you provide in your write-up for this competency in your summary of experience – rather than being hypothetical or general.

Level 2 Purchase and Sale is therefore about practical experience of the purchase or sale of all types of residential property and of the associated decision-making process, marketing, reporting, and completion of the transaction.[7]

Examples of the type of level 2 experience that would typically be included in a summary of experience are:

*At (**example**) I arranged viewings and liaised with my client and the prospective purchaser once an offer was received at market value. I verified the purchaser's identity and the availability and source of funds and notified my client of the offer. Once the offer was accepted, I prepared the Memorandum of Sale and issued this to all parties, liaising with the parties' solicitors to help conclude the sale.*

Questions relating to this example could include:

- How did you arrange viewings?
- How did you liaise regarding the offer?
- How did you verify the purchaser's identity?
- How did you verify the source of funds for the purchase?
- Tell me about the Customer Due Diligence that you carried out.
- Tell me about the Memorandum of Sale that you produced.
- Describe your role liaising with legal advisers to help conclude the sale.

*At (**example**) my firm was instructed to market an unfurnished modern three-bedroom apartment. I explained to the seller that for a small additional charge my firm could arrange for the marketing material to include computer-generated photographs of the property furnished and staged, to enable prospective purchasers to envisage use of the floorspace and wall space. This virtual service is affordable for clients as no outlay is required on furniture and contents. The client agreed so I arranged this service and ensured that the staged photographs were included in the printed and online marketing material.*

Questions relating to this example could include:

- Why did you suggest that the computer-generated images could enhance the marketing material?
- How did you explain this proposal to the client?
- How did you obtain the computer-generated images of the staged apartment?
- Describe your role marketing the property.
- What was the cost of the computer-generated images?
- How did the staged photographs enhance the marketing material?

*At (**example**) I conducted a viewing of a one-bedroom flat in a popular residential area of the city. The prospective buyer was a* *buy-to-let investor. The flat did not have a parking space. Using my local knowledge, I explained that application could be made to the council for a resident's parking permit and that some unrestricted on-street parking was available nearby. I also explained that the area was well-served by public transport and that many residents did not have cars. The buyer decided to proceed, making an offer which was accepted by the seller.*

Questions on this example could include:

- How did you prepare for the viewing?
- How did you ensure your safety whilst lone working?
- Describe how you conducted the viewing.
- How did you know that the flat did not have a parking space?
- How did you know that many local residents did not have cars?
- Talk me through the residents' parking options?
- Describe your role regarding the buyer's offer, and the seller's acceptance of the offer.
- What was the method of sale?
- What was the outcome of this instruction; did the sale complete?

How Can You Demonstrate Level 1?

Although the assessors will focus on your highest level, you may be asked some level 1 questions, focussing on the knowledge behind your practical level 2 (and potentially level 3) examples.

Level 1 requires candidates to demonstrate knowledge and understanding of how various types of property are sold (or a similar interest is acquired for a client) and the different types of interests that may be placed on the market. Candidates should also demonstrate an understanding of the economics of the residential property market and of the appropriate legal framework around the purchase and sale of residential properties.[8]

Awareness of 'hot topics' is also required so it is important to keep up to date with news and developments relevant to the Purchase and Sale competency. A useful way of keeping up to date is to read the regular market updates published by the RICS and major agencies. Some suggested sources are included at the end of this chapter.

As with all competencies, one way of enhancing your level 1 knowledge and understanding in your summary of experience is to explain how you gained your knowledge. This can be through continuing professional development (CPD; formal or informal), through your studies during a degree, and through work experience. Think about your CPD; does any of your CPD relate to the Purchase and Sale competency? Perhaps, for example, you have spent time reading and making notes on a residential market report that could be logged as informal CPD. Candidates' CPD logs are available to assessors and they can question candidates on this, so logging relevant CPD can support your submission.

An example level 1 summary of experience could include:

I understand the impact of location, design, and specification on sale price and market; e.g., solar panels and electric car charging points can improve a property's EPC rating and enhance its market appeal. I understand the stages of the conveying process and that the parties are not legally committed to the transaction until contracts have been exchanged. I am familiar with my firm's due diligence procedures and understand the importance of identifying and reporting suspected money laundering. Through my work experience and CPD I am familiar with the methods of sale, particularly private treaty and informal tender. I am also familiar with consumer protection laws, the Estate Agents Act 1979; Property agency and management principles, Global, 1st edition, 2024; and Conflicts of interest (Global), 1st edition, 2017. For example, I understand that agents must work with due skill, care, and diligence.

Questions on this example could include:

- Tell me about the Estate Agents Act 1979.
- What are the two estate agents redress schemes?
- What are the advantages/disadvantages of private treaty/informal tender/formal tender/auction?
- Briefly explain the legal conveyancing process.
- What is meant by exchange of contracts?
- What factors can affect the property market?
- Tell me about your duty of care as an estate agent.

The following are further examples of level 1 questions:

- What is overage?
- What is meant by completion?
- What information can you obtain from the Land Registry?
- What is a conditional contract?

- What types of agency agreement are you aware of?
- Tell me about sole selling rights/sole agency/joint sole agency/multiple agency/sub-agency.
- Tell me some key terms to include in terms of engagement.
- Tell me about estate agency redress schemes.
- Explain the role of the National Trading Standards Estate and Letting Agency Team.

Conclusion

Purchase and Sale is a skilled area of work with legal obligations and professional standards that reflect the value and significance of residential property transactions for the client buyer or seller. Candidates must be familiar with the key RICS publications, the law, and their own firm's procedures relating to, for example, money laundering. The duty of care must be clearly understood, and experience should demonstrate a range of property and transaction types. This chapter signposts key areas but candidates should explore the resources at the end of this chapter and carry out their own research to confidently satisfy the requirements of this competency.

Reference List

1 RICS (2016) *Real estate agency and brokerage* 3rd Edition 2016 (Global) [Online] Available at: https://www.rics.org/profession-standards/rics-standards-and-guidance/sector-standards/real-estate-standards/real-estate-agency-and-brokerage (Accessed 26 August 2024).

2 RICS (2016) *Real estate agency and brokerage* 3rd Edition 2016 (Global) [Online] Available at: https://www.rics.org/profession-standards/rics-standards-and-guidance/sector-standards/real-estate-standards/real-estate-agency-and-brokerage (Accessed 26 August 2024).

3 RICS (2016) *Real estate agency and brokerage* 3rd Edition 2016 (Global) [Online] Available at: https://www.rics.org/profession-standards/rics-standards-and-guidance/sector-standards/real-estate-standards/real-estate-agency-and-brokerage (Accessed 26 August 2024).

4 Wilcox J, Forsyth J (2022) *Real estate – the basics Chapter 10 real estate transactions* Abingdon: Routledge.

5 RICS (2017) UK residential real estate agency 6th Edition [Online] Available at: https://www.rics.org/profession-standards/rics-standardsa nd-guidance/sector-standards/real-estate-standards/uk-residential-real-estate-agency (Accessed 27 August 2024).

6 National Trading Standards Estate and Letting Agency Team (2023) *Material information in property listings (sales)* Guidance for Estate Agents

[Online] Available at: https://www.nationaltradingstandards.uk/uploads/
Material%20Information%20in%20Property%20Listings%20(Sales)%20
v1.0.pdf (Accessed 21 August 2024).

7 RICS (2024) *Residential pathway guide* [Online] Available at: https://www.
rics.org/join-rics/sector-pathways (Accessed 26 August 2024).

8 RICS (2024) *Residential pathway guide* [Online] Available at: https://www.
rics.org/join-rics/sector-pathways (Accessed 26 August 2024).

Further Reading and Resources

GOV.UK (no date) *Find an energy certificate* [Online] Available at: https://
www.gov.uk/find-energy-certificate (Accessed 12 February 2024).

Law Society Standard Conditions of Sale (5th Edition – 2018 Revision)
[Online] Available at: https://www.lawsociety.org.uk/topics/property/stand-
ard-conditions-of-sale (Accessed 26 August 2024).

Leasehold Advisory Service: https://www.lease-advice.org (Accessed 26 August
2024).

Lemen J (2019) *Hot topic highlight – countering bribery and corruption,
money laundering and terrorist financing* Property Elite Blog & Podcast
[Online] Available at: https://www.property-elite.co.uk/post/hot-topic-high-
light-countering-bribery-and-corruption-money-laundering-and-terrorist-
financing (Accessed 12 February 2024).

Lemen J (2019) *Hot topic highlight – methods of sale* Property Elite Blog &
Podcast [Online] Available at: https://www.property-elite.co.uk/post/hot-
topic-highlight-methods-of-sale (Accessed 24 January 2024).

Lemen J (2023) *Hot topic highlight – how to advise a client post-completion*
Property Elite Blog & Podcast [Online] Available at: https://www.property-
elite.co.uk/post/hot-topic-highlight-how-to-advise-a-client-post-completion
(Accessed 24 January 2024).

Lemen J (2023) *Hot topic highlight – a practical guide to comparable evidence
research* Property Elite Blog & Podcast [Online] Available at: https://www.
property-elite.co.uk/post/comparable-evidence-tips (Accessed 8 March 2024).

Ministry of Housing, Communities and Local Government & Department
for Levelling Up, Housing and Communities (2019) *How to buy a home*
HM Government [Online] Available at: https://www.gov.uk/government/
publications/how-to-buy-a-home (Accessed 24 January 2024).

Ministry of Housing, Communities and Local Government & Department
for Levelling Up, Housing and Communities (2019) *How to sell a home*
HM Government [Online] Available at: https://www.gov.uk/government/
publications/how-to-sell-a-home (Accessed 24 January 2024).

National Trading Standards Estate and Letting Agency Team (NTSELAT)
[Online] Available at: https://www.nationaltradingstandards.uk/work-areas/
estate-agency-team/ (Accessed 12 February 2024).

National Trading Standards Estate and Letting Agency Team (2023) *Material
information in property listings (sales)* Guidance for Estate Agents [Online]

Available at: https://www.nationaltradingstandards.uk/uploads/Material%20 Information%20in%20Property%20Listings%20(Sales)%20v1.0.pdf (Accessed 21 August 2024).

RICS (no date) *Property agency and management* [Online] Available at: https://www.rics.org/profession-standards/rics-standards-and-guidance/ sector-standards/real-estate-standards/property-agency-and-management (Accessed 20 January 2025).

RICS (2024) *UK residential market survey* [Online] Available at: https:// www.rics.org/news-insights/market-surveys/uk-residential-market-survey (Accessed 12 February 2024).

Savills (2024) *Residential property market forecasts* [Online] Available at: https:// www.savills.co.uk/insight-and-opinion/research-consultancy/residential-market-forecasts.aspx (Accessed 12 February 2024).

The Postlip Community: https://www.postliphall.org.uk/about-us.html (Accessed 26 August 2024).

Wilcox J, Forsyth J (2022) *Real estate – the basics* (In particular, Chapters 7, 9, 10 & 14) Abingdon: Routledge.

Wright J (2023) *How to buy a house* Which? [Online] Available at: https:// www.which.co.uk/money/mortgages-and-property/first-time-buyers/ buying-a-home/how-to-buy-a-house-a8zHm0a1JZsP (Accessed 25 January 2024).

7 Market Appraisal

Introduction

Market Appraisal is a core technical RICS APC competency, which can be selected to level 2 or level 3 for Residential pathway candidates. However, candidates are free to decide whether to select the competency; it is not compulsory even though it is on the core list.

The RICS pathway guide sets out the relevant knowledge (level 1), practical application (level 2), and reasoned advice (level 3) for this competency. However, as with all competencies, candidates do not need to have encountered everything listed, as this will depend on their experience and role.

Market appraisals are usually an essential aspect of the disposal or letting of a property, and a major influence on the client's decision-making process in what, for the client, is likely to be a major asset and investment. The competency therefore particularly complements the Purchase and Sale and Leasing and Letting competencies. This competency should also be read in tandem with other competencies, such as Inspection, Measurement, Health and Safety, Building Pathology, and Valuation.

This chapter will explain what candidates should know in relation to Market Appraisal, covering the main requirements of level 1, with guidance on levels 2 and 3.

Should You Select This Competency?

Market Appraisal is on the list of core technical competencies, but you can decide whether to select it. Candidates who do opt for Market Appraisal can choose either level 2 or level 3 as their highest level. As with all technical competencies, check the pathway guide carefully

DOI: 10.1201/9781032705095-7

and think about your role. Generally, candidates working in an agency role, advising on asking prices for properties being marketed, will have a good foundation for this competency.

The pathway guide outlines the requirements of each level and the sections later in this chapter will help to identify suitable examples for each level. However, for level 2, candidates must provide examples of market appraisals carried out, and involvement in the preparation of reports to clients. This can relate to the sales or rental markets. The Market Appraisal competency can also support Valuation and Loan Security Valuation, as some of the techniques used – for example, the analysis of comparable evidence – will overlap. These competencies are also complementary as they can demonstrate awareness of the context and interaction of roles in a property transaction.

Level 3 is more in depth, with reasoned advice. For example, did the market appraisal consider the viability of a site or the need for renovations, or did advice consider different options for sale or development? If you can provide specific examples of reasoned advice to your employer or to a client, consider selecting the competency to level 3.

Market Appraisal Skills

Surveyors carrying out market appraisals will usually need to combine inspection and measurement skills with the ability to analyse comparable evidence and to apply market and economic factors to provide accurate advice on asking price and marketing strategy. As with all competencies, client requirements need to be checked carefully and reflected in the terms of engagement and any concerns arising from desktop research, such as market uncertainty and locational constraints, need to be notified to the client. Relevant experience may include preparation of terms of engagement, so ensure that you are familiar with your firm's terms and the instruction process.

It is very important that you are familiar with the Blue Book's content on market appraisals. It is particularly important to understand that a market appraisal is not a formal valuation. Rather, it is advice on the appropriate asking price or asking rent, which does not deter potential purchasers but avoids inducing the client to sell or let below the market value. The distinction between the asking price or rent and a realistic sale price or rent needs to be clearly explained to the client and confirmed in writing. If the proposed transaction is a lease of the property, the recommended lease terms should also be confirmed to the client. A key point is that an estate agent providing a market appraisal will be judged as a reasonably competent estate agent in the event of a negligence claim, whereas misrepresenting a market appraisal as a formal valuation may result in the agent being judged as a valuer carrying out a formal Red Book valuation.[1]

The Glossary in UK residential real estate agency, 6th edition, 2017 (the Blue Book), defines a market appraisal as "An estimate of market price or rent based on market evidence and knowledge of the local market".[2] Key aspects, therefore, are knowledge of the local market and the ability to research and analyse comparable evidence to advise on asking price and a realistic sale price or rent.

RICS real estate agency and brokerage, 3rd edition 2016 (now archived, but containing useful information), and the Blue Book explain that the term 'appraisal' is sometimes used for valuations in non-UK jurisdictions. This clarifies an area of confusion for candidates; the Blue Book confirms that market appraisals are advice on the asking price or rent, not a formal valuation. Agents carrying out market appraisals are not carrying out Red Book valuations; rather, they should be familiar with the Blue Book and with RICS Comparable evidence in real estate valuation, 1st edition, 2019, in particular.

Candidates selecting Market Appraisal need to understand their local market conditions and be aware of changes to it and factors that may influence it. Comparable evidence needs to be considered in relation to the market. For example, has the market improved for sellers, or are prices falling since the date of the comparable transaction? Remember that there will usually be a delay, potentially for several months, between the price being agreed between the buyer and seller and the legal sale process completing, during which the market can change significantly without the price of the comparable evidence necessarily being renegotiated, so comparable evidence can be dated even if it appears to be relatively recent. Use of internal and external databases will be helpful, as will conversations with fellow agents and awareness of market trends. You should keep up to date with internal and external market reports, trends, and market factors (for instance, political events), and economic factors such as mortgage interest rates, which may be evidenced by your own firm's experience of changing market conditions.

The RICS Residential Market Surveys are of particular relevance to Residential pathway candidates. These indicate current and future UK residential sales and lettings market conditions. Surveyors can participate in the survey, which provides 30 minutes of informal continuing professional development (CPD). The survey is used by the government and other key institutions and is a source of information for the media. Candidates should keep up to date with these monthly surveys and consider how the national and regional market trends identified might apply or vary locally, even down to individual streets. For example, at the time of writing, the most recent market survey was January 2024. This identified data consistent with a gradual recovery in buyer demand. The same survey noted that the number of market appraisals was above that of the previous year.[3] Participation in the survey can also provide an opportunity to raise the profile of individual surveyors and firms, as regional surveyors' comments on their experience of the month's sales and lettings market are presented. The fact that the media may report on market trends can pose a challenge to surveyors carrying out market appraisals as sellers may be aware of generalised trends through media reports, but unaware of specific local variations. It is therefore important that surveyors remain professional and objective and explain their reasoning when providing a market appraisal.

At the end of this chapter, in the 'Further Reading and Resources' section, there is a link to the RICS market survey page.

Market reports and indices are also available from HM Land Registry; major firms of surveyors, such as Savills and Cushman & Wakefield; platforms such as Rightmove and Zoopla; and financial institutions such as Halifax and Nationwide.

RICS Professional Standards and Practice Information

This list of RICS Professional Standards and Practice Information relevant to the Market Appraisal competency is not exhaustive, and it will be subject to change as the RICS updates its publications and processes (see below). However, it should be a helpful indication of the relevant documentation. It is important to check for further standards and information relevant to your role, and for updates to those listed below. Examples are:

- Surveying safely, 2nd edition, 2018;
- Property agency and management principles, Global, 1st edition, 2024;

- RICS Real estate agency and brokerage, 3rd edition, 2016 (archived)
- UK Residential real estate agency, 6th edition, 2017;
- Comparable evidence in real estate valuation, 1st edition, 2019 (reissued as a professional standard in 2023).

The latter document – 'Comparable evidence in real estate valuation', 1st edition, 2019 – refers to valuation in its title, but its principles apply to the selection and analysis of comparable evidence for a market appraisal. The real estate market is not always transparent, as full details of a comparable transaction may not be available, or there may be a delay between a transaction being agreed and the details becoming publicly available. Agents carrying out market appraisals need to be aware of this and address it where necessary, for example, by explaining any uncertainties in the appraisal to the client. Within this context, comparable evidence needs to be as similar as possible to the subject property, recent, the result of an open market transaction, and in the context of an active market.[4] A full list of the characteristics of ideal comparable evidence can be found in the professional standard.

Other key aspects of the comparable evidence professional standard, which candidates should understand and be able to apply, include:

- Factors affecting the value of residential property, such as location, aspect, and lease terms;
- Sources of comparable evidence, and the need to verify the information obtained;
- Hierarchy of evidence – agents may need to use their judgement to prioritise some types of comparable evidence over others. The comparable evidence professional standard outlines three categories of comparable evidence:
  - Category A – direct comparables, listed in order of priority from contemporary, completed transactions of near-identical properties, to asking prices at the bottom of Category A.
  - Category B – general market data, such as indices and data on supply and demand. This information is stated to provide guidance rather being a direct indication of value.
  - Category C – other sources, e.g., interest rates.
- Recording comparable evidence – comparable evidence should be recorded in a format that enables clear and accurate analysis. Comparable evidence tables or matrices work well, and the professional

standard contains a useful list of the likely headings that should be applied to the summary and analysis of the evidence. Candidates should ensure that they are familiar with these and consider the format of their firm's comparable evidence records.

- Once the comparable evidence has been researched and compiled into suitable records, it will need to be analysed. This involves the conversion of the information into useful data that supports the agent's appraisal of the asking price and recommended sale price.[5]

At the time of writing in 2024, the RICS was consolidating its lettings, sales, and management agency standards and guidance. It is expected that Real estate agency and brokerage, 3rd edition, 2016, UK residential real estate agency, 6th edition, 2017 and Real estate management 3rd edition 2016 will be superseded by new professional standards. There is a link to the relevant RICS page in the Further Reading and Resources section at the end of this chapter. It is very important that you keep up to date with changes to RICS publications. However, any publications superseded by the new professional standards will still be relevant if they applied at the date of your examples in your summary of experience, so you will need to be familiar with both the archived, and new, consolidated documents.

Relevant Laws

As market appraisal is part of an estate or letting agent's role, refer to Chapters 6 (Purchase and Sale) and 8 (Leasing and Letting) for relevant laws.

How Can You Demonstrate Level 3?

Your assessors will start at the highest level you have declared, which will be either level 2 or level 3. At level 3 assessors will expect you to present specific examples of reasoned advice that you have provided to a client or your employer as a result of a market appraisal, perhaps considering and explaining the options available, to demonstrate a deeper level of understanding than is needed at level 2.

Check the pathway guide carefully and think about whether you can provide your own examples to reflect the examples given in the guide. The guide is not exhaustive, and you do not have to provide an example of each bullet-point, but the guide does provide a useful indication of the type of knowledge and experience that you need to demonstrate.

Examples of the type of level 3 experience that could be included in a summary of experience are:

*At (**example**) a portfolio of vacant properties suitable for the rental market was being marketed by my firm for disposal as a whole. However, the portfolio was not generating interest having been on the market for two years and the client now needed to achieve a quick sale. I carried out my market appraisal and concluded that the properties would generate more interest if offered for sale individually, as this would expand the potential market to include owner-occupiers and smaller buy-to-let investors. This would also expand the potential availability of finance for prospective buyers. I advised the client regarding suitable asking prices, rental, and sale prices for each unit, using the comparable method. The client accepted my advice, and the properties were marketed for sale individually by private treaty, generating significant interest and selling for a total exceeding the original portfolio valuation.*

Questions based on this example could include:

- Describe the portfolio to me.
- Why was the portfolio not generating interest?
- Talk me through your market appraisal.
- Talk me through your advice to the client.
- Why did you think the properties would generate more interest individually?
- What were the local market trends regarding investment portfolio sales?
- What were the local market trends regarding owner-occupiers/ buy-to-let investments?
- How did the availability of finance affect your advice regarding owner-occupiers/small-scale buy-to-let investors?

*At (**example**) I carried out a market appraisal of a modern house of modular construction in a rural area. The house had an energy efficiency rating of B. Having reviewed the available comparable evidence in the immediate vicinity and in an expanded search area, I advised the sellers that there was a shortage of comparable evidence due to the unusual nature of the property. I therefore provided a best- and worst-case market appraisal. I also advised that local trends* *indicated strong demand and rising prices in rural areas post-COVID and that the high energy-efficiency rating would appeal to buyers. I recommended initially marketing the property at the upper range of my appraisal. The seller accepted my advice, and the property sold at the upper end of my appraisal.*

Questions on this example could include:

- Talk me through your advice to the client.
- What is modular construction?
- What was the significance of the EPC B-rating?
- Describe the local market trends at the time.
- How did you research/analyse your comparable evidence?
- Why did you extend the search area?
- Why did you advise on best-case and worst-case asking prices?
- Talk me through your hierarchy of evidence/analysis of the comparable evidence.
- How did you apply RICS Comparable evidence in real estate valuation, 1st edition, 2019?
- How did you record your comparable evidence research/analysis?

*At (**example**) I was approached by a client for advice on whether to sell or rent a one-bedroom flat. I researched comparable evidence for both market value and market rent. Through my analysis of the comparable evidence, market report research, and local knowledge and experience, I advised that the sales market was slowing down, and prices were falling, but that there was strong rental demand for this type of property with rising rents. I advised the client to rent out the property to generate an income whilst allowing time for the sales market to recover. The client accepted my advice, and my firm successfully negotiated a 12-month assured shorthold tenancy of the property.*

Questions on this example could include:

- Talk me through your advice on the sales market.
- Talk me through your advice on the rental market.
- How did you research the comparable evidence for the sales/rental market?
- How did your comparable evidence research support your advice?
- Explain your analysis of the sales/rental comparable evidence.
- How did you identify the sales/rental market conditions?
- What market reports did you refer to, to support your advice?

- What RICS guidance or professional standards did you refer to when researching/analysing the sales/rental comparables?
- What factors affected the sales/rental markets?

How Can You Demonstrate Level 2?

Level 2 Market Appraisal is about practical experience of the preparation of sale and rental market appraisals. You will be expected to demonstrate experience of market appraisal methods and application of appraisal standards and guidance.[6]

Examples of the type of level 2 experience that could be included in a summary of experience are:

*At (**example**) I prepared a market appraisal for the sale of a detached family house. I carried out my desktop research, inspected the property, researched comparable evidence on my firm's internal database and on external databases, before compiling a table of comparable evidence. I analysed and adjusted the comparable evidence in accordance with RICS Comparable evidence in real estate valuation, 1st edition, 2019. I provided my market appraisal in a written report to the client and my firm was instructed to market the property for sale.*

Questions on this example could include:

- Talk me through your desktop research.
- Which databases did you search?
- Describe how you researched your comparable evidence.
- Talk me through your analysis of the comparable evidence.
- How did you comply with RICS Comparable evidence in real estate valuation, 1st edition, 2019?
- What did you include in your report to the client?

*At (**example**) I provided a market appraisal of a leasehold flat. The seller was considering whether to sell or remortgage to raise funds for further investment. I checked the lease terms and noted an escalating ground rent. I provided my market appraisal and reported that the escalating ground rent may limit the market for the property, particularly as there were new leasehold properties for sale in the locality, at a peppercorn rent. My client decided not to sell, but to remortgage. In accordance with UK residential real estate agency, 6th edition, 2017, I informed the client that my market appraisal was not a formal valuation.*

Questions on this example could include:

- How did you check the lease terms?
- Tell me about the escalating ground rent.
- Why would the escalating ground rent potentially limit the market?
- How would the peppercorn rents at the new local development potentially impact on the asking price/price achievable for the subject property?
- How did you comply with UK residential real estate agency, 6th edition, 2017?

How Can You Demonstrate Level 1?

Although the assessors will focus on your highest level, you may be asked some level 1 questions, focusing on the knowledge behind your practical level 2 (and potentially level 3) examples. Level 1 requires candidates to demonstrate their knowledge and understanding of the purposes of market appraisals, together with appraisal methods and limitations, and relevant standards and guidance.[7]

As mentioned, awareness of 'hot topics' and local, regional, and national market data and trends is also required so it is important to keep up to date with news, market reports and surveys, and developments relevant to the Market Appraisal competency.

One way of enhancing your level 1 knowledge and understanding is to explain how you gained your knowledge. This can be through CPD (formal or informal), through your studies during a degree, and through work experience such as shadowing a colleague. Think about your CPD; does any of your CPD relate to the Market Appraisal competency? Perhaps, for example, you have spent time reading and making notes on market reports that could be logged as informal CPD. Candidates' CPD logs are available to assessors and they can question candidates on this, so logging relevant CPD can support your submission.

An example level 1 submission could include:

I understand that market appraisals must be properly researched and supported by evidence to help clients to make informed decisions regarding sales or lettings. I am familiar with RICS Comparable evidence in real estate valuation, 1st edition, 2019, and I understand that there is a hierarchy of evidence. I recognise that a market appraisal is not a formal valuation and that clients should be informed that an appraisal is an estimate of the appropriate asking price or rent, in accordance with UK residential real estate agency, 6th edition, 2017, and Real estate agency and brokerage, 3rd edition, 2016.

Questions on this example could include:

- Why must market appraisals be properly researched?
- How can market appraisals be researched?
- Tell me about RICS Comparable evidence in real estate valuation, 1st edition, 2019.
- How can you ensure that clients are made aware of the difference between a market appraisal and a formal valuation?
- Tell me about hierarchies of evidence.
- What are the categories of comparable evidence?
- Tell me about UK residential real estate agency, 6th edition, 2017.

The following are further examples of level 1 questions:

- What market reports/indices are you aware of?
- What is the difference between a market appraisal and a formal valuation?
- Is a market appraisal the same as a formal valuation?
- What factors affect the sales/rental markets?
- What factors are currently affecting the market in your locality?

Conclusion

The Market Appraisal competency complements other related competencies, such as Purchase and Sale, Leasing and Letting, Valuation, and Loan Security Valuation. Candidates must understand their local markets and be aware of trends and social, political, and economic factors that affect the market and price of residential property for sale or to let. The competency offers candidates the opportunity to support and further demonstrate understanding of the residential sales and rentals markets, and their ability to research and analyse comparable evidence.

Reference List

1 RICS (2017) *UK residential real estate agency* 6th Edition [Online] Available at: https://www.rics.org/profession-standards/rics-standards-and-guidance/sector-standards/real-estate-standards/uk-residential-real-estate-agency (Accessed 27 August 2024).

2 RICS (2017) *UK residential real estate agency* 6th Edition [Online] Available at: https://www.rics.org/profession-standards/rics-standards-and-guidance/sector-standards/real-estate-standards/uk-residential-real-estate-agency (Accessed 27 August 2024).

3 RICS (2024) *January 2024 UK residential market survey* [Online] Available at: https://www.rics.org/news-insights/market-surveys/uk-residential-market-survey (Accessed 3 March 2024).

4 RICS (2019) *Comparable evidence in real estate valuation* 1st Edition [Online] Available at: https://www.rics.org/profession-standards/rics-standards-and-guidance/sector-standards/valuation-standards/comparable-evidence-in-real-estate-valuation (Accessed 27 August 2024).

5 RICS (2019) *Comparable evidence in real estate valuation* 1st Edition [Online] Available at: https://www.rics.org/profession-standards/rics-standards-and-guidance/sector-standards/valuation-standards/comparable-evidence-in-real-estate-valuation (Accessed 27 August 2024).

6 RICS (2024) *Residential pathway guide* [Online] Available at: https://www.rics.org/join-rics/sector-pathways (Accessed 26 August 2024).

7 RICS (2024) *Residential pathway guide* [Online] Available at: https://www.rics.org/join-rics/sector-pathways (Accessed 26 August 2024).

Further Reading and Resources

Estate Agents Act 1979: Available at: https://www.legislation.gov.uk/ukpga/1979/38.

Faulkner K (2023) *Hot topic highlight – market trends and analysis* Property Elite Blog & Podcast [Online] Available at: https://www.property-elite.co.uk/post/market-trends (Accessed 8 March 2024).

HM Land Registry UK House Price Index [Online] Available at: https://www.gov.uk/government/publications/about-the-uk-house-price-index/about-the-uk-house-price-index#:~:text=The%20UK%20House%20Price%20Index%20(%20UK%20HPI%20)%20captures%20changes%20in,and%20Wales%20since%20January%201995 (Accessed 11 March 2024).

Lemen J (2023) *Hot topic highlight – a practical guide to comparable evidence research* Property Elite Blog & Podcast [Online] Available at: https://www.property-elite.co.uk/post/comparable-evidence-tips (Accessed 8 March 2024).

Property Checklist: Available at: https://propertychecklists.co.uk.

RICS (no date) *Property agency and management* [Online] Available at: https://www.rics.org/profession-standards/rics-standards-and-guidance/sector-standards/real-estate-standards/property-agency-and-management (Accessed 20 January 2025).

RICS (2024) *UK residential market survey* [Online] Available at: https://www.rics.org/news-insights/market-surveys/uk-residential-market-survey (Accessed 3 March 2024).

Savills (2024) *Residential property market forecasts* Available at: https://www.savills.co.uk/insight-and-opinion/research-consultancy/residential-market-forecasts.aspx (Accessed 12 February 2024).

8 Leasing and Letting

Introduction

Leasing and Letting is a core technical RICS APC competency, which can be selected to level 2 or level 3 for Residential pathway candidates. However, candidates are free to decide whether to select the competency; it is not compulsory even though it is on the core list.

The RICS pathway guide sets out the relevant knowledge (level 1), practical application (level 2), and reasoned advice (level 3) for this competency. However, as with all competencies, candidates do not need to have encountered everything listed, as this will depend on their experience and role.

Leasing and Letting is an important area of work for many surveyors and it impacts on other areas. For example, a sales agent may be involved in the acquisition or disposal of a let property, or a block manager may have to liaise with landlords regarding consent to sublet. This competency should therefore be read in tandem with several other competencies relevant to Leasing and Letting, such as Communication and Negotiation, Health and Safety, Inspection, Landlord and Tenant, Building Pathology, Property Management, Valuation, and Market Appraisal.

This chapter will explain what candidates should know in relation to Leasing and Letting, covering the main requirements of level 1, with guidance on levels 2 and 3.

Should You Select This Competency?

As a core technical competency, you can select Leasing and Letting as one of your competencies. If selected, you can choose whether to take the competency to level 2 or level 3.

DOI: 10.1201/9781032705095-8

If you have experience of leasing and letting residential premises, consider selecting this competency. Check the pathway guide and think about tenancies that you have negotiated and followed through to completion; in relation to each, think about what you did to achieve the outcome, how you did it, and any reasoned advice or unusual circumstances that you encountered. This will help you to decide whether to select the competency and if so, whether to choose level 2 or level 3.

The pathway guide outlines the requirements of each level and the sections later in this chapter will help to identify suitable examples for each level. However, in brief, for level 2, you must provide examples of lettings achieved, with brief explanations of your role and the processes followed.

Level 3 is more in depth, with reasoned advice. For example, did you provide detailed advice regarding the suitability of a prospective tenant? If you can provide specific examples of reasoned advice to your employer or to a client, consider selecting the competency to level 3.

The overlap between Leasing and Letting, and the Landlord and Tenant and Property Management competencies can be very confusing. These competencies are complementary, so some examples will be suitable for more than one of them. In brief:

- Leasing and Letting focuses on the transaction, or 'doing the deal', i.e., finding a property or successfully marketing it, and negotiating the contractual relationship between the landlord and the tenant. This can include managing the landlord/tenant relationship during or at the end of the tenancy.
- Landlord and Tenant focuses on processes and issues that may arise during the lease or tenancy, e.g., rent reviews, enfranchisement, and dispute resolution.
- Property Management covers management matters arising between the client and agent, including statutory compliance. As well as covering both lettings and block management, the competency focuses on the owner/occupier/agent relationship.[1]

You should find it helpful to study the pathway guide carefully, together with the relevant chapters in this book, to help you to distinguish between the competencies and to identify knowledge and experience suitable for each. It is possible that some of the residential competencies will be combined in future, once the RICS has completed its pathway and competency review.

Leasing and Letting Skills

As mentioned above, this competency focusses on transactions, i.e., on 'doing the deal', from marketing the property to let if acting for the landlord or selecting the property to rent if acting for the tenant, through to completion. It therefore relates to the tenant-finding aspect, or the successful property search if acting for the tenant and you will need to understand your local market if selecting this competency. It can extend to managing the landlord and tenant relationship during or at the end of the tenancy. Leasing and Letting does not relate to the sale and purchase of long residential leases, which are covered by the Purchase and Sale competency (see Chapter 6).

UK residential real estate agency, 6th Edition, 2017 (the Blue Book), is of particular importance. It is a professional statement, so compliance is mandatory. The Blue Book contains both general content on, for example, ethics, and consumer protection, and chapters specifically aimed at agents acting for landlords. It also outlines key stages when acting for a landlord letting a property or a tenant in a property search. The detail of the Blue Book is not repeated here, and candidates should familiarise themselves with it. Key areas include:

- Acting for landlords;
- Acting for tenants;
- Advertising and marketing;
- Compliance with professional standards and ethics;
- Compliance with relevant legislation, such as the Immigration Act 2014 (Right to Rent checks), the Equality Act 2010, and the Consumer Protection from Unfair Trading Regulations 2008;
- Duty of care;
- Ending the instruction;
- Health and safety;
- Licensing of houses in multiple occupation (HMOs);
- Managing acceptance of offers;
- Matters that may impact on 'lettability';
- Securing instructions;
- Terms of engagement;
- Types of tenancy.

The Blue Book also contains a glossary in the Appendix, which you may find helpful.

Most surveyors working in leasing and letting will have experience of Assured Shorthold Tenancies, under the Housing Act 1988. This is a tenancy which is the tenant's only or principal home and for which the annual rent is not less than £250 (£1,000 in London) and does not exceed £100,000. However, there are other types of residential tenancies, including:

- Assured tenancies under the Housing Act 1988;
- Company lets;
- Contractual (common law) tenancies;
- Rent Act regulated tenancies (uncommon, but still occasionally encountered).

There are other types of occupation, such as licences (for example, a lodger), short-term Airbnb-type lets, and holiday lets. Awareness of the types of occupation that exist, and which may remove housing stock from the rental market, enhances understanding of the sector.

Street v Mountford [1985] AC809 gave us the legal principle that it is the reality of the relationship between the owner and the occupier of a property that determines whether the arrangement is a lease/tenancy or a licence, not the label on the agreement. Therefore, a 'licence' could actually be a tenancy if the arrangement has the characteristics of a lease/tenancy:

- Exclusive possession (i.e., the tenant has the right to exclude everyone else from the property);
- Certainty of term (i.e., the arrangement is for a fixed period, or it is periodic [e.g., weekly, monthly]);
- Rent is not an essential characteristic, but it can evidence a periodic tenancy.

In view of this, correct documentation and a proper understanding of the difference between a lease and a licence is important. A licence, for example, does not confer the same protection (e.g., security of tenure) as can benefit a tenant.

Regarding advertising and marketing properties to let, you should be aware of the need to provide information that is material to consumers' decision-making (Consumer Protection from Unfair Trading Regulations 2008). The National Trading Standards Estate and Letting Agency Team has published useful guidance for letting agents and you will find a link in the Further Reading and Resources section at the end of this chapter. Material information includes:

Part A – information that is always material, e.g., rent, deposit, council tax;

Part B – information to be established for all properties, e.g., number and types of room, electricity and water supplies, broadband, and parking;

Part C – information that may need to be established, e.g., easements, flood risk, planning permission.[2]

RICS Professional Standards and Practice Information

This list of RICS Professional Standards and Practice Information relevant to the Leasing and Letting competency is not exhaustive, and it will be subject to change as the RICS updates its publications and processes. However, it should be a helpful indication of the relevant documentation. It is important to check for further standards and information relevant to your role, and for updates to those listed below. Examples (which include some useful archived publications) are:

* Health and safety for residential property managers, 1st edition, 2016;
* Real estate agency and brokerage, 3rd edition, 2016 (archived);
* Real estate management, 3rd edition, 2016 (archived);
* Property agency and management principles, Global, 1st edition, 2024;
* Surveying safely, 2nd edition, 2018;
* UK residential real estate agency, 6th edition, 2017 (the Blue Book).

The Private Rented Sector Code of Practice 2015 has become rather dated and has now also been archived by the RICS. Nevertheless, you should be familiar with it if it applied to examples in your summary of experience.

At the time of writing in 2024, the RICS was consolidating its lettings, sales, and management agency standards and guidance. It is expected that Real estate agency and brokerage, 3rd edition, 2016; UK residential real estate agency, 6th edition, 2017; and Real estate management, 3rd edition, 2016, will be superseded by the new professional standards.

There is a link to the relevant RICS page in the Further Reading and Resources section at the end of this chapter. It is very important that you keep up to date with changes to RICS publications. However, any publications superseded by the new professional standards will still be relevant if they applied at the date of examples in your summary of experience, so you will need to be familiar with both the archived, and new, consolidated documents.

Relevant Laws

Candidates should have a good understanding of the main legal requirements relating to leasing and letting. Matters such as prescribed information, licensing of HMOs, deposit protection, energy performance certificates, fees charged to tenants, landlords' repairing/safety obligations, membership of redress schemes, and client money-handling are all critical. The list below is not exhaustive, but it indicates the legislation that candidates should be aware of; it is important that all candidates are familiar with the law relating to their specific area of practice and keep up to date with changes.

- Bribery Act 2010;
- Business Protection from Misleading Marketing Regulations 2008;
- Consumer Contracts (Information, Cancellation and Additional Charges) Regulations 2013;
- Consumer Protection from Unfair Trading Regulations 2008;
- Consumer Rights Act 2015;
- Deregulation Act 2015;
- Electrical Safety Standards in the Private Rented Sector (England) Regulations 2020;
- Equality Act 2010;
- Estate Agents Act 1979;
- Gas Safety (Installation and Use) Regulations 1998;
- Homes (Fitness for Human Habitation) Act 2018;
- Housing Acts 1988, 1996 and 2004;
- Housing and Planning Act 2016;
- Immigration Act 2014;
- Landlord and Tenant Act 1985;
- Landlord and Tenant Act 1987;
- Misrepresentation Act 1967;
- Smoke and Carbon Monoxide Alarm (England) Regulations 2015;

- Smoke and Carbon Monoxide Alarm (Amendment) Regulations 2022;
- Tenant Fees Act 2019;
- Town & Country Planning (Control of Advertisements) (England) Regulations 2007;
- Unfair Contract Terms Act 1977.

In early 2025, the Renters' Rights Bill was being debated by Parliament. At the time of writing, this was not yet law and candidates should monitor the progress and implementation of the significant reforms proposed by this Bill, which include:

- A new landlord's Private Rented Sector Database to support compliance;
- A new Private Rented Sector Landlord Ombudsman;
- Removal of fixed term tenancies – instead all tenancies will be periodic;
- Rationalisation of rent review processes and rights;
- A right for tenants to request a pet at the property, with landlords being unable to unreasonably refuse consent;
- Abolition of section 21 (Housing Act 1988) 'no-fault evictions';
- Revised landlord's possession grounds;
- A ban on discrimination against prospective tenants in receipt of benefits or with children;
- A ban on landlords accepting offers above the advertised rent, therefore banning rental bidding.

Another possible development concerns the regulation of property agents (ROPA). At the time of writing, letting agents and management agents in England do not need to be licensed and there is no minimum qualification required. ROPA was proposed as a means of addressing this, to help improve standards and protect landlords and tenants. Proposals include:

- Appointment of a regulator;
- Creation of a single ombudsman or redress scheme;
- Licensing of letting agency businesses;
- Staff carrying out certain activities should be qualified and licensed.

Candidates should be aware of requirements for letting agents to join a redress scheme, and of the enforcement role provided by the National

Trading Standards Estate and Letting Agency Team. The link is at the end of this chapter. In an extreme situation, landlords and agents could be prohibited from letting and managing residential property, via a banning order under the Housing and Planning Act 2016.

How Can You Demonstrate Level 3?

Your assessors will start at the highest level you have declared, which will be either level 2 or level 3. At level 3 the RICS expects you to present specific examples of reasoned advice that you have provided to a client or your employer in relation to leasing and letting, perhaps considering and explaining the options available, to demonstrate a deeper level of understanding and the ability to deal with more complex cases than is needed at level 2.

Check the pathway guide carefully and think about whether you can provide your own examples to reflect the examples given in the guide. The guide is not exhaustive, and you do not have to provide an example of each bullet-point, but the guide does provide a useful indication of the type of knowledge and experience that you need to demonstrate.

Level 3 requires reasoned advice in all types of leasing and letting transactions, with the ability to deal with complex cases (with assistance), and provision of holistic market and lettings advice.[3]

Examples of the type of level 3 experience that could be included in a summary of experience are:

*At (**example**) I provided rental market appraisals for letting a three-bedroom house as a single-family home and as a house in multiple occupation with three separate room lets. I recommended that the landlord consider letting the property as a house in multiple occupation as there was local demand from young professionals and the HMO would generate a higher yield.*

Questions on this example could include:

*   Why did you provide rental market appraisals for a single-family home and HMO?
*   What advice did you provide regarding renting the property as an HMO?
*   What advice did you provide regarding the market?
*   Talk me through the options that you considered.
*   How did you establish the demand from young professionals?

- What is an Article 4 direction?
- What are the planning/licensing rules regarding HMOs?

*At (**example**) I marketed a two-bedroom house to let on behalf of a private sector landlord. Interest in the property had been limited and the landlord wished to let the property quickly. A disabled prospective tenant was in receipt of Universal Credit, but the Local Housing Allowance rate for a single person was considerably lower than the local market rent for a two-bedroom house. I liaised with the prospective tenant and established that she was entitled to an additional allowance for a carer. I recommended that the landlord proceed with the tenant (subject to receipt of a holding deposit, references, and Right to Rent checks) because Universal Credit provided a reliable source of income for the tenant, and she could afford the rent due to her additional allowance.*

Questions on this example could include:

- What advice did you provide regarding references?
- Why was interest in the property limited?
- How could the limited interest in the property have been addressed?
- What is the Local Housing Allowance rate?
- How does the Equality Act 2010 relate to housing?
- Why did you recommend that Universal Credit is a reliable source of income?
- Tell me about caps on holding deposits.
- How did you carry out Right to Rent checks?
- What legislation applies to Right to Rent checks?
- What references did you seek?

*At (**example**) I negotiated the letting of a one-bedroom house. The prospective tenant failed the referencing due to affordability. As the prospective tenant had received a very good reference from his previous landlord, I recommended that the client landlord proceed subject to provision of a deed of guarantee from a suitable guarantor. The client accepted this advice, and I completed the tenancy agreement with the tenant and a deed of guarantee with the guarantor.*

Questions on this example could include:

- Tell me about the affordability checks carried out when referencing a tenant.
- What references did you obtain for the prospective tenant?

- Why did the prospective tenant fail the affordability check?
- What advice did you provide regarding the guarantor?
- Why did you recommend a guarantor?
- What are the benefits of obtaining a guarantor?
- How did you ensure that the guarantee was legally binding?
- Why did you use a deed of guarantee?

How Can You Demonstrate Level 2?

Level 2 Leasing and Letting is about applying your knowledge and skills to leasing/letting and demonstrating practical experience of decision-making, marketing, reporting, and completion of the transaction. You should also be able to demonstrate knowledge and understanding of other property transaction types, and why decisions were made to proceed along the chosen leasing or letting route.[4]

Examples of activities and knowledge comprised within this level are:

*At (**example**) I prepared the tenancy agreement for letting a two-bedroom house. I ensured that the correct information was included for the landlord's name and address for service under section 48 of the Landlord and Tenant Act 1987, the rent, tenancy duration, deposit, and deposit protection scheme. I also included an extra clause in the tenancy agreement prohibiting the parking of commercial vehicles on the drive, in accordance with the landlord's instructions and the restrictive covenant that applied to the property.*

Questions on this example could include:

- Talk me through the main clauses of the tenancy agreement.
- Describe your role in drafting the tenancy agreement.
- How did you comply with the landlord's instructions?
- Why did the landlord instruct you to prohibit parking commercial vehicles?
- What is a restrictive covenant?
- What is a possible consequence of breach of a restrictive covenant?

*At (**example**) I prepared an inventory before the tenancy started. I inspected the property thoroughly and noted its condition and cleanliness. I recorded all my observations on my firm's inventory software on my tablet. I photographed each room and uploaded the photos so that they were embedded in the inventory. I tested all services to ensure* *that they were in working order and I ensured that smoke and carbon monoxide detectors were installed and functioning. I sent the inventory to my supervisor to provide to the tenant at check-in.*

Questions on this example could include (note this example could be used for the Data Management and Inspection competencies):

- Talk me through the inventory software that you used.
- Why did you prepare an inventory?
- Why did you test services/smoke detectors/carbon monoxide detectors?
- How did you ensure that the inventory covered all necessary areas/features of the property?
- What safety measures did you take when lone working at the property?

How Can You Demonstrate Level 1?

Although the assessors will focus on your highest level, you may be asked some level 1 questions, focussing on the knowledge behind your practical level 2 (and potentially level 3) examples. Level 1 requires knowledge and understanding of how various types of property are let, the different types of interests that may be placed on the market, an understanding of the economics of the market, and the appropriate legal frameworks. This includes understanding of the impact of the terms of a lease on marketability and value.[5]

As mentioned, awareness of 'hot topics' is also required so it is important to keep up to date with news and developments relevant to the Leasing and Letting competency.

A level 1 summary of experience could include:

I am aware of the law relating to leasing and letting; e.g., the Tenant Fees Act 2019 limits security deposits to five weeks rent (six weeks if the annual rent is £50,000 or more), and the Immigration Act 2014 requires landlords to check that prospective tenants have the right to rent property in the UK.

The following are examples of level 1 questions:

- Tell me about the Tenant Fees Act 2019.
- What fees are permitted to charge to a tenant?
- What is the maximum deposit a landlord can charge?
- What RICS guidance applies to leasing and letting?

- Give me some examples of laws applicable to leasing and letting.
- What prescribed information must be issued to a tenant before the tenancy starts?
- What is a consequence of failing to serve the prescribed information on a tenant?
- Tell me about the rental market in your locality.
- What is a 'right to rent' check?
- Tell me about the Immigration Act 2014.
- What is an inventory?
- Why is an inventory necessary?
- How may an assured shorthold tenancy be terminated?

Conclusion

The Leasing and Letting competency is usually suitable for candidates working as letting agents or otherwise employed in the rented sector. It requires marketing, communication, and negotiation skills to 'close the deal', combined with the legal and technical knowledge necessary to comply with the many legal requirements associated with a new tenancy. It can also involve management of the tenancy and terminating the transaction, at the end of the tenancy. The competency is highly compatible with the Landlord and Tenant and Property Management competencies, which can complement each other and help demonstrate breadth of knowledge and experience.

Reference List

1 RICS (2024) *Residential pathway guide* London: RICS.
2 National Trading Standards Estate and Letting Agency Team (2023) *Material information in property listings (lettings)* [Online] Available at: https://www.nationaltradingstandards.uk/uploads/Material%20Information%20in%20Property%20Listings%20(Lettings)%20v1.0.pdf (Accessed 22 August 2024).
3 RICS (2024) *Residential pathway guide* [Online] Available at: https://www.rics.org/join-rics/sector-pathways (Accessed 26 August 2024).
4 RICS (2024) *Residential pathway guide* [Online] Available at: https://www.rics.org/join-rics/sector-pathways (Accessed 26 August 2024).
5 RICS (2024) *Residential pathway guide* [Online] Available at: https://www.rics.org/join-rics/sector-pathways (Accessed 26 August 2024).

Further Reading and Resources

Gov.uk (no date) *Tenancy agreements: A guide for landlords (England and Wales)* [Online] Available at: https://www.gov.uk/tenancy-agreements-a-guide-for-landlords/tenancy-types (Accessed 26 July 2024).

Ministry of Housing, Communities & Local Government (2025) *Guide to the Renters' Rights Bill* [Online] Available at: https://www.gov.uk/government/publications/guide-to-the-renters-rights-bill/82ffc7fb-64b0-4af5-a72e-c247 01a5f12a (Accessed 18 January 2025).

National Residential Landlords Association: www.nrla.org.uk.

National Trading Standards Estate and Letting Agency Team (NTSELAT) Available at: https://www.nationaltradingstandards.uk/work-areas/estate-agency-team/ (Accessed 12 February 2024).

National Trading Standards Estate and Letting Agency Team (2023) *Material information in property listings (lettings)* [Online] Available at: https://www.nationaltradingstandards.uk/uploads/Material%20Information%20in%20Property%20Listings%20(Lettings)%20v1.0.pdf (Accessed 22 August 2024).

Propertymark: https://www.propertymark.co.uk/about-us/propertymark-protected.html.

Propertymark (2024) *Lords tell UK Government to get on with agent regulation'* [Online] Available at: https://www.propertymark.co.uk/resource/lords-tell-uk-government-to-get-on-with-agent-regulation.html (Accessed 11 April 2024).

RICS (no date) *Property agency and management* [Online] Available at: https://www.rics.org/profession-standards/rics-standards-and-guidance/sector-standards/real-estate-standards/property-agency-and-management (Accessed 18 January 2025).

Shelter (no date) *Banning orders against landlords and letting agents* [Online] Available at: https://england.shelter.org.uk/professional_resources/legal/housing_conditions/private_sector_enforcement/banning_orders_againstlandlords_and_letting_agents#reference-2 (Accessed 23 August 2024).

Shelter (no date) *Commonhold property* [Online] Available at: https://england.shelter.org.uk/professional_resources/legal/home_ownership/leasehold_and_commonhold/commonhold_property (Accessed 23 August 2024).

Shelter (Home Page): https://england.shelter.org.uk.

Shelter (Professional Resources): https://england.shelter.org.uk/professional_resources/legal.

The Property Institute: https://www.tpi.org.uk.

Wilcox J & Forsyth J (2022) *Real estate; The Basics* Abingdon: Routledge.

9 Landlord and Tenant

Introduction

Landlord and Tenant is an optional technical RICS APC competency. Candidates can decide whether to select the competency, and, if selected, they can declare it to either level 2 or level 3, depending on the candidate's experience.

The RICS pathway guide sets out the relevant knowledge (level 1), practical application (level 2), and reasoned advice (level 3) for this competency. However, as with all competencies, you do not need to have encountered everything listed, as this will depend on your experience and role.

This competency should be read in tandem with several other competencies relevant to Landlord and Tenant, such as Conflict Avoidance, Management and Dispute Resolution Procedures, Legal and Regulatory Compliance, Communication and Negotiation, Valuation, Leasing and Letting, Property Management, and Purchase and Sale.

This chapter will explain what candidates should know in relation to Landlord and Tenant, covering the main requirements of level 1, with guidance on levels 2 and 3.

Should You Select This Competency?

As mentioned above, as an optional technical competency, Landlord and Tenant can be selected to level 2 or level 3.

Landlord and tenant work is a specialism requiring knowledge and experience of the complex landlord and tenant relationship, and relevant law and practice, combined with good communication and negotiation skills. Examples of landlord and tenant work include leasehold enfranchisement, lease extensions, the right to manage, rent reviews, service charge disputes, and applications to the First-tier Tribunal

DOI: 10.1201/9781032705095-9

(Property Chamber). Level 3 focuses particularly (but is not limited to) strategic advice, negotiations, and disputes. Experience of applying knowledge in practice, such as the preparation of statutory notices, may indicate level 2 as the suitable level.

The pathway guide outlines the requirements of each level and the sections later in this chapter will help to identify suitable examples for each level.

The overlap between Landlord and Tenant, and the Leasing and Letting and Property Management competencies can be very confusing. Some examples will be suitable for more than one of these competencies, each of which is complementary in terms of the knowledge and skills required. In brief:

- Leasing and Letting focuses on the transaction, or 'doing the deal', i.e., finding a property or successfully marketing it, and negotiating the contractual relationship between the landlord and the tenant. This can include managing the landlord/tenant relationship during or at the end of the tenancy.
- Landlord and Tenant focuses on processes and issues that may arise during the lease or tenancy, e.g., rent reviews, enfranchisement, and dispute resolution.
- Property Management covers management matters arising between the client and agent, including statutory compliance. As well as covering both lettings and block management, the competency focuses on the owner/occupier/agent relationship.[1]

You should find it helpful to study the pathway guide carefully, together with the relevant chapters in this book, to help you to distinguish between the competencies and to identify knowledge and experience suitable for each. It is possible that some of the residential competencies will be combined in future, once the RICS has completed its pathway and competency review.

Landlord and Tenant Skills

This competency concerns the management of relationships through the professional representation of either the landlord or the tenant with regard to long residential leases, or short-term tenancies.

Competencies can appear to be very similar, and to overlap, and (as mentioned), this competency is particularly related to Leasing and Letting and Property Management. A helpful way to consider the Landlord and Tenant competency is to think about the respective rights and responsibilities of landlords and tenants. These can be, for example, through express and implied lease covenants, or through statutory rights and obligations. It is very important, therefore, to understand the contents of the leases or tenancy agreements that you deal with, and the laws that affect them.

Candidates' experience is likely to cover a wide range of scenarios. The below list is not exhaustive, but it should help to identify the type of example that is suitable for this competency. Matters covered could include:

In relation to long residential leases:

- Advising on enfranchisement rights under the Leasehold Reform Act 1967 or the Leasehold Reform, Housing and Urban Development Act 1993;
- Advising on lease extensions (Leasehold Reform Act 1967 or the Leasehold Reform, Housing and Urban Development Act 1993);
- Advising on tenants' rights of first refusal (Landlord and Tenant Act 1987);
- Advising on the forfeiture of leases;
- Advising on the right to manage (Commonhold and Leasehold Reform Act 2002);
- Applications to the First-tier Tribunal (Property Chamber), and preparation for and representation at hearings, for example, regarding the reasonableness of service charges (sections 19 and 27A of the Landlord and Tenant Act 1985);
- Appointment of a manager by the First-tier Tribunal (Property Chamber), (Landlord and Tenant Act 1987);
- Carrying out consultations under section 20 of the Landlord and Tenant Act 1985;
- Other matters e.g., recognised tenants' associations;
- Instructing solicitors in relation to disputes;
- Variation of leases (Landlord and Tenant Act 1987).

In relation to short residential tenancies:

- Advising on and negotiating deposit disputes;
- Advising on compliance with legal requirements, e.g., notification of landlord's name and address for service of notices (section 48

Landlord and Tenant Act 1987 – this section also applies to long residential leases);

* Advising on mandatory and discretionary grounds for possession (section 8 and Schedule 2 Housing Act 1988);
* Advising on recovery of possession and issuing notice to quit under section 21 Housing Act 1988;
* Advising on security of tenure (section 5 Housing Act 1988);
* Checking rent review clauses, valuing for rent reviews, preparing rent review notices (section 13 Housing Act 1988);
* Negotiating and implementing break clauses;
* Negotiating lease surrenders. These may be express (documented in a deed of surrender) or implied by the conduct of the parties.

With any landlord and tenant matter, the lease or tenancy agreement is the starting point. Surveyors should always read the relevant lease clauses before advising. However, the lease is not the full picture, and the law can intervene in the landlord and tenant relationship. This can:

* Change the way that the lease works (for example, section 19(1)(a) Landlord and Tenant Act 1927 requires landlords to act reasonably if they receive a request for consent to assign or sublet, and section 1 Landlord and Tenant Act 1988 requires landlords to respond to requests for consent to assignment or subletting, within a reasonable time);
* Provide additional statutory rights (for example, section 5 Housing Act 1988 creates a statutory periodic tenancy when an assured tenancy or an assured shorthold tenancy fixed term expires);
* Create additional procedures, such as the requirement to use the prescribed form of demand for ground rent (section 166 Commonhold and Leasehold Reform Act 2002) and for summaries of rights to be provided with service charge and administration charge demands;
* Impose additional obligations (for example, the duty to consult with leaseholders regarding qualifying works and qualifying long-term agreements, under section 20 Landlord and Tenant Act 1985);
* Clarify how a procedure under the lease must be implemented. For instance, there is extensive case law on break clauses (the website of the charity 'Shelter' provides very useful advice – see the link at the end of this chapter);
* Result in enforcement action (so this competency also relates to Legal/Regulatory Compliance and Conflict Avoidance, Management

and Dispute Resolution Procedures). Enforcement could include a banning order against a landlord and/or agent in an extreme situation, preventing them from letting or managing residential property.

The Landlord and Tenant competency therefore often covers situations in which something has gone wrong in the landlord and tenant relationship; perhaps there is uncertainty regarding service charges, or perhaps the landlord or the tenant wants to change or manage the relationship. Surveyors can become involved directly – resolving the situation or ensuring compliance with legal requirements – or indirectly, recommending specialist advisers or briefing and liaising with solicitors. This idea of changing and managing the landlord and tenant relationship demonstrates the wide range of situations in which candidates may gain knowledge and experience.

As with each competency, the examples in the RICS pathway guide are not prescriptive, so it is not necessary to have experience of each of the bullet-points listed in the guide; rather, these provide guidance on the nature of the professional knowledge and experience expected of a surveyor at the specified level.

Remember that if you say that you understand or are aware of RICS Professional Standards and Practice Information and relevant laws in your summary of experience, ensure that you can answer questions on these! When writing your summary of experience, you can also indicate your understanding of the content of the document that you are referring to. For example, if you mention the Service Charge Residential Management Code, you can briefly outline something that you understand from the document.

In addition to RICS publications, it is important to have a thorough knowledge of relevant law. Examples are listed in the section below. Be aware of 'hot topics' and other sources of information, for example, government publications and resources such as the '.gov' website and the Leasehold Advisory Service website. Links are provided at the end of this chapter.

RICS Professional Standards and Practice Information

This list of RICS (and other) publications relevant to the Landlord and Tenant competency is not exhaustive, and it will be subject to change as the RICS updates its publications. Publications can also become out of date as legislation changes, so it is important to stay abreast of legal developments. However, this list should be a helpful indication of the relevant documentation. As mentioned, it is important to check for further standards and information relevant to your role, and for updates to those listed below.

Examples are:

- Association of Retirement Housing Managers (ARHM) Private Retirement Housing Code of Practice (there are separate codes of each of England, Scotland, and Wales);
- Private Rented Sector Code of Practice 2015 (this has now been archived, but it could still apply to earlier examples in your summary of experience);
- Property agency and management principles, Global, 1st edition, 2024;
- RICS Real estate management, 3rd edition, 2016 (archived);
- Service charge, residential management code, 3rd edition, 2016;
- UK Residential real estate agency, 6th edition, 2017 (the Blue Book).

At the time of writing in 2024, the RICS was consolidating its lettings, sales, and management agency standards and guidance. It is expected that Real estate agency and brokerage, 3rd edition, 2016; UK residential real estate agency, 6th edition, 2017; and Real estate management, 3rd edition, 2016, will be superseded by the new professional standards. There is a link to the relevant RICS page in the Further Reading and Resources section at the end of this chapter. It is very important that you keep up to date with changes to RICS publications. However, any publications superseded by the new professional standards will still be relevant if they applied at the date of examples in your summary of experience, so you will need to be familiar with both the archived, and new, consolidated documents.

Relevant Laws

This list is not exhaustive, but it indicates the legislation that you should be aware of; it is important that you check the law relating to your specific area of practice and keep up to date with changes. Please also refer to Chapter 8 (Leasing and Letting), Chapter 10 (Property Management), and Chapter 13 (Legal/Regulatory Compliance):

- Building Safety Act 2022;
- Commonhold and Leasehold Reform Act 2002;

- Homes (Fitness for Human Habitation) Act 2018;
- Housing Act 1985;
- Housing and Planning Act 2016;
- Landlord and Tenant (Covenants) Act 1995;
- Landlord and Tenant Act 1927;
- Landlord and Tenant Act 1985;
- Landlord and Tenant Act 1987;
- Landlord and Tenant Act 1988;
- Leasehold and Freehold Reform Act 2024;
- Leasehold Reform (Ground Rent) Act 2022;
- Leasehold Reform Act 1967;
- Leasehold Reform, Housing and Urban Development Act 1993;
- Tenant Fees Act 2019.

At the time of writing in 2024, there were significant changes expected to both the long residential leasehold sector and short residential tenancies. Candidates should monitor professional journals and media reports for updates. The Leasehold and Freehold Reform Act 2024 received the Royal Assent in 2024. This Act, when it takes effect, will (amongst other changes):

- Ban the sale of new leasehold houses;
- Enable long residential leaseholders of flats and houses to extend their leases to 990 years (instead of one 50-year extension for houses, and multiple 90-year extensions for flats);
- Introduce standard format service charge bills;
- Require self-managing landlords to join a redress scheme;
- Simplify the lease extension and enfranchisement processes.

Two further proposals may also take effect:

- The Renters (Reform) Bill was expected to reform short-term tenancies. It did not become law before the general election in 2024, but at the time of writing, reform is still expected from the subsequent government, via the Renters' Rights Bill. It is therefore important to keep up to date. One proposal is to abolish 'no-fault' evictions under section 21 of the Housing Act 1988.
- Regulation of Property Agents (ROPA) may require licensing of lettings and management agents, with minimum qualifications for relevant professionals. See Chapter 8 for more information.

It is also worth checking the Law Commission's reports on the residential leasehold sector. The Law Commission researches and carries out public consultations on key issues, which inform recommendations to the government regarding changes to the law. The reports undertaken as part of its 13th Programme of Law Reform covered:

- The right to manage (Commonhold and Leasehold Reform Act 2002);
- Commonhold;
- Leasehold enfranchisement.

The reports help to provide context for leasehold reform.

How Can You Demonstrate Level 3?

Your assessors will start at the highest level you have declared, which will be either level 2 or level 3. At level 3 RICS expects you to present specific examples of reasoned advice that you have provided to a client or your employer in relation to a landlord and tenant matter, perhaps considering and explaining the options available, to demonstrate a deeper level of understanding than is needed at level 2.

Check the pathway guide carefully and think about whether you can provide your own examples to reflect the examples given in the guide. The guide is not exhaustive, and you do not have to provide an example of each bullet-point, but the guide does provide a useful indication of the type of knowledge and experience that you need to demonstrate.

Questions on level 3 examples will focus on your reasoned advice, and options that you may have considered. However, assessors may also want to check your knowledge and understanding and the processes and procedures that you followed.

Examples of the type of level 3 experience that would typically be included in a summary of experience are:

*At (**example**) I advised the landlord residents' management company (RMC) that aesthetic improvements to the communal areas were not recoverable from the service charge under the lease. I also advised that leaseholders had the right under S27A of the Landlord and Tenant Act 1985 to challenge the expenditure at the First-tier Tribunal (Property Chamber). I suggested that the company's non-service charge account, in which the ground rents received by the RMC were held, could be used to fund the improvements.*

Questions based on this example could include:

- Tell me about the improvements.
- Why were the costs not recoverable?
- Explain the leaseholders' rights under S27A of the Landlord and Tenant Act 1985.
- Talk me through your advice to the client.
- Why did you advise that the ground rents could be a source of funding?
- What were the risks of a S27A application by leaseholders?

*At (**example**) leaseholders disputed the proposed installation of emergency lighting in the communal areas. I advised the landlord to make an application to the First-tier Tribunal (Property Chamber) under S27A of the Landlord and Tenant Act 1985 for a determination as to whether the cost, if incurred, would be a service charge cost. I represented the client at the Tribunal, which determined that the costs could be recovered via the service charge. The work was carried out as required by the fire risk assessment.*

Questions on this example could include:

- Tell me about the fire risk assessment.
- Why was a fire risk assessment necessary?
- Tell me about S27A of the Landlord and Tenant Act 1985.
- How did you prepare to represent your client at the Tribunal?
- Talk me through your advice regarding the application.
- Why did the leaseholders object to the work?
- Why did you advise the client to apply to the Tribunal?
- On what lease clauses did the Tribunal base its decision?

*At (**example**) a leaseholder with significant service charge arrears refused to engage in negotiations or mediation. I recommended to the landlord client that solicitors be instructed to recover the debt. I briefed the solicitor regarding the lease terms, provided details of the arrears, and liaised between the client and the solicitors throughout the recovery process. The leaseholder defended the claim but was required by the court to engage in mediation. I supported the client at the mediation, at which the matter was settled and ratified by a Consent Order.*

Questions relating to this example could include:

- Over what period did the arrears arise?
- Why was the leaseholder in arrears?
- What pre-legal steps did you take to recover the arrears?
- Why did you advise that solicitors be instructed?
- What advice did you provide regarding alternative dispute resolution?
- How did you support the client at the mediation?
- What was the outcome?

*At (**example**) my client decided to sell the freehold of a block of flats. I advised that the Landlord and Tenant Act 1987 required the landlord to first offer the building to leaseholders, and I explained the process that applied. I recommended that solicitors be instructed to prepare the necessary notices and oversee the process.*

Questions on this example could include:

- Tell me about the right of first refusal.
- Why did the property qualify for these rights?
- What are the consequences of failing to comply with the right of first refusal?
- Talk me through your advice.
- Why did you recommend that solicitors be instructed?
- What was the outcome?

*At (**example**) leaseholders were unhappy with the landlord's management. There were also disputes and difficult relationships amongst leaseholders themselves. I recommended that the leaseholders set up a tenants' association and apply for recognition from the landlord under S29 Landlord and Tenant Act 1985. I arranged several meetings of leaseholders' representatives to encourage communication and collaboration amongst leaseholders. I supported leaseholders through creation of the association and successfully applied to the landlord for recognition.*

Questions on this example could include:

- What advice did you give regarding the association?
- Why did you recommend setting up a tenant's association?

- How did you apply for recognition?
- What were the benefits of setting up a recognised tenants association?
- How did you improve relationships between leaseholders?

*At (**example**) I was approached by a landlord regarding a long-term, vulnerable, assured shorthold tenant with rent arrears. I advised the landlord that a S21 Housing Act 1988 notice to quit could be used to gain possession if required and that legal action could be taken to recover the arrears if the deposit was insufficient; however, communication with the tenant would be advisable to try to resolve the matter. The landlord did not want to evict a vulnerable tenant, so I recommended that I meet with the tenant and a support worker, or a family member. The landlord and tenant both agreed with this approach. At the meeting I was able to resolve the situation and obtain payment of the arrears, whilst retaining the long-term tenant.*

Questions on this example could include:

- What do you mean by a 'vulnerable tenant'?
- Tell me about S21 Housing Act 1988.
- Why did the landlord want to retain the tenant?
- What advice did you provide to the landlord?
- Talk me through your advice regarding terminating the tenancy.
- What other options did you consider to try to resolve the situation?
- How did you negotiate a solution?
- Did you/how did you negotiate a solution that could protect the client against future arrears?

How Can You Demonstrate Level 2?

Level 2 Landlord and Tenant is about practical experience of landlord and tenant issues, law, and practice, in relation to short or long residential leases. Typical level 2 questions will start with, 'How have you...', 'Tell me about an example when you...', or 'Describe your role...'. Remember, all the assessors' questions should be based upon the examples that you provide in your write-up for this competency in your summary of experience – rather than being hypothetical or general. However, assessors may also ask for more examples of relevant work that you have carried out, especially if they want additional evidence of your practical experience.

Examples of the type of level 2 experience that would typically be included in a summary of experience are:

At (**example**) *I reviewed the lease for a new client. I prepared a schedule of key lease clauses and reported that service charges were payable quarterly in advance on the usual quarterdays.*

Questions on this example could include:

- How did you review the lease?
- Talk me through the schedule that you prepared.
- Describe your role when taking on a new client.
- What are the benefits of collecting service charges in advance?
- What are the usual quarterdays?

At (**example**) *I prepared the S20 Landlord and Tenant Act 1985 consultation notices for qualifying works. I ensured that the correct time periods were observed. When a leaseholder nominated a contractor to provide an estimate in response to the Notice of Intention, I checked that the contractors were competent and insured. I reviewed the estimates received and issued the Statement of Estimates. The client subsequently instructed me to accept the lowest estimate, which was from the nominated contractor, so I did not need to issue a Notice of Reasons.*

Questions on this example could include:

- What were the landlord's repairing obligations under the lease?
- Talk me through the consultation process that you carried out.
- Why did you need to consult with leaseholders?
- What are the potential consequences of failing to consult with leaseholders?
- What notice periods did you observe?
- Why did you not need to issue a Notice of Reasons?
- What is the role of the First-tier Tribunal (Property Chamber) in relation to S20 consultation?
- What are qualifying works?
- How did you check that the notices contained the correct information?

At (**example**) *the joint tenants (a couple) separated and wanted to end the tenancy during the two-year fixed term. I checked the tenancy agreement and noted that there was no break clause. I informed my supervisor and the landlord. The landlord's policy in this situation was to accept a surrender of the tenancy and to relet without delay, to mitigate potential losses. I explained the surrender process to the tenants, who subsequently vacated the property. I arranged an independent* *check-out report and attended the property to accept the keys from the tenant, to surrender the tenancy.*

Questions on this example could include:

- Why did you check whether there was a break clause?
- What is a break clause?
- Tell me about joint and several liability.
- What is joint and several liability?
- What is surrender of a tenancy?
- How did you explain the surrender process to the tenants?
- Can a surrender be achieved by a landlord or a tenant unilaterally?
- Why was it important that you accepted return of the keys in this situation?
- What is an express surrender?
- What is implied surrender?
- What is surrender by operation of law?

How Can You Demonstrate Level 1?

Although the assessors will focus on your highest level, you may be asked some level 1 questions, focussing on the knowledge behind your practical level 2 (and potentially level 3) examples. Level 1 requires candidates to demonstrate their knowledge and understanding of the law and practice in relation to landlord and tenant.[2]

A level 1 summary of experience could include, for example:

I am familiar with the Housing Acts 1988, 1996, and 2004 and with the main clauses of an assured shorthold tenancy agreement. I understand that an assured shorthold tenant has security of tenure, and that these tenancies can only be ended using one of the prescribed methods. I understand that landlords have an implied repairing covenant under S11 Landlord and Tenant Act 1985 and that Warren v Keen 1953 (as outlined in the Private Rented Sector Code of Practice) helps define a 'tenant-like manner'.

Questions on this summary of experience could include:

- What is an assured shorthold tenancy?
- How does an assured shorthold tenancy differ from an assured tenancy?
- Which sections of the Housing Act 1988 relate to regaining possession?

- What are the mandatory/discretionary grounds for possession under Schedule 2 of the Housing Act 1988?
- Give me two examples of clauses that you would expect in an assured shorthold tenancy agreement.
- Tell me about section 21 of the Housing Act 1988.
- What happens at the end of a fixed-term assured shorthold tenancy?
- What key changes did the Housing Act 1996 make?
- What are a landlord's repairing obligations under S11 Landlord and Tenant Act 1985?
- When does S11 Landlord and Tenant Act 1985 apply?
- Tell me about Warren v Keen 1953.

Conclusion

Residential landlord and tenant work is a skilled area requiring thorough legal and technical knowledge combined with communication and negotiation skills. The competency relates to the landlord and tenant relationship, so it requires the ability to manage not just the legal rights and constraints around that relationship, but also the personal aspect. For candidates with the necessary experience, it complements and supports several other mandatory and technical competencies. Experience can be gained in either (or both) long residential leases or short-term lettings, so the Landlord and Tenant competency covers a wide scope of work. The competency can be a suitable option for candidates with a good understanding of landlord and tenant law, and an interest in this changing, politicised, and sometimes controversial sector.

Reference List

1 RICS (2024) *Residential pathway guide* [Online] Available at: https://www.rics.org/join-rics/sector-pathways (Accessed 26 August 2024).
2 RICS (2024) *Residential pathway guide* [Online] Available at: https://www.rics.org/join-rics/sector-pathways (Accessed 26 August 2024).

Further Reading and Resources

Association of Retirement Housing Managers (no date) *Association of retirement housing managers (ARHM) private retirement housing code of practice* [Online] Available at: https://www.arhm.org/code-of-practice/#:~:text=The%20

Code%20can%20be%20used,a%20matter%20of%20good%20practice (Accessed 23 August 2024).

Law Commission: https://www.lawcom.gov.uk/project/leasehold-enfranchisement/.

RICS (no date) *Property agency and management* [Online] Available at: https://www.rics.org/profession-standards/rics-standards-and-guidance/sector-standards/real-estate-standards/property-agency-and-management (Accessed 20 January 2025).

Shelter (no date) *Using break clauses to end fixed term tenancies* [Online] Available at: https://england.shelter.org.uk/professional_resources/legal/renting/how_a_tenant_can_end_a_tenancy/using_break_clauses_to_end_fixed_term_tenancies#reference-9 (Accessed 23 August 2024).

Shelter (no date) *Banning orders against landlords and letting agents* [Online] Available at: https://england.shelter.org.uk/professional_resources/legal/housing_conditions/private_sector_enforcement/banning_orders_against_landlords_and_letting_agents#reference-2 (Accessed 23 August 2024).

Shelter (no date) *Council tenant right to buy process* [Online] Available at: https://england.shelter.org.uk/professional_resources/legal/home_ownership/right_to_buy/council_tenant_right_to_buy_process#:~:text=If%20the%20landlord%20refuses%20the,tenant%20receiving%20the%20RTB2%20form (Accessed 23 August 2024).

The Leasehold Advisory Service: https://www.lease-advice.org.

The Property Institute: https://www.tpi.org.uk.

Wilcox J, Forsyth J (2022) *Real estate – the basics* Abingdon: Routledge.

10 Property Management

Introduction

Property Management is a core technical competency. The RICS pathway guide sets out the relevant knowledge (level 1), practical application (level 2) and reasoned advice (level 3) for this competency. However, as with all competencies, you do not need to have encountered everything listed, as this will depend on your experience and role.

This competency should be read in tandem with several other competencies relevant to Property Management, such as Health and Safety, Landlord and Tenant, Leasing and Letting, Building Pathology, Legal/Regulatory Compliance, Inspection, Housing Maintenance, Repairs and Improvements, and Purchase and Sale.

This chapter will explain what candidates should know in relation to Property Management, covering the main requirements of level 1, with guidance on levels 2 and 3.

Should You Select This Competency?

Property Management concerns the activities and relationship between the client (principal) and agent, and it includes compliance with the many statutory requirements that apply. Experience can be gained in the private and/or social housing sectors. Although the focus of this chapter is on a property manager's role and the agency relationship, property managers can be employed in-house, e.g., by institutional build-to-rent landlords and social housing bodies, in which case you should consider the management objectives, compliance obligations, organisational structure, and processes of the organisation, and the relationship between the organisation and its residents.

DOI: 10.1201/9781032705095-10

You are not required to select this competency, but if selected, you can declare it to level 2 or level 3. As with all technical competencies, check the pathway guide and think about property management-related tasks that you have carried out; in relation to each, think about what you did, and how and why you did it. What was your role? Did you follow a process, having regard to the terms of engagement with the client, the terms of the lease/tenancy agreement, and the law? Did you have to consider various options to address or resolve a situation, or provide your reasoned advice? This will help you to decide whether to choose level 2 or level 3.

The pathway guide outlines the requirements of each level and the sections later in this chapter will help to identify suitable examples for each level. However, in brief, for level 2, candidates must provide examples of property management-related experience, covering a range of tasks (and tenures) to demonstrate how you applied your knowledge in practice.

Level 3 is more in depth, with reasoned advice. Examples of the type of experience required are shown later in this chapter. If you can provide specific examples of reasoned advice to your employer or to a client, consider selecting the competency to level 3.

The overlap between Property Management, and the Leasing and Letting, and Landlord and Tenant competencies can be very confusing. These competencies are complementary, so some examples will be suitable for more than one of them. In brief:

- Leasing and Letting focuses on the transaction, or 'doing the deal', i.e., finding a property or successfully marketing it, and negotiating the contractual relationship between the landlord and the tenant. This can include managing the landlord/tenant relationship during or at the end of the tenancy;
- Landlord and Tenant focuses on processes and issues that may arise during the lease or tenancy, e.g., rent reviews, enfranchisement, and dispute resolution;
- Property Management covers management matters arising between the client and agent, including statutory compliance. As well as covering both lettings and block management, the competency focuses on the owner/occupier/agent relationship.[1]

You should find it helpful to study the pathway guide carefully, together with the relevant chapters in this book, to help you to distinguish between the competencies and to identify knowledge and experience suitable for each. It is possible that some of the residential competencies will be combined in future, once the RICS has completed its pathway and competency review.

Property Management Skills

Specific property management skills will depend on your role. Experience can be gained in freeholds, short residential tenancies (for example, a six-month assured shorthold tenancy) and long residential leases, and in both the private sector and the social housing sector.

As this competency focuses on management duties and the client/principal/agent relationship, a good starting point is the terms of engagement. Understanding your firm's terms of engagement ensures that you are aware of your management role and responsibilities, and of the extent of your authority. This can help to manage client and tenant/leaseholder expectations. This is an important point; a management agent (i.e., a letting agent or leasehold block managing agent) is instructed by the client, who appoints the agent to carry out specified duties of the landlord under the lease/tenancy agreement and the law. However, the agent also needs to collaborate with the 'customer' – the tenant/leaseholder – as the tenant occupier is the 'end-user' of the agent's management service. The agent needs to ensure that they act in the client landlord's interests, and, if necessary, make tenants/leaseholders aware of the extent of their authority, seeking further instructions from the client where needed.

In view of this, client requirements need to be checked carefully and reflected in the terms of engagement. Any limitations should be notified to the client, especially where standard terms of engagement are used. It is normal for management agents' terms of engagement to cover routine management services, with further instructions and an additional fee payable for other non-routine matters. For example, the management fee is likely to cover the management time involved in arranging a routine repair. The contractor's repairing invoice will usually be charged to the client and, if appropriate, paid from the service charge. If the manager is instructed by the client to arrange major cyclical maintenance, such as external redecoration, the manager is likely to require specific instructions and to charge an additional fee. It is therefore important that candidates are familiar with the firm's terms of engagement and fee structure. The agent also needs to understand that if instructed to carry out major cyclical maintenance (to continue the example), the lease must be reviewed, service charge budgets and funds must be checked, and there are likely to be other statutory requirements, such as section 20 Landlord and Tenant Act 1985 consultation on major works.

The Landlord and Tenant Act 1985 is also relevant to agents' own fees: if the terms of engagement create a qualifying long-term agreement under section 20 of the Act, the statutory consultation process must be followed before the agent is appointed. Failure to do so could leave the landlord unable to recover fees via the service charges (at the time of writing, the landlord would be unable to recover more than £100 per unit in any one accounting period).

The Tenant Fees Act 2019 intervenes in agents' fee structures. Whereas it was previously common to charge fees to both landlord and tenant in relation to short residential tenancies, the fees and charges that can now be passed on to tenants (other than rents and payments for utilities, council tax, TV licence, and communication services) are:

- Charges for changes to the tenancy agreement;
- Charges in relation to early termination of the tenancy agreement (if the termination is at the tenant's request);
- Fees for late payments of rent;
- Fees for replacement keys or security devices, such as electronic fobs;
- Refundable holding deposits (capped at one weeks rent);
- Refundable security deposits (capped at five weeks rent if the annual rent is less than £50,000, or six weeks rent if the annual rent is £50,000 or more).

The Act contains further detailed restrictions on permitted charges so you should familiarise yourself with these. Any other fees and charges will be prohibited payments. The consequences of prohibited payments are potentially onerous; landlords cannot serve a valid section 21 Housing Act 1988 notice requiring possession until any unlawful fees, charges, or deposits have been repaid to the tenant.

In response to the loss of an income stream, some residential letting agents have diversified into other areas such as block management (i.e., long residential leasehold management), commercial leases, sales, and short-term (holiday) lets. Another commonly acknowledged consequence is that the loss of an income stream from tenants has caused agents to pass more charges on to landlords, with a consequent rise in rents. Candidates working in lettings management should be aware of whether and how the Act affected their firm's business and fee structure and their relationship with landlord clients.

Managers must establish the status of the client and occupier, so it is important that candidates understand the tenure of the managed property:

- Commonhold (a type of freehold) – these are very rare;
- Freehold (usually houses);
- Long residential leases (usually flats, but occasionally houses);
- Short residential tenancies (flats or houses).

Often, more than one will apply, for example:

- A freehold house may be part of an estate maintained by a management company that owns the communal areas (e.g., carparks, shared gardens and grounds, private roads, and paths);
- A leaseholder who owns a flat with a long residential lease may decide to sublet it to a tenant using an assured shorthold tenancy agreement.

The property manager therefore needs to understand the nature of the landlord/client's ownership, and the status of the tenant/occupier. The property manager's role can be particularly complex if the client landlord is a leaseholder, as the manager may be managing a subtenancy. Headlease covenants may therefore need to be checked. For example: is head landlord consent to subletting required; is head landlord consent needed for other management matters, such as alterations? Perhaps the property is to be refurbished or reconfigured before it is let, in which case head landlord consent may be required under the headlease.

Perhaps the simplest situation is a landlord who owns the freehold. However, there may still be management constraints: for example, is mortgagee (lender) consent required before the property can be let, or are there any restrictive covenants that could affect the tenant (such as prohibiting parking of commercial vehicles – a common source of complaint)?

Regardless of tenure, the Property Management competency requires good communication and customer care skills, to manage different clients (landlords) and end-users (leaseholders and tenants).

Landlords may be experienced and knowledgeable expert investors, or lay-people, with little or no understanding of their roles. The mandatory Client Care competency is therefore relevant here.

The leases or tenancy agreements are critical, and managers must be familiar with them. It is the manager's role to ensure that the client landlord complies with its obligations in the documents. Checking the lease or tenancy agreement is usually the first step when undertaking a management task or addressing an issue. However, the lease or tenancy agreement is just the starting point, and legislation can affect the landlord and tenant relationship, and therefore also the client and agent relationship. For example, a manager may receive a request from a tenant for consent to sublet. The manager will need to check the lease/tenancy agreement and if consent is a prerequisite to subletting, the manager may need to seek instructions and advise the client landlord that under section 1 Landlord and Tenant Act 1988, a response must be provided within a reasonable time. It can be seen, therefore, that this competency is closely allied to the Landlord and Tenant, and Leasing and Letting competencies and there may be similarities between suitable examples for each.

Many surveyors will be appointed as agents for residents' management company (RMC) clients. It is important, once again, to check tenure. Is the RMC client also the freeholder or are they a leaseholder under a headlease? Alternatively, the RMC could be a party to the lease, named as the manager in the lease. This can affect the management duties. An agent acting for a RMC also needs to consider whether the agent will accept any limited company roles and duties. For example, will the agent be company secretary (if a secretary is to be appointed)? Will the agent arrange preparation and filing of the annual accounts and confirmation statement?

Having considered terms of engagement, tenure, the lease or tenancy agreement, and the law, there is a further matter to review: professional standards and guidance. There is a list of relevant legislation, and RICS and other guidance and professional standards later in this chapter and managers must be familiar with those that are relevant to their area of practice.

Duties of a Property Manager

RICS Real estate management, 3rd edition, 2016, (now archived), was a mandatory professional statement. However, the statement still provides a useful framework for ethical and professional property management.

Managers must be honest, fair, transparent, and professional and carry out work with skill, care, and diligence. Topics covered in this statement, with which candidates should be familiar in relation to their area of practice, include:

- Access;
- Alterations and improvements;
- Assignment and underletting (the latter is also known as subletting);
- Changes to lease terms;
- Client due diligence;
- Disputes;
- Enforcement and breach of covenant;
- Insurance;
- Inventories and schedules of condition;
- Lease termination;
- Rent arrears;
- Rent reviews;
- Repairs;
- Service charges;
- Sustainability.[2]

More specifically, typical duties for a property manager dealing with short residential tenancies will include:

- Checking the market and providing strategic advice;
- Compliance with housing standards;
- Arranging inventories;
- Preparing and completing tenancy agreements;
- Deposit collection and protection;
- Inspections;
- Issuing prescribed information;
- Managing void periods;
- Planned preventative maintenance (overlapping with the Housing Maintenance, Repairs and Improvements competency);
- Reactive and emergency maintenance (overlapping with the Housing Maintenance, Repairs and Improvements competency);
- Rent collection and managing arrears;
- Rent reviews;
- Safety compliance (for example, gas, electrical, fire, and carbon monoxide safety);
- Tenancy termination.

The duties of a long leasehold manager are likely to include:

*   Advising the landlord on leaseholder rights, for example, lease extensions and enfranchisement under the Leasehold Reform, Housing and Urban Development Act 1993;
*   Advising the landlord on their own rights, for example, to apply to the First-tier Tribunal (Property Chamber) regarding service charges (S27A Landlord and Tenant Act 1985);
*   Dealing with changes of ownership of flats;
*   Ground rent collection if applicable (section 166 of the Commonhold and Leasehold Reform Act 2002 applies);
*   Health and safety compliance (for example, arranging asbestos surveys, risk assessments and fire risk assessments);
*   Inspections;
*   Insurance (depending on authorisation) including building reinstatement cost assessments, liability insurance, renewal, and claims;
*   Lease compliance, e.g., dealing with consents, and breaches of covenant;
*   Legal compliance, e.g., section 20 Landlord and Tenant Act 1985 consultation;
*   Liaising with professional advisers, such as accountants and solicitors;
*   Managing service charge bank accounts, ensuring compliance with section 42 Landlord and Tenant Act 1987 and client money-handling rules;
*   Monitoring leaseholder compliance with lease covenants;
*   Planned preventative maintenance management (overlapping with the Housing Maintenance, Repairs and Improvements competency);
*   Reactive maintenance;
*   Service charge budgets, collection, and accounting.

Strategic Property Management

In addition to the day-to-day running of blocks of flats, individual units, or portfolios on behalf of landlords, property management may involve monitoring the performance of properties as investment assets and providing strategic advice. For example, property managers may review the yield and profitability of a property or a portfolio of properties. They may also advise on disposal and reinvestment of the proceeds, or refurbishment/development to expand or change the property's target market and maximise the return on the investment.

Covenants

Property managers need to understand the covenants affecting the freehold and in the lease (or clauses of a tenancy agreement). A covenant is a promise in a deed or lease, and it may be a positive covenant to do something (e.g., to pay service charges or rent) or restrictive/negative, not to do something (e.g., not to obstruct communal areas). Some obligations will be express (i.e., documented in the lease or tenancy agreement) or they may be implied by law. Generally, the tenant or leaseholder will have more covenants than the landlord, and a key part of a property manager's role is ensuring that all parties comply with their obligations. Property managers must therefore understand the leases and tenancy agreements that they are managing, whilst being aware that there may be additional implied covenants.

Two key landlord's implied covenants are:

- Quiet enjoyment (the tenant must be allowed to use their property for the purpose for which it has been let, without unlawful disturbance or disruption). The quiet enjoyment covenant will usually be expressly stated in the lease or tenancy agreement, but if not, it will be implied.
- Repairing obligations in short residential tenancies, under Section 11 Landlord and Tenant Act 1985.

Commonhold

So far, the focus of this competency has been on long leasehold and lettings management. In these cases, management will be on behalf of the landlord, who will be a freeholder or head leaseholder. If the landlord is a head leaseholder, the surveyor/agent needs to manage the occupational leases, with regard to compliance with the head lease covenants.

However, property management could include management of commonhold properties. Commonholds were introduced by the Commonhold and Leasehold Reform Act 2002, as an alternative to long residential leasehold tenure. Commonhold is a type of freehold and the owner of each flat in a commonhold block will have a share in the commonhold association that is responsible for managing the block. Commonhold associations may appoint a managing agent to manage on their behalf, so in some ways there are similarities with an RMC. However, the key difference with a commonhold block is that there is no separate landlord and therefore no separation between the freehold and leasehold ownership (known as estates in land). Commonhold is rare, although the government at the time of writing in 2024 is trying to promote it. Candidates should have a basic understanding of commonhold, although most will not have direct experience of commonhold management. There are links to further reading on the topic at the end of the chapter.

Termination of the Agency Agreement

Management contracts may be terminated, either by the client, or through legal intervention. In the case of short residential tenancies, banning orders prohibit landlords and agents who commit offences from letting or managing residential properties. Banning order offences include unlawful eviction or harassment under the Protection from Eviction Act 1977, and failure to comply with Houses in Multiple Occupation (HMO) management regulations under the Housing Act 2004. Applications for banning orders can only be made by a local authority to the First-tier Tribunal (Property Chamber), after conviction for a banning order offence.[3]

In the case of long residential leases, one or more leaseholders have the right to apply to the First-tier Tribunal (Property Chamber) under the Landlord and Tenant Act 1987 for the appointment of a manager. This is a fault-based right; if the leaseholder(s) can satisfy the Tribunal that the manager or landlord is not meeting their management obligations under the lease, the law, or professional standards, the Tribunal can appoint a new manager to manage the property.

Leaseholders also have the right via a Right to Manage Company under the Commonhold and Leasehold Reform Act 2002 to take over the management of their block, without needing to prove any fault on the part of the landlord or manager. If leaseholders follow the correct process, and if the leaseholders and the building qualify, the manager's contract will end when the leaseholders take over the management. The outgoing agent may be able to negotiate a new contract with the Right to Manage Company, but this is not guaranteed.

Furthermore, leaseholders may enfranchise, buying the freehold of their block. If the block and the leaseholders qualify, and the correct process is followed, the landlord cannot prevent this form of compulsory purchase, so once again the agent could lose the management contract.

Redress Schemes and the Regulation of Property Agents

Candidates should be aware of proposals to regulate property agents (Regulation of Property Agents). At the time of writing in 2024, these proposals have been around for several years but have not yet become law. However, there is still some sector pressure for regulation, and if this proceeds, individuals in certain roles may be required to have minimum qualifications, and firms carrying out property management work may need to be licenced. There is a link to further information at the end of this chapter.

In the meantime, property management firms must belong to one of two redress schemes offering independent complaints resolution:

* The Property Ombudsman;
* The Property Redress Scheme.

Chapter 14 contains more information on redress schemes.

Leasehold Reform and Renters Reform

At the time of writing in 2024, legislation was also going through Parliament reforming both the short residential lettings and long leasehold sectors. The latter became law (Leasehold and Freehold Reform Act 2024) just before the 2024 general election. The Renters (Reform) Bill did not become law before the general election though there are still plans to progress reforms via a new Renters' Rights Bill.

Candidates should keep up to date with changes and there are useful links at the end of this chapter.

The above is a brief outline of relevant areas. It is not exhaustive so you should consider your role, and your understanding of the law, and of professional guidance and standards that apply to it. It may also be helpful to refer to Chapter 2 (Inspection), Chapter 8 (Leasing and Letting), Chapter 9 (Landlord and Tenant), Chapter 12 (Housing Maintenance, Repairs, and Improvements), and Chapter 13 (Legal/Regulatory Compliance). Several mandatory competencies will also be relevant, for example, Client Care.

RICS Professional Standards and Practice Information

This list of RICS (and other) publications relevant to the Property Management competency is not exhaustive, and it will be subject to change as the RICS updates its publications and processes. However, it should be a helpful indication of the relevant documentation. It is important to check for further standards and information relevant to your role, and for updates to those listed below. Examples are:

- Association of Retirement Housing Managers (ARHM) Private Retirement Housing Code of Practice (there are separate codes of each of England, Scotland, and Wales);
- Client money handling UK, 1st edition, 2019;
- Health and safety for residential property managers, 1st edition, 2016;
- ICAEW Tech 03/11 Residential service charge accounts;
- Private Rented Sector Code of Practice 2015 (this has now been archived by the RICS but may still be relevant to older examples);
- Property agency and management principles, Global, 1st edition, 2024;
- Real estate management, 3rd edition, 2016 (archived);
- Service charge, residential management code, 3rd edition, 2016;
- Surveying safely, 2nd edition, 2018;
- UK Residential real estate agency, 6th edition, 2017 (the Blue Book).

At the time of writing in 2024, the RICS was consolidating its lettings, sales, and management agency standards and guidance. It is expected that Real estate agency and brokerage, 3rd edition 2016; UK residential real estate agency, 6th edition, 2017; and Real estate management, 3rd edition 2016, will be superseded by the new professional standards. There is a link to the relevant RICS page in the Further Reading and Resources section at the end of this chapter. It is very important that you keep up to date with changes to RICS publications. However, any publications superseded by the new professional standards will still be relevant if they applied at the date of examples in your summary of experience, so you will need to be familiar with both the archived, and new, consolidated documents.

Relevant Laws

This list is not exhaustive, but it indicates the legislation that you should be aware of. It is important that you check the law relating to your specific area of practice and keep up to date with changes. The links at the end of this chapter also provide further detail of some of these laws:

- Building Safety Act 2022;
- Commonhold and Leasehold Reform Act 2002;

- Control of Asbestos Regulations 2012;
- Defective Premises Act 1972;
- Deregulation Act 2015;
- Equality Act 2010;
- Fire Safety Act 2021;
- Higher-Risk Buildings (Management of Safety Risks etc.) (England) Regulations 2023;
- Homes (Fitness for Human Habitation) Act 2018;
- Housing Acts 1988, 1996, and 2004;
- Housing and Planning Act 2016;
- Housing and Planning Act 2016 (Banning Order Offences) Regulations 2018;
- Immigration Act 2014;
- Landlord and Tenant Acts 1985, 1987, and 1988;
- Leasehold and Freehold Reform Act 2024;
- Leasehold Reform (Ground Rent) Act 2022;
- Leasehold Reform Act 1967;
- Leasehold Reform, Housing and Urban Development Act 1993;
- Occupiers Liability Acts 1957 and 1984;
- Protection from Eviction Act 1977;
- Regulatory Reform (Fire Safety) Order 2005;
- Rent Act 1977;
- Social Housing (Regulation) Act 2023;
- Tenant Fees Act 2019;
- The Building Safety (Leaseholder Protections) (England) Regulations 2022;
- The Client Money Protection Schemes for Property Agents (Approval and Designation of Schemes) Regulations 2018.

There is also a lot of case law relating to residential management, particularly regarding long leasehold management and service charges. It is outside the scope of this book to provide detailed case law, but reading professional updates and case analysis will help to keep you up to date with the key decisions of the courts and tribunals. In addition to RICS news and updates, other organisations such as Shelter, Propertymark, and The Property Institute are good sources of information, and the Leasehold Advisory Service has clear and thorough explanations of the law relating to long residential leases (and park homes). You will find links at the end of this chapter.

How Can You Demonstrate Level 3?

Your assessors will start at the highest level you have declared, which will be either level 2 or level 3. At level 3 the RICS expects you to present specific examples of reasoned advice that you have provided to a client or your employer, perhaps considering and explaining the options available, to demonstrate a deeper level of understanding than is needed at level 2.

Check the pathway guide carefully and think about whether you can provide your own examples to reflect the examples given in the guide. The guide is not exhaustive, and you do not have to provide an example of each bullet-point, but the guide does provide a useful indication of the type of knowledge and experience that you need to demonstrate.

Level 3 requires provision of reasoned advice. Examples of the type of level 3 experience that could be included in a summary of experience are:

*At (**example**) leaseholders were concerned about an unprotected vertical drop of approximately two meters from the car park into a stream. I advised that a risk assessment was required as the communal areas of the block of flats are a place of work for health and safety purposes. I arranged a risk assessment, which recommended that railings be erected to prevent falls down the drop. The client accepted this recommendation, and I arranged for the work to be carried out. I advised that consultation with leaseholders was not required as the cost did not exceed the S20 Landlord and Tenant Act 1985 threshold of £250 for any leaseholder.*

Questions on this example could include:

- Why did you advise that a risk assessment was required?
- What are the landlords' obligations regarding risk assessment?
- What legislation applies to health and safety in blocks of flats?
- Tell me about the consultation process.
- How did you check whether the cost of the risk assessment/railings could be charged to the service charges?

*At (**example**) I provided strategic advice to a private rented sector portfolio landlord. I recommended a phased disposal of leasehold flats in two Regency-period blocks, subject to high service charges and maintenance and management concerns. I also recommended that* *the properties be replaced with modern freehold houses, to minimise maintenance and property management requirements and costs, enable direct landlord control over the property management, and potentially maximise returns on investment. I advised the landlord to first obtain tax advice on the implications of disposal and purchase. The landlord accepted my advice and proceeded with the disposals and re-investment.*

Questions on this example could include:

- Why did you recommend a phased disposal?
- Why did you recommend that specialist tax advice be obtained?
- Talk me through your advice to the client.
- What were the tax implications?
- What were the property management concerns?
- How did your advice potentially maximise the return on investment?
- Why did you recommend purchase of modern freehold houses?
- What options did you consider regarding the portfolio?
- Why was control over property management decisions a factor?
- Tell me about SMART portfolio objectives.

*At (**example**) I advised an investor new to the sector. I explained landlords' legal duties in relation to short residential tenancies. The investor instructed my firm to source and manage suitable properties. I recommended investing in one- and two-bedroom properties in a range of popular locations attracting different target markets, to maximise yield and minimise void periods. I explained the three management service levels offered by my firm. The investor selected the highest level of management service, and I ensured that suitable terms of engagement were signed before management commenced.*

Questions on this example could include:

- What advice did you provide regarding landlords' legal duties?
- What was the investor's budget?
- Why did you recommend investing in one- and two-bedroom properties?
- What other options did you consider (e.g., HMOs)?
- What target markets did you recommend?
- Why did you recommend these target markets?
- Why did you recommend minimising void periods?
- Did you recommend freehold or leasehold properties? Why?

- What factors did you need to consider in relation to leasehold properties?
- Tell me about the three management service levels.
- What management service level did you recommend in order to meet the client's objectives?
- Tell me about the terms of engagement that you signed.

How Can You Demonstrate Level 2?

Level 2 Property Management is about practical experience of applying the principles of property management to provide solutions to issues affecting owners and occupiers.[4] Typical level 2 questions will start with, 'How have you...', 'Tell me about an example when you...', or 'How did you provide good client care when...'. Remember, all the assessors' questions should be based upon the examples that you provide in your write-up for this competency in your summary of experience – rather than being hypothetical or general. However, assessors may also ask for more examples, especially if they want additional evidence of your practical experience.

Examples of the type of level 2 experience that could be included in a summary of experience are:

*At (**example**) I prepared the service charge budget. I checked the lease and the service charge schedules. I reviewed the expenditure incurred during the current financial year, the client reserve account balance, inflation, and the estimated expenditure for the forthcoming year. I presented the budget to the client residents' management company directors, and then to leaseholders in a leaseholder meeting. The budget was approved, and I issued service charge demands in compliance with the lease and sections 47 and 48 of the Landlord and Tenant Act 1987. I also issued Service Charges Summaries of Rights and Obligations, in accordance with S153 Commonhold and Leasehold Reform Act 2002.*

Questions on this example could include:

- Tell me about the service charge clauses in the leases.
- Tell me about the service charge schedules.
- Describe how you prepared the budget.
- Why did you consider the expenditure incurred during the current financial year/the client reserve account balance/inflation/the estimated expenditure for the forthcoming year?
- How did you ensure a realistic and accurate service charge budget?

- How did you manage the impact of the service charge budget on the relationship between the landlord and the leaseholders?

*At (**example**) the landlord instructed my firm to arrange external redecoration of the block. I explained that my firm's terms of engagement stated that the cost of arranging major works and carrying out the statutory consultation procedure is not a routine management task within my firm's management fee and that an additional charge would be payable. I confirmed that I would arrange for my firm to provide a fee estimate.*

Questions on this example could include:

- How did you explain your firm's fee structure to the client? What was their response?
- Describe the block – how large was it and what redecoration was required?
- What was the frequency of external redecoration under the lease?
- Tell me about the statutory consultation procedure.
- What laws apply to the statutory consultation procedure?
- What management tasks were included in your firm's routine management fee?
- What tasks required payment of an additional fee?
- How are additional fees calculated for carrying out statutory consultation/management of major works?
- How did you arrange the fee estimate?

*At (**example**) the tenant was concerned about security due to a neighbour's anti-social behaviour. The client did not want to lose the tenant and had agreed to provide a video doorbell to act as a deterrent and to enable the tenant to see and record anyone coming to the door. I liaised with the tenant, arranged for reimbursement of the cost when the tenant had bought the doorbell, and provided a receipt. The tenant reported that she felt safer as a result and remained in the property.*

Questions on this example could include:

- What type of anti-social behaviour was occurring?
- Why did the client want to retain this tenant?
- What were the benefits/potential disadvantages of the video doorbell?
- Why did the client agree to provide the doorbell?

- How did you liaise with the tenant?
- How did you arrange reimbursement of the cost?

How Can You Demonstrate Level 1?

Although the assessors will focus on your highest level, you may be asked some level 1 questions, focussing on the knowledge behind your practical level 2 (and potentially level 3) examples. Level 1 requires candidates to demonstrate their knowledge and understanding of property management and the relationship between owner and occupier.[5] This includes thorough technical knowledge, which will depend on your area of practice.

As with all competencies, one way of enhancing your level 1 knowledge and understanding is to explain how you gained your knowledge. This can be through formal or informal Continuing Professional Development (CPD), through your degree studies, and through work experience such as shadowing a colleague. Think about your CPD; does any of your CPD relate to the Property Management competency?

An example of a level 1 submission is:

I understand my firm's terms of engagement and the duties that fall within this. I am familiar with my firm's standard assured shorthold tenancy agreement. I understand that I must manage properties in accordance with the terms of engagement, tenancy agreement, the law, and professional standards such as Property agency and management principles, Global, 1st edition, 2024. For example, I understand that when carrying out property inspections I must give the tenant sufficient notice in accordance with the tenancy agreement and that I must not disturb the tenant's right to quiet enjoyment of the property. I am familiar with the Housing Acts 1988 and 1996 and am aware of the Renters' Rights Bill, which may make significant changes to the law relating to short residential tenancies if it comes into force.

Questions on this submission could include:

- Tell me about your firm's terms of engagement.
- Tell me about your firm's standard assured shorthold tenancy agreement.
- What other types of tenancies are you aware of?
- What is an assured shorthold tenancy?
- What laws apply to the management of short residential tenancies?

- How much notice are you required to give to tenants before inspecting?
- Tell me about the Housing Act 1988/1996.
- Tell me about the Renters' Rights Bill.

Conclusion

The Property Management competency can complement several other mandatory and technical competencies. It requires understanding of a property manager's role, and technical and legal knowledge combined with good communication skills. Selecting this competency can therefore help you to demonstrate a range of management expertise in residential lettings and/or block management. If you select this competency, it is important to ensure that you are familiar with your firm's terms of engagement, RICS publications, and the many laws that regulate property management in practice.

Reference List

1 RICS (2024) *Residential pathway guide* [Online] Available at: https://www.rics.org/join-rics/sector-pathways (Accessed 26 August 2024).
2 RICS (2016) *Real estate management* 3rd Edition [Online] Available at: https://www.rics.org/profession-standards/rics-standards-and-guidance/sector-standards/real-estate-standards/real-estate-management (Accessed 27 August 2024).
3 Shelter (2024) *Banning orders against landlords and letting agents* [Online] Available at: https://england.shelter.org.uk/professional_resources/legal/housing_conditions/private_sector_enforcement/banning_orders_against_landlords_and_letting_agents (Accessed 25 April 2024).
4 RICS (2024) *Residential pathway guide* [Online] Available at: https://www.rics.org/join-rics/sector-pathways (Accessed 26 August 2024).
5 RICS (2024) *Residential pathway guide* [Online] Available at: https://www.rics.org/join-rics/sector-pathways (Accessed 26 August 2024).

Further Reading and Resources

Association of Retirement Housing Managers (no date) *Association of retirement housing managers (ARHM) private retirement housing code of practice* [Online] Available at: https://www.arhm.org/code-of-practice/#:~:text=The%20Code%20can%20be%20used,a%20matter%20of%20good%20practice (Accessed 23 August 2024).
Da Silva M (2024) *The pressure to enact Regulation of Property Agents is building* Property Industry Eye [Online] Available at: https://propertyindustryeye.com/

the-pressure-to-enact-regulation-of-property-agents-is-building-propertymark/ (Accessed 24 July 2024).

Department for Levelling Up, Housing and Communities, and Ministry of Housing, Communities and Local Government (2018) *Banning orders for landlords and property agents under the housing and planning 2016* [Online] Available at: https://www.gov.uk/government/publications/banning-orders-for-landlords-and-property-agents-under-the-housing-and-planning-act-2016 (Accessed 25 April 2024).

Department for Levelling Up, Housing and Communities (2023) *Guide to the Leasehold and Freehold Reform Bill* [Online] Available at: https://www.gov.uk/guidance/guide-to-the-leasehold-and-freehold-reform-bill (Accessed 26 April 2024).

Dharmasena J (2024) *The impact of the leasehold and freehold reform Bill on local authorities* Inside Housing [Online] Available at: https://www.insidehousing.co.uk/comment/the-impact-of-the-leasehold-and-freehold-reform-bill-on-local-authorities-85713 (Accessed 25 April 2024).

ICAEW (2024) *Accounting for service charges and service charge accounts* [Online] Available at: https://www.icaew.com/technical/corporate-reporting/accounting-for-specific-sectors/service-charges-and-service-charge-accounts# (Accessed 23 August 2024).

Leasehold Advisory Service: https://www.lease-advice.org/

Lemen J (2023) An A-Z of legal and regulatory compliance for APC *RICS Built Environment Journal* [Online] Available at: https://ww3.rics.org/uk/en/journals/built-environment-journal/apc-legal-regulatory-compliance-core-building-surveying-competency.html (Accessed 13 May 2024).

Lemen J (2023) *Hot topic highlight – service charges, pay now, argue later?* Property Elite Blog & Podcast [Online] Available at: https://www.property-elite.co.uk/post/service-charge-case (Accessed 5 March 2025).

National Residential Landlords Association: https://www.nrla.org.uk/news/renters-reform-bill-what-achieved-so-far#:~:text=The%20Renters%20(Reform)%20Bill%20has,what%20this%20means%20for%20landlords.

Propertymark: https://www.propertymark.co.uk/.

Propertymark (2024) *Lords tell UK government to get on with agent regulation* [Online] Available at: https://www.propertymark.co.uk/resource/lords-tell-uk-government-to-get-on-with-agent-regulation.html (Accessed 11 April 2024).

RICS (2024) *Client money* [Online] Available at: https://www.rics.org/regulation/regulatory-schemes/client-money (Accessed 27 August 2024).

RICS (2024) *RICS client money protection scheme* [Online] Available at: https://www.rics.org/regulation/regulatory-schemes/client-money/cmp-scheme (Accessed 27 August 2024).

RICS (2024) *Property agency and management* [Online] Available at: https://www.rics.org/profession-standards/rics-standards-and-guidance/

sector-standards/real-estate-standards/property-agency-and-management (Accessed 20 January 2025).

Shelter (2024) *Banning orders against landlords and letting agents* [Online] Available at: https://england.shelter.org.uk/professional_resources/legal/housing_conditions/private_sector_enforcement/banning_orders_against_landlords_and_letting_agents (Accessed 25 April 2024).

Shelter (2024) *Commonhold property* [Online] Available at: https://england.shelter.org.uk/professional_resources/legal/home_ownership/leasehold_and_commonhold/commonhold_property (Accessed 27 August 2024).

The Property Institute: https://www.tpi.org.uk.

UK Parliament (2024) *Renters Reform Bill* Parliamentary Bills [Online] Available at: https://bills.parliament.uk/bills/3462 (Accessed 25 April 2024).

UK Parliament (2024) *Leasehold and Freehold Reform Bill* Parliamentary Bills [Online] Available at: https://bills.parliament.uk/bills/3523 (Accessed 25 April 2024).

Wilcox J, Forsyth J (2022) *Real estate – the basics* Abingdon: Routledge.

11 Building Pathology

Introduction

Building Pathology is a core technical RICS APC competency, available to select to level 2 or level 3 for Residential pathway candidates.

The RICS pathway guide sets out the relevant knowledge (level 1), practical application (level 2), and reasoned advice (level 3) for this competency. However, as with all competencies, candidates do not need to have encountered everything listed, as this will depend on their experience and role.

This competency should be considered in tandem with mandatory competencies such as Health and Safety, Sustainability, and Inclusive Environments, and technical competencies such as Inspection, Valuation, Property Management, Housing Maintenance, Repairs and Improvements, Legal/Regulatory Compliance, and Maintenance Management.

This chapter will explain what candidates should know in relation to Building Pathology, covering the main requirements of level 1, with guidance on levels 2 and 3.

Should You Select This Competency?

As a core technical competency, you can decide whether to select Building Pathology as one of your competencies. If selected, you can decide whether to declare the competency to level 2 or level 3.

Building pathology is an inherent part of many residential surveyors' roles, regardless of the surveyor's specialist area of expertise. For example, a surveyor with a property management role may identify a defect on an inspection and refer the matter to a building surveyor for diagnosis, prognosis, and advice on remediation. Similarly, valuers

DOI: 10.1201/9781032705095-11

need to have a good understanding of building pathology to identify matters that may affect the value of a property, possibly recommending further specialist advice if necessary. Surveys may also be carried out for planned preventative maintenance purposes, snagging, and stock condition surveys, for example.

As with all technical competencies, you should check the pathway guide and think about your knowledge and experience of building construction, defects, and remedies. In particular, think about specific examples in practice to help decide whether to choose level 2 or level 3. In general, building surveyors carrying out surveys of residential properties will typically select level 3, whereas surveyors in other roles (e.g., property management) may perhaps prefer level 2.

The pathway guide outlines the requirements of each level and the sections later in this chapter will help to identify suitable examples for each level. However, in brief, for level 2, candidates must provide examples of building surveys carried out, or instances in which they have 'followed the trail' to identify a defect and analysed its cause. Level 3 is in more depth, with reasoned advice. For example, did the building survey identify a serious defect that required detailed advice on the cause(s), and on the options for remedying the defect, or recommendations for further or specialist investigations? If you can provide specific examples of reasoned advice to your employer or to a client, consider selecting the competency to level 3.

Building Pathology Skills

Building Pathology requires knowledge and understanding of the structure, materials, function, and use of residential buildings, to identify and remedy defects and failures. This is a very large topic; some key areas are briefly outlined below but it is important to remember that the list is not exhaustive or prescriptive. However, it should help candidates to identify the type of knowledge required, when read in conjunction with the pathway guide and considered in relation to the candidates' experience and locality. Candidates must consider the range of residential property designs, construction, use, and defects encountered in practice and provide examples, at the level selected.

It is also important that candidates are familiar with the relevant RICS standards and guidance, and with other resources such as the Health and Safety Executive and Building Research Establishment (BRE) websites.

In addition, candidates will benefit from understanding the context and purpose of a survey or inspection, for instance, the landlord's maintenance responsibilities if preparing a planned preventative maintenance schedule, or the tenant's express and implied covenants if preparing a schedule of dilapidations or tenancy check-out report.

Key Areas

Asbestos: This overlaps with the Health and Safety competency in particular, although other competencies such as Inspection and Legal/ Regulatory Compliance are also relevant. Asbestos is a naturally occurring mineral. Its use in building construction was widespread, particularly due to its fire resistance, but asbestos-containing materials (ACMs) have been prohibited in new construction since late 1999. It continues to be very common and ACMs are typically encountered in panels, roofing, insulation, textured ceilings, and floor tiles, amongst other materials.

Asbestos surveyors have a specialist role, but all surveyors need to be aware of the nature of, and risks posed by, asbestos. RICS publications (see the list below), the *Mandatory Competencies* book in this *APC Essentials* series, and the Health and Safety Executive website are all useful sources of information, including on licensable and non-licensable work with asbestos.

Aluminium composite materials (also abbreviated to ACMs): Candidates should be aware of the likely presence, safety, and financial implications of aluminium composite materials. You should refer to Chapter 4 (Valuation), which includes information on cladding and fire safety.

Bamboo: It is common to find that homeowners have planted bamboo as a decorative garden feature. However, bamboo rhizomes are incredibly strong, and while they can't puncture or lift solid ground or sound foundations, they can potentially grow into gaps or cracks in walls, floors, and drains as they search for new ground to colonise. Therefore, it should be treated as seriously as Japanese knotweed.

Building Regulations: Building Regulations set minimum standards under the Building Act 1984 and the Building Regulations 2010. The Building Regulations are supported by Approved Documents alphabetised from A to S, and the additional number 7 relating to materials and workmanship (it should be noted that 'workmanship' is not a very inclusive term.). The Approved Documents cover key areas such as Structure (Approved Document A), Electrical Safety (Approved Document P), and Infrastructure for Charging Electric Vehicles (Approved Document S – also relevant to the Sustainability competency). Candidates should be familiar with the Building Regulations applicable to their area of practice, with the process of obtaining consent, and with the consequences of failing to obtain consent. Building Regulations are also relevant to other competencies such as Health and Safety, Legal/Regulatory Compliance, and Inclusive Environments.

Building Research Establishment (BRE): This provides a range of built environment services, including training, testing, the Building Research Establishment Environmental Assessment Method (BREEAM) (see 'Sustainability' below), and the BRE Digest publications.

Construction: Candidates should understand the different construction methods and materials that they encounter in their locality, and the component parts of a residential property. This includes traditional and non-traditional construction (mundic, for example). In relation to these, candidates should consider relative merits and potential issues: sustainability, strength, fire resistance, maintenance requirements, availability of materials, cost, and aesthetics, for example.

Cracking: Candidates should understand the causes of cracking in residential properties, be able to identify the severity of a crack and whether it is likely to be historic or progressive, and know how to monitor a crack. Candidates declaring Building Pathology to level 3 need to provide reasoned advice, for example, on whether a remedy or further investigation is necessary. The BRE Digest 251 classifies cracks and is generally considered to be a good starting point for surveyors. In general, categories 0, 1, and 2 (hairline, to less than 5 mm) are aesthetic and unlikely to cause significant structural issues. Categories 3 and 4 (between 5mm and 25mm) cause serviceability issues such as penetrating damp. Category 5 cracks exceeding 25mm width are likely to need structural intervention.[1] Causes of cracks include subsidence (particularly caused by trees), settlement of new properties, heave, and thermal movement.

Damp: Damp is a very common defect, which candidates are highly likely to encounter in practice. It can cause considerable damage to a property, and significant health problems, particularly respiratory diseases, for occupiers. Damp (excess water or moisture in a home) takes different forms:

• Condensation – this is a complex subject, but simply put, it occurs when water vapour in the air condenses into a liquid on contact with cold surfaces. Condensation is a very common problem and can cause severe issues. A typical sign of condensation is black mould, and it often occurs in corners, or behind furniture, where there is poor air circulation. Condensation can be improved by increasing heating and ventilation and reducing humidity, e.g., by drying clothes outside and by opening windows to allow moisture to evaporate.

- Flooding – see below.
- Leaks – identifying and rectifying the source, such as leaking boilers and heating systems, burst or damaged pipes, is critical.
- Penetrating damp – this is water that finds its way into the property from outside by penetrating the outer envelope. Again, the source needs to be identified and remedied. This could be, for example, a gap around a window frame, defective rainwater goods, or broken or missing roof tiles.
- Rising damp – usually caused by a defective damp proof course. This is often misdiagnosed. General academic consensus puts the incidence of rising damp in all damp properties as low as 5%.[2] The remaining 95% is caused by other problems such as bridged wall ties and blocked cavities.

Defects: A defect is generally a deficiency in design or construction, but it may be expressly defined, e.g., in a contract. Defects may be patent or latent. A patent defect is generally detectable during the works, at practical completion, or in the defects liability period. A latent defect, in contrast, would not generally be detectable during an inspection.[3] Building defects may give rise to claims for breach of contract, negligence, or under the Defective Premises Act 1972.

Flooding: Media stories of extreme flooding are now very familiar, and this is an issue about which clients, lenders, and insurers are becoming increasingly aware. Flooding has a variety of sources, e.g., surface water flooding, groundwater flooding, water breaching riverbanks, run-off from hills, and coastal flooding. Due to the range of sources, flooding can occur in unexpected places, in extreme cases even on hilltops and hillsides miles from any river. Flood damage, or flood resilience measures, may be apparent during a survey, and the latter may also be recommended depending on risk. Flood risk is also likely to impact on value and on the availability of insurance (see the link to 'Flood Re' in the further resources at the end of this chapter).

Home Survey Standard: Many candidates will be very familiar with the Home Survey Standard UK, 1st edition, 2019 (effective 1st

March 2021). This professional standard was brought in to create a framework to maintain the consistency and quality of residential surveys. There are three levels of home surveys under the Standard:

- Level 1 is the least comprehensive survey, designed to provide a report on the condition of the property at an economic price. It is usually best suited to modern homes of conventional construction, in satisfactory condition, and is not generally appropriate for older, more complex or neglected properties.
- Level 2 is an intermediate level of survey with a more extensive inspection than level 1. It is generally suited to a broader range of conventionally built homes but is still likely to be unsuitable for more complex, older/historic or neglected properties.
- Level 3 is the most comprehensive survey that will suit any domestic property.[4]

Appendices A and B of the Home Survey Standard provide very useful information on the three levels and on benchmarking inspections. The RICS also provides a helpful online Surveyor's Toolkit.

At the time of writing, the Home Survey Standard was under review, so it is important to refer to the version current at the date of your examples.

There are links to further information at the end of this chapter.

Inspection techniques, equipment, and testing: This is closely related to the Inspection competency and encompasses routine tasks such as use of a damp meter to measure the moisture content of timber, and more specialist inspection and testing, such as:

- Asbestos sampling and testing;
- Borescopes to inspect areas that are difficult to access;
- Drones to inspect building components at height;
- Thermal imaging cameras to detect temperature differences and patterns that reveal the existence of water.[5]

Insulation: Candidates should be familiar with the different types of insulation, e.g., cavity wall insulation, spray foam insulation, and external wall insulation, and issues that may be encountered with them. Regulating the energy efficiency and temperature of homes and reducing heat loss and carbon emissions are also related to the Sustainability competency.

Japanese knotweed: Japanese knotweed is a bamboo-like plant that can grow and spread very quickly. It is not native to the UK, and it can be difficult and expensive to remediate. Although not directly a building defect, surveyors should be able to recognise Japanese knotweed, even if its presence needs to be verified by a specialist. Surveyors carrying out pre-purchase surveys or loan security valuations, for example, need to alert clients to the presence of Japanese knotweed and to advise on its implications for the transaction to help the client to make informed decisions. The RICS professional standard Japanese Knotweed and Residential Property advises that Japanese knotweed rarely causes structural damage to residential properties, but it can damage more lightweight structures such as garden walls, paths, and drains.[6]

Mould: Mould is always present in our homes. However, when spores land on areas with excessive moisture (e.g., condensation, rising or penetrating damp, or leaks) the spores grow, potentially producing mycotoxins implicated in illness suffered by residents.[7] Nutrients in building materials can encourage this growth. The tragic death in 2020 of two-year-old Awaab Ishak, due to a respiratory condition caused by severe mould in his home, illustrates the seriousness of the problem.

There are links to information on mould in the Further Reading and Resources section at the end of this chapter.

Movement: This covers subsidence (particularly caused by trees), settlement of new properties, heave, and thermal movement. See also cracking above. Candidates should be familiar with the types of movement, their causes, and remedies, such as underpinning and cementitious grouting.[8]

Non-traditional construction: Candidates should be familiar with the types of non-traditional housing construction in their area. Any property that is not built with brick or stone with a slate or tiled roof is considered non-standard construction. Non-traditional construction of houses has been around since the 19th century, although these methods particularly reflect post–World War I and World War II shortages of housing, materials, and skilled labour.

For example:

- **Timber frame houses** – these are a non-standard method of construction that, quite literally, have timber frames.
- **British Iron and Steel Federation (BISF) housing** – this is steel-framed housing built by the BISF between 1945 and 1948 to help address the post-war housing shortage. These are not defective

under the Housing Act 1985, but surveyors should be alert to issues such as steel corrosion, poor thermal performance, and risk of asbestos-containing materials.[9]

* **Mundic** – this means iron pyrites in the Cornish language, and it relates to mining waste used in building materials in Devon and Cornwall, mainly in the first half of the 20th century. These materials can deteriorate in certain conditions, affecting value and mortgageability, so a three-stage specialist test may be required to establish a property's condition. The RICS has produced guidance 'The Mundic Problem', 3rd edition, 2015, which contains detailed information and there is further information in the links at the end of this chapter.

See also RAAC, below.

RAAC: RAAC is reinforced autoclaved aerated concrete. It was generally used from the 1950s to the 1990s but may have been used into the 2000s. RAAC is a lightweight concrete with no aggregate, which was generally used in public buildings, with use in residential buildings limited to roof-top plant rooms and some wall panels.[10] Despite this, RAAC is still an issue for the residential sector, as evidenced by a BBC report that hundreds of homes in Aberdeen require demolition and rebuilding due to RAAC.[11]

The problem posed by RAAC is that it can fail if it was not properly formed or installed, or if it has not been maintained; e.g., water ingress can cause corrosion. The RICS has produced an advice and FAQ webpage – see the link in the resources at the end of this chapter.

Sustainability: Candidates should refer to the requirements of Sustainability as a mandatory and technical competency, as the related knowledge and experience is also relevant to Building Pathology. Relevant aspects include sustainable construction and design, insulation, renewable energy, technology, and water conservation. Candidates should also be aware of assessment methodologies, such as BREEAM. See also Flooding above.

Timber decay: There are two common forms of rot caused by the growth and spread of fungal spores in the presence of moisture:

* Dry rot (Serpula lachrymans), which requires only 20% moisture content to grow;
* Wet rot – with the exception of Serpula lachrymans, all white rots and brown rots are referred to as wet rots. There are several fungi

that cause this, commonly Coniophora puteana (cellar fungus). Wet rot grows when the moisture content reaches around 50%. White rots cause wood to become lighter in colour and fibrous in texture without cross-cracking. Brown rots cause the wood to become darker in colour, and to crack along and across its grain.

Insect infestation is another common cause of timber decay. Most candidates will have encountered woodworm (a generic term for wood-boring beetles). The Common Furniture Beetle is prevalent in the UK and, as with rot, infestation is associated with moisture content, as female furniture beetles favour a minimum moisture content of 28% but can be found in timber as low as 12% moisture.[12] Damage is caused to timber when larvae bore into wood before emerging from flight holes, leaving behind piles of dust called frass. Remember that the frass is an indication of the insects maturing from the larvae stage and exiting the timber between April and September, dependent on the temperature. The larvae may remain in the wood for up to five years, so only a proportion of the population may emerge in any one season. BRE Digest 327 provides advice on treating active infestations.

Remediation for timber decay may include chemical treatment, removal and replacement of affected timber, and remediation of the source of high moisture content, but specialist advice may be required.

RICS Professional Standards and Practice Information

This list of RICS Professional Standards and Practice Information relevant to the Building Pathology competency is not exhaustive, and it will be subject to change as the RICS updates its publications and processes. However, it should be a helpful indication of the relevant documentation. It is important to check for further standards and information relevant to your role, and for updates to those listed below. Examples are:

- Asbestos UK, 4th edition, 2021;
- Flat roof coverings, 2nd edition, 2011 (for information - archived);
- Home survey standard, 1st edition, 2019 (effective 1st March 2021);
- Japanese knotweed and residential property, 1st edition, 2022;
- Planned preventative maintenance, 1st edition, 2022;

- Residential retrofit standard, 1st edition, 2024;
- RICS Consumer guide – Flooding;
- RICS Consumer guide – Spray foam insulation;
- Surveying assets in the built environment, 1st edition, 2017;
- Surveying safely, 2nd edition, 2018;
- The various VPGA sections of the UK National Supplement, e.g., UK VPGA 11;
- VPGA 8 of the 2022 and 2024 versions of RICS Valuation – Global Standards (the Red Book);
- VPS 2 of the Red Book (note that the Red Book is being updated at the time of writing in 2024 and the revised version is likely to be current at the date of your submission, in which case VPS 4 is important).

Relevant Laws

Again, this list is not exhaustive, but it indicates the legislation that candidates should be aware of. It is important that you check the law relating to your specific area of practice and keep up to date with changes. RICS publications can also be a good source of information on laws relating to specific building pathology matters:

- Building Act 1984
- Building Regulations 2010;
- Building Safety Act 2022;
- Control of Asbestos Regulations 2012;
- Defective Premises Act 1972;
- Environmental Protection Act 1990;
- Fire Safety Act 2021;
- Homes (Fitness for Human Habitation) Act 2018;
- Housing Act 1985;
- Housing Act 2004;
- Landlord and Tenant Act 1985;
- Latent Damage Act 1986;
- Occupiers' Liability Act 1957;
- Occupiers' Liability Act 1984;
- Party Wall etc. Act 1996;
- Social Housing (Regulation) Act 2023.

Relevant case law includes Hart v Large: a surveyor was negligent when he failed to identify significant damp issues. There is recommended reading on this case in the Further Reading and Resources section at the end of this chapter.

How Can You Demonstrate Level 3?

Your assessors will start at the highest level you have declared, which will be either level 2 or level 3. At level 3 the RICS expects you to present specific examples of reasoned advice that you have provided to a client or your employer in relation to building pathology, perhaps considering and explaining the options available, to demonstrate a deeper level of understanding than is needed at level 2.

Check the pathway guide carefully and think about whether you can provide your own examples to reflect the examples given in the guide. The guide is not exhaustive, and you do not have to provide an example of each bullet-point, but the guide does provide a useful indication of the type of knowledge and experience that you need to demonstrate.

Level 3 requires reasoned advice and recommendations. You should check the pathway guide carefully, but examples of level 3 include: preparing reports; explaining the causes of failure, and the likely results of failure, together with appropriate remedial measures; formulating the necessary remedial/preventative works in a schedule of works; referring specialist work on to the relevant specialists; discussing in detail examples of unusual defects encountered; and explaining the different types of report and how they meet clients' needs.[13]

Examples of the type of level 3 experience that could be included in a summary of experience are:

*At (**example**) I carried out a level 2 survey for the purchaser of a flat in a purpose-built block built fifteen years ago. As a result of my inspection, I identified a leak from the flat roof, water-damage to the timber frame, and evidence of decay to wooden window frames. I applied condition rating 3 to the defects. I recommended that the client's legal advisers investigate further with the management company regarding planned repairs and availability of funds.*

Questions on this example could include:

- Why was a level 2 survey selected for the property?
- How did you identify the leaking roof/water-damage/evidence of decay?
- How did you follow the trail?
- What remedies did you recommend?
- Why did you apply condition rating 3 to the defects?

- Tell me about condition rating 1/2/3.
- Talk me through your advice to the client.
- Why did you recommend that the management company be approached?

*At (**example**) I inspected a Regency property following a report of fungus on a skirting board on an exterior wall on the first floor. I identified the fruiting bodies associated with dry rot (Serpula lacrymans). I also noted that there was excessive movement to the floor of the room, accompanied by cuboidal cracking and visible mycelium. This alerted me to the likely presence of dry rot. Using my damp meter, I measured a moisture content of 26% in the timber floorboards and joists. From my external inspection I suspected that water ingress from defective gutters was a contributory factor. I recommended that the client appoint a timber treatment specialist to carry out further investigations, to identify the extent of the problem, and to advise on suitable remedies.*

Questions on this example could include:

- Describe the symptoms of dry rot.
- How did the construction of the property likely contribute to the outbreak of dry rot?
- Tell me about the excessive movement in the floor – how did you determine this?
- What was the significance of the damp metre reading?
- In what way were the gutters defective?
- What advice did you provide to the client?
- Why did you recommend specialist investigations?
- What advice did you give about the continued use of the suspect floor?
- How was this advice communicated?

How Can You Demonstrate Level 2?

Level 2 Building Pathology is about practical experience and application of knowledge to carry out building surveys, and 'following the trail' to diagnose and explain defects.

Examples of the type of level 2 experience that would typically be included in a summary of experience are:

*At (**example**) I identified damaged brickwork, and that cement mortar had been used for the pointing, which was inappropriate for this period property. I reported that the cement mortar was harder and less* *porous than the bricks, contributing to the spalling. I also reported that replacing the cement mortar with a more suitable lime mortar would help to avoid this problem.*

Questions on this example could include:

- What was the age of the property?
- What do you mean by 'spalling'?
- Why was cement mortar inappropriate for the property?
- What was the evidence to support this?
- Why would lime mortar be more appropriate?
- Describe the damage to the brick work.
- What problems can be caused by spalling?

*At (**example**) I was asked to inspect a managed top-floor attic flat in a converted former chapel. The leaseholders had reported leaks from the skylights causing water to run down the panes and damage the plaster and paintwork. During my inspection I noted that the vents in the sky-lights were closed, that there were no other sources of ventilation, and that cooking and laundry drying in the affected rooms was creating humidity and condensation. I reported that the skylights were not leak-ing and that the issue was condensation. I provided my firm's informa-tion to the leaseholders on how to reduce and manage condensation.*

Questions on this example could include:

- Talk me through your inspection.
- How did you identify condensation?
- Did you use a humidity meter?
- Talk me through how you used a humidity meter.
- How high above the floor were the skylights?
- What was the evidence of there being no leaks from the skylights?
- Could the skylight vents be opened?
- What causes condensation?
- How can condensation be reduced or prevented?
- Which Building Regulation Approved Document applies to ventilation?

How Can You Demonstrate Level 1?

Although the assessors will focus on your highest level, you may be asked some level 1 questions, focussing on the knowledge behind your practical level 2 (and potentially level 3) examples. Level 1 requires candidates to demonstrate their knowledge and understanding of building defects including collection of information, measurements, and tests.[14] In addition to RICS publications, it is important to have a thorough knowledge of relevant law, some of which is outlined above. Be aware of other sources of information, for example, government publications and resources such as isurv, the '.gov', BRE, and HSE websites.

An example level 1 summary of experience submission could be as follows:

Through my role as a surveyor I understand the requirements of RICS level 1, 2, and 3 surveys. I have gained knowledge of traditional and non-traditional construction methods (e.g., mundic). I am familiar with common building defects such as wet rot, dry rot, damp, and cracking and I understand the importance of following the trail to diagnose building defects. Through CPD, I have gained knowledge of Japanese knotweed and understand the issues it can present. I am aware of hazardous materials, such as asbestos and I am familiar with RICS publications such as Japanese knotweed and residential property, 1st edition, 2022, and the RICS Consumer Guide Spray Foam Insulation.

Level 1 questions could include:

- What are the requirements of level 1/2/3 surveys?
- Tell me about the condition ratings in the Home Survey Standard.
- What is the Home Survey Standard?
- What is traditional construction?
- What types of non-traditional construction are you aware of?
- What is mundic?
- What are the issues with mundic?
- What are the symptoms of dry rot?
- Which BRE Digest applies to cracking?
- What is a common cause of penetrating damp?
- What problems can Japanese knotweed cause?
- What are the issues with spray foam insulation?
- When was asbestos banned in construction?

As with each competency, keeping up to date, developing your knowledge, and being aware of 'hot topics' are also required so it is important to read news and professional updates relevant to the Building Pathology competency. This can be a frequently reported topic, for example, following the Grenfell Tower tragedy, and regarding other issues such as RAAC.

One way of enhancing your level 1 knowledge and understanding is to explain how you gained your knowledge. This can be through CPD (formal or informal), through your studies during a degree, and through work experience such as shadowing a colleague. Think about your CPD; does any of your CPD relate in the Building Pathology competency? If necessary, sign-up for relevant CPD or identify reliable sources such as RICS Modus for informal reading to help fill any gaps in your knowledge.

Conclusion

Building Pathology is a large area with specialist skills and knowledge, and it is relevant to every residential surveyor's role. Building Pathology therefore plays a fundamental role in surveying practice, as demonstrated by its status as a core competency. It also applies to other competencies, such as Valuation, Legal/Regulatory Compliance, and Inspection. Assessors will expect candidates to demonstrate knowledge and understanding, and practical experience of identifying a range of defects. Candidates carrying out building surveys and valuations in particular may feel that they have the necessary knowledge and experience of building construction, defects, and remedies to declare this competency.

Detailed knowledge is required for candidates selecting Building Pathology to level 3, particularly those focusing on building surveying as their main area of practice. However, this knowledge is useful for all surveyors. For example, valuers need to identify defects and their effect on value, and property managers need to identify defects during inspections and refer them to specialists for further investigation and remediation. For those candidates not selecting Building Pathology, this knowledge can be demonstrated in other competencies, such as Inspection, Legal/Regulatory Compliance, Property Management, Maintenance Management, and Housing Maintenance, Repairs, and Improvements.

Reference List

1 Kenny T (2017) *Pathology: identifying structural movement cracking up* isurv RICS [Online] Available at: https://www.isurv.com/info/390/features_archive/11148/pathology_identifying_structural_movement (Accessed: 6 June 2024).

2 Malone J (2016) *The incidence of true rising damp vs induced rising damp* Building Defect Analysis [Online] Available at: https://buildingdefectanalysis.co.uk/damp/the-incidence-of-true-rising-damp-vs-induced-rising-damp/ (Accessed 24 August 2024).

3 RICS (2024) *What is a 'defect'?* isurv [Online] Available at: https://www-isurv-com (Accessed 1 July 2024).

4 RICS (2019) *Home survey standard* 1st Edition (Effective from 1st March 2021) [Online] Available at: https://www.rics.org/profession-standards/rics-standards-and-guidance/sector-standards/building-surveying-standards/home-surveys/home-survey-standards (Accessed 2 July 2024).

5 Teledyne Flir (2019) *How to detect a water leak with thermal imaging* [Online] Available at: https://www.flir.co.uk/discover/professional-tools/how-to-detect-a-water-leak-with-thermal-imaging/ (Accessed 24 July 2024).

6 RICS (2022) *Japanese knotweed and residential property* UK 1st Edition Professional Standard [Online] Available at: https://www.rics.org/profession-standards/rics-standards-and-guidance/sector-standards/valuation-standards/japanese-knotweed-and-residential-property (Accessed 27 August 2024).

7 Singh J (2019) *Spore law: how to control mould and prevent hazards to health* RICS News and Insights [Online] Available at: https://www.rics.org/news-insights/spore-law-how-to-control-mould-and-prevent-hazards-to-health (Accessed 14 August 2024).

8 Rainforth E (2023) *Mainmark – cementitious grouting used to re-level and stabilise London Residential Housing instead of traditional underpinning* The Subsidence Forum [Online] Available at: https://www.subsidenceforum.org.uk/2023/05/17/case-studies/ (Accessed 24 July 2024).

9 Lemen J (2024) *Hot topic highlight – BISF housing* Property Elite Blog & Podcast [Online] Available at: https://www.property-elite.co.uk/post/bisf-housing (Accessed 2 July 2024).

10 RICS (2024) *RAAC: advice and FAQs* [Online] Available at: https://www.rics.org/news-insights/current-topics-campaigns/raac-advice-and-faqs (Accessed 2 July 2024).

11 Banks K, McDonald P (2024) Hundreds of Aberdeen RAAC homes to be demolished *BBC News* [Online] Available at: https://www.bbc.co.uk/news/articles/cgm7wmvky4ro (Accessed 24 August 2024).

12 Setherton G (no date) *A complete guide to treating Woodworm* Permagard Products Ltd [Online] Available at: https://www.permagard.co.uk/advice/how-to-treat-woodworm#:~:text=Female%20Furniture%20beetles%20tend%20to,becomes%20for%20them%20to%20feed (Accessed 2 July 2024).

13 RICS (2024) *Residential pathway guide* [Online] Available at: https://www.rics.org/join-rics/sector-pathways (Accessed 26 August 2024).

14 RICS (2024) *Residential pathway guide* [Online] Available at: https://www.rics.org/join-rics/sector-pathways (Accessed 26 August 2024).

Further Reading and Resources

Some of the links provided are at an introductory level, but they provide useful overviews and will help you to revise and address gaps in your knowledge. Candidates with access to the RICS database 'isurv' will find the Building Surveying and Pathology sections, and the Building Defects Database very helpful.

Anderson A, Porter M, Cusack K (2021) *RICS home survey standard and Hart v Large* RICS Available at: https://www.rics.org/news-insights/rics-home-survey-standard-and-hart-v-large (Accessed 24 July 2024).

Building Research Establishment: https://bregroup.com.

Building Research Establishment Environmental Assessment Method (BREEAM): https://breeam.com.

Callister R (2024) *The A-Z of building regulations drawings with building regs checklist* Urbanist Architecture [Online] Available at: https://urbanist architecture.co.uk/building-regulations-drawings/ (Accessed 15 May 2024).

Cornwall Council (no date) *A guide to mundic block* [Online] Available at: https://www.cornwall.gov.uk/housing/private-housing/cornwall-responsible-landlord-scheme/a-guide-to-mundic-block/# (Accessed 2 July 2024).

Daas V (2024) *Building materials: the next frontier for decarbonisation* RICS News & Insights [Online] Available at: https://www.rics.org/news-insights/building-materials-the-next-frontier-for-decarbonisation (Accessed 13 May 2024).

Department for Levelling Up, Housing and Communities, Department of Health and Social Care, UK Health Security Agency (2023) *Understanding and addressing the health risks of damp and mould in the home* [Online] Available at: https://www.gov.uk/government/publications/damp-and-mould-understanding-and-addressing-the-health-risks-for-rented-housing-providers/understanding-and-addressing-the-health-risks-of-damp-and-mould-in-the-home--2#:~:text=airways%20and%20lungs.-,The%20respiratory%20effects%20of%20damp%20and%20mould%20can%20cause%20serious,wheeze%20and%20shortness%20of%20breath&text=increased%20risk%20of%20airway%20infections,airways%20with%20the%20fungus%20Aspergillus (Accessed 6 June 2024).

Department for Levelling Up, Housing and Communities, and Ministry of Housing, Communities and Local Government (2023) *Guidance the merged approved documents* [Online] Available at: https://www.gov.uk/guidance/building-regulations-and-approved-documents-index (Accessed 13 May 2024).

Energy Saving Trust: energysavingtrust.org.uk/energy-at-home/reducing-home-heat-loss.

Flood Re: https://www.floodre.co.uk.

Hopps R (no date) *Cracking in houses* The Hopps Partnership Blog [Online] Available at: https://thehoppspartnership.co.uk/cracking-in-houses/ (Accessed 6 June 2024).

Hopps R (no date) *What is damp?* The Hopps Partnership Blog [Online] Available at: https://thehoppspartnership.co.uk/what-is-damp/ (Accessed 6 June 2024).

Lemen J (2023) *An A-Z of building pathology for APC* RICS Built Environment Journal [Online] Available at: https://ww3.rics.org/uk/en/journals/built-environment-journal/apc-building-pathology-core-building-surveying-competency.html (Accessed 15 May 2024).

Lemen J (2022) *Hot topic highlight RICS guidance note planned preventative maintenance* Property Elite Blog & Podcast [Online] Available at: https://www.property-elite.co.uk/post/hot-topic-highlight-rics-guidance-note-planned-preventative-maintenance-of-commercial-and-resident (Accessed 4 July 2024).

Lemen J (2021) *Hot topic highlight – Hart v Large* Property Elite Blog & Podcast [Online] Available at: https://www.property-elite.co.uk/post/hot-topic-highlight-hart-v-large (Accessed 24 July 2024).

Lemen J (2023) *An A-Z of the building regulations* APC Series Estates Gazette [Online] Available at: https://www.property-elite.co.uk/post/eg-building-regulations (Accessed 15 May 2024).

Lemen J (2023) An A-Z of building pathology for APC *Built Environment Journal RICS* [Online] Available at: https://ww3.rics.org/uk/en/journals/built-environment-journal/apc-building-pathology-core-building-surveying-competency.html (Accessed 1 July 2024).

Lemen J (2023) *Hot topic highlight – pitch fibre drains* Property Elite Blog & Podcast [Online] Available at: https://www.property-elite.co.uk/post/pitch-fibre-drains (Accessed 13 May 2024).

Lemen J (2023) *Hot topic highlight – why can chimney breasts be problematic?* Property Elite Blog & Podcast [Online] Available at: https://www.property-elite.co.uk/post/hot-topic-highlight-why-can-chimney-breasts-be-problematic (Accessed 13 May 2024).

Lemen J (2023) *Hot topic highlight – an introduction to structural movement and cracking* Property Elite Blog & Podcast [Online] Available at: https://www.property-elite.co.uk/post/hot-topic-highlight-an-introduction--to-structural-movement-and-cracking (Accessed 13 May 2024).

Lemen J (2024) *Hot topic highlight – spray foam insulation* Property Elite Blog & Podcast [Online] Available at: https://www.property-elite.co.uk/post/spray-foam (Accessed 13 May 2024).

Lemen J (2024) *Hot topic highlight – BISF housing* Property Elite Blog & Podcast [Online] Available at: https://www.property-elite.co.uk/post/bisf-housing (Accessed 13 May 2024).

Lemen J (2024) *Hot topic highlight – cavity wall insulation (CWI)* Property Elite Blog & Podcast [Online] Available at: https://www.property-elite.co.uk/post/cavity-wall-insulation (Accessed 1 July 2024).

Ministry of Housing, Communities & Local Government, Department of Health & Social Care, UK Health Security Agency (2024) *Understanding and addressing the health risks of damp and mould in the home* [Online] Available at: https://www.gov.uk/government/publications/damp-and-mould-understanding-and-addressing-the-health-risks-for-rented-housing-providers/understanding-and-addressing-the-health-risks-of-damp-and-mould-in-the-home--2 (Accessed 24 August 2024).

Non Standard House Construction Admin (2020) *Quick find – list of several common non-traditional houses UK* [Online] Available at: https://

nonstandardhouse.com/quick-find-common-non-traditional-houses-uk/ (Accessed 24 August 2024).

Property Care Association (2024) *Homeowner help and guidance* [Online] Available at: https://www.property-care.org/home (Accessed 13 May 2024).

RICS (2017) *How to: identify and treat dry rot and wet rot* RICS [Online] Available at: https://www.ricsfirms.com/residential/maintenance/interior/how-to-identify-treat-dry-rot-wet-rot/ (Accessed 2 July 2024).

RICS (2022) *Investigation of moisture and its effect on traditional buildings joint position statement* [Online] Available at: https://www.rics.org/profession-standards/rics-standards-and-guidance/sector-standards/building-surveying-standards/investigation-of-moisture-and-its-effect-on-traditional-building (Accessed 6 June 2024).

RICS (2022) *RICS consumer guide: flooding* [Online] Available at: https://www.ricsfirms.com/residential/maintenance/exterior/rics-consumer-guide-flooding/ (Accessed 2 July 2024).

RICS (2023) *RICS release new spray foam consumer guide* Press Release [Online] Available at: https://www.rics.org/news-insights/rics-release-new-spray-foam-consumer-guide (Accessed 13 May 2024).

RICS (2024) *RICS home surveys* [Online] Available at: https://www.rics.org/profession-standards/rics-standards-and-guidance/sector-standards/building-surveying-standards/home-surveys (Accessed 2 July 2024).

RICS (2024) *Home survey standard* [Online] Available at: https://www.rics.org/profession-standards/rics-standards-and-guidance/sector-standards/building-surveying-standards/home-surveys/home-survey-standards#:~:text=Review%20of%20the%20standard%202024%2D5&text=RICS%20aims%20to%20deliver%20a,consumer%20sentiment%20and%20sector%20developments (Accessed 22 July 2024).

RICS (2024) *RAAC: advice and FAQs* [Online] Available at: https://www.rics.org/news-insights/current-topics-campaigns/raac-advice-and-faqs (Accessed 2 July 2024).

Roberts v J Hampson & Co [1988]; [1989] 2 EGLR 181; 2 All ER 504 Isurv [Online] Available at: https://www.isurv.com/directory_record/5280/roberts_v_j_hampson_and_co (Accessed 24 July 2024).

Robinson B (2022) *Hot topic highlight – dampness in buildings Part 1* Property Elite Blog & Podcast [Online] Available at: https://www.property-elite.co.uk/post/hot-topic-highlight-dampness-in-buildings-part-1 (Accessed 13 May 2024).

Robinson B (2023) *Hot topichHighlight – dampness in buildings Part 2* Property Elite Blog & Podcast [Online] Available at: https://www.property-elite.co.uk/post/hot-topic-highlight-dampness-in-buildings-part-2 (Accessed 13 May 2024).

Robinson B (2023) *Hot topic highlight – dampness in buildings Part 3* Property Elite Blog & Podcast [Online] Available at: https://www.property-elite.co.uk/post/hot-topic-highlight-dampness-in-buildings-part-3 (Accessed 13 May 2024).

Shah H (2023) *Hot topic highlight – steel v concrete construction* Property Elite Blog & Podcast [Online] Available at: https://www.property-elite.co.uk/post/hot-topic-highlight-steel-v-concrete-construction (Accessed 13 May 2024).

Singh J (2019) *Spore law: how to control mould and prevent hazards to health* RICS News and Insights [Online] Available at: https://www.rics.org/news-insights/spore-law-how-to-control-mould-and-prevent-hazards-to-health (Accessed 14 August 2024).

Singh J (2019) Controlling mould *RICS Built Environment Journal* [Online] Available at: https://ww3.rics.org/uk/en/journals/built-environment-journal/controlling-mould.html (Accessed 24 August 2024).

12 Housing Maintenance, Repairs, and Improvements

Introduction

Housing Maintenance, Repairs, and Improvements is a core technical RICS APC competency, available to select to level 2 or level 3 for Residential pathway candidates. This means that candidates have the option to declare level 2 or 3, but it is not compulsory to select the competency.

The RICS pathway guide sets out the relevant knowledge (level 1), practical application (level 2), and reasoned advice (level 3) for this competency. However, as with all competencies, candidates do not need to have encountered everything listed, as this will depend on their experience and role.

This competency is closely related to several others that complement the knowledge and skills needed and reflect the context in which housing maintenance, repairs, and improvements are required, for example:

- Building Pathology;
- Health and Safety;
- Inspection;
- Landlord and Tenant;
- Leasing and Letting;
- Legal/Regulatory Compliance;
- Maintenance Management;
- Property Management.

This chapter will explain what candidates should know in relation to Housing Maintenance, Repairs, and Improvements, covering the main requirements of level 1, with guidance on levels 2 and 3.

DOI: 10.1201/9781032705095-12

Should You Select This Competency?

As a core technical competency, you can decide whether to select Housing Maintenance, Repairs, and Improvements. If you do select the competency, you can choose whether to declare it to level 2 or level 3.

The Housing Maintenance, Repairs, and Improvements competency is particularly relevant to candidates managing properties, for example, under long residential leases or short residential tenancies, or carrying out building surveys. The competency relates to the assessment of maintenance and repairing issues to managed estates, advising and implementing strategies to meet housing needs.[1] As with all competencies, check the pathway guide and think about instances in which you have dealt with maintenance, repairs, and improvements. In relation to each, think about the work that you arranged, how and why you arranged it, what your role was, and the issues you addressed. This will help you to decide whether to choose the competency and if so, whether to select level 2 or level 3.

The pathway guide outlines the requirements of each level and the sections later in this chapter will help to identify suitable examples for each level. However, in brief, for level 2, candidates need to apply their knowledge to assess housing condition and prepare reports and cost estimates.[2] Level 3 is more in depth, with reasoned advice. For example, what was the maintenance strategy and why was it adopted, was there a serious defect that required a detailed remediation plan and budget, who was responsible for the work, what options were considered for remedying and funding the defect, what recommendations were made for further or specialist investigations, and what were the legal implications for your client? If you can provide specific examples of in-depth knowledge and reasoned advice to your employer or to a client, consider selecting the competency to level 3.

Housing Maintenance, Repairs, and Improvements Skills

This competency is relevant to a wide range of surveying roles, for example:

- Assessing and co-ordinating the safety aspects of works;
- Compliance with/advising on the legal liability of your client;

- Organising and managing repairs, both proactively and reactively;
- Planning and budgeting repairs;
- Surveying a building's condition.

Housing maintenance, repairs, and improvements are all essential to meeting residents' housing needs. Maintenance means keeping a property in good condition. Repairs are likely to be needed to keep a property in good condition. For a repair to be necessary, an item must be in disrepair; i.e., it has deteriorated and is not functioning as intended. 'Improvements' mean that an item has been enhanced. So, for example, maintaining the interior communal areas of a block of flats will require periodic redecoration, usually at intervals specified in the lease. If the redecoration were to be enhanced by fitting new plaster cornices and a ceiling rose, this would be an improvement. However, if the communal areas already have cornices and a ceiling rose that have deteriorated, perhaps becoming chipped or cracked, they will need repair to maintain them in good condition.

Responsibility for maintenance, repairs, and improvements arises from:

- Statutes;
- The common law;
- The lease or tenancy agreement as a contract.

This area can be a source of conflict between landlords and tenants as they may have differing motivations and objectives. Budget constraints, repairing responsibilities, identifying whether improvements are permitted under a lease, and managing expectations can all present a challenge.

It is useful to separate different types of managed estate and deal with each individually. The following is a brief outline of some relevant topics to help you to understand the wider context of the competency, but it is not exhaustive or prescriptive and it is important that you focus on your own area of practice and ensure that you are familiar with – and refer to – relevant laws, guidance, and professional standards.

Long Residential Leases

A long residential lease generally has a term exceeding 21 years. In the long residential leasehold sector, profit tends not to be the motivating factor, as service charges are intended to cover expenditure without any profit element for the landlord, particularly if the landlord is a residents' management company. However, landlords and leaseholders may have very different views of what is necessary and reasonable, and of affordability, so careful budgeting and planning is essential to ensure that blocks are properly maintained to preserve the safety, security, and value of the block as an asset, and to meet residents' housing needs.

Some leases will permit the creation of reserve funds, allowing block managers to save towards future works, ideally in accordance with a planned preventative maintenance (PPM) schedule. However, some do not, thereby creating funding problems for very expensive work and this may affect your advice. For example, temporary repairs designed to last until the full funding is obtained may be required.

The budget process in the lease needs to be followed. Usually, the budget will be set before the start of a financial year, and it should include an allowance for maintenance, together with any planned projects for the year. When obtaining budget costs for the work, it may be necessary to allow a contingency for inflation and for unforeseen works.

Leaseholders will be invoiced, usually in advance, with payments typically monthly, quarterly, biannually, or annually. In view of this, cash flow is important, and managers must ensure that they:

- Have funds available through the routine service charge funds;
- Know whether additional funds can be demanded during the financial year;
- Know the procedure for dealing with budget surpluses and shortfalls at the end of the financial year.

Improvements may not be permitted in the lease; in which case the cost of the improvement cannot usually be recovered from leaseholders via the service charges. However, it is not that straightforward. Because standards – for example, Building Regulations and minimum energy efficiency standards – can change over time, an original component may have to be replaced with an upgraded model: an improvement. For example:

- Replacing single-glazed windows installed in the 1970s will usually require the replacement windows to be double-glazed and to meet current Building Regulations;

- Renovating at least 50% of the surface of a roof may require the whole roof to be upgraded to the requirements of Part L of the Building Regulations.

The landlord will usually be responsible for maintaining the structure and exterior, and the communal areas, but the lease needs to be checked carefully as this is not always straightforward. For example, responsibility for maintaining windows frequently varies between leases.

There is a common law obligation implied upon landlords to keep communal areas in repair (Liverpool City Council v Irwin [1977] AC 239).

Statutes also play a role in the maintenance and repair of blocks of flats owned under long residential leases, with the Landlord and Tenant Act 1985 (as amended), in particular, affecting the maintenance of a building. For example:

- Section 19 states that costs incurred can only be recovered via a service charge to the extent that they are reasonably incurred and if the services or works are of a reasonable standard. This section has a broader application than just maintenance, but surveyors arranging maintenance, repairs, and improvements need to be aware that it must be reasonable to do the work, which must be done to a reasonable standard, for a reasonable price. The amount that the landlord can charge the leaseholder may be limited to a reasonable payment for the work done. Waaler v Hounslow LBC [2017] EWCA Civ 45 makes some interesting points on reasonableness: if a landlord's course of action leads to a reasonable outcome, the costs of pursuing that course of action will have been reasonably incurred, even if there was another cheaper, reasonable outcome. Furthermore, the context of works cannot be ignored, especially if the works (such as improvements) are optional. Three factors should be considered:

  - The extent of the leaseholders' interests (i.e., the unexpired terms of the leases);
  - Leaseholders' opinions on the works;
  - The financial impact of the works on the kinds of people who own the leases in the block.[3]

- Section 20 requires landlords to consult with leaseholders before carrying out major works to a building or premises, which will cost any one leaseholder over £250. 'Major works' include improvements. Consultation must also be carried out for qualifying long-term agreements. These are agreements for a period exceeding 12 months that will cost any one leaseholder more than £100 in the accounting period; e.g., a five-year lift service and maintenance contract would require consultation with leaseholders if the financial threshold is exceeded.

Potential issues concerning maintenance, repairs, and improvements could include, for example:

- Budget constraints;
- Disputes regarding permitted expenditure under the lease;
- Inaccurate or disputed apportionment of service charges;
- Lack of clarity, and misunderstanding regarding repairing responsibilities;
- Resistance towards reserve fund contributions;
- The intervention of legislation.

Landlords' repairing obligations need to be considered parallel to leaseholder obligations. Leaseholders with a long residential lease will typically covenant to repair the interior, services (e.g., pipes, wires) that exclusively serve the flat, and possibly windows, whether the glass, frames, or both. Each lease must be checked carefully to ascertain repairing responsibilities, which will usually reflect the demise.

Many long residential leases will include a Jervis v Harris clause, which can be a useful means of enforcing repairing obligations against a leaseholder. This is a clause that enables a landlord to enter to inspect the property upon giving notice to the leaseholder. The landlord can then issue notice of repairs to the leaseholder, to be commenced within a timeframe specified in the lease. If the leaseholder fails to comply, the landlord can carry out the repairs, charge the cost to the leaseholder, and recover the cost from the leaseholder as a debt.

Short Residential Tenancies

Focussing now on the private rented sector, landlord motivations will likely be profit-driven, balanced with the need to maintain the capital and rental value of the investment. A landlord carrying out maintenance, repairs, and improvements will need to consider whether the work:

* Is a legal requirement, e.g., under the lease or statute;
* Will enhance the asset's rental market appeal;
* Will increase the asset's market rental value;
* Will maintain or increase the asset's capital value.

Section 11 of the Landlord and Tenant Act 1985 implies important repairing obligations on the landlords of residential tenancies. Under section 11, landlords must repair the structure and the exterior, and the installations for water, gas, electricity and sanitation, space heating, and heating water. Section 11 also implies a right for the landlord to enter into the property to carry out repairs provided at least 24 hours' notice has been given to the tenant. However, the landlord does not have to carry out repairs that result from the tenant's failure to use the premises in a tenant-like manner.

Warren v Keen [1954] 1 QB 15 provides useful guidance for residential tenancies: tenants need to take care of the property, doing the small, routine jobs that a reasonable tenant would do, such as unblocking sinks and turning the water off if absent from the property during the winter. Tenants must not damage the property, but if they do, they must repair the damage. Beyond this, tenants are not liable for disrepair through fair wear and tear and lapse of time. Therefore, landlords need to factor into their maintenance budgets, fair wear and tear, and the lifespan of the component parts of a residential let.

Landlords are not generally in breach of a repairing obligation unless they have notice of it; for example, the tenant has notified the landlord of the repair, or perhaps because the landlord has inspected the property and was, or should have been, aware of the defect. Landlords also have a reasonable time in which to effect the repair. This is a complex area and legal advice may be required.

Section 33 of the Deregulation Act 2015 relates to 'retaliatory evictions' if a tenant has complained about the condition of their property. The section applies provided the tenant has made a written complaint, the landlord has not responded adequately, and the tenant reported the issue to the local authority. The effect of section 33 is that the landlord cannot serve a valid section 21 Housing Act 1988 notice terminating the tenancy (section 21 is often referred to as a 'no fault eviction'.).

The Homes (Fitness for Human Habitation) Act 2018 amended the Landlord and Tenant Act 1985. Rented homes must be fit for human habitation at the start of and throughout a tenancy. It applies to both the private rented sector and social landlords. Tenants can take legal action against landlords who fail to comply. There is a link to further information at the end of this chapter.

Social Housing

Candidates with social housing experience can apply their knowledge and skills to this aspect of the residential sector. There is some similarity with the private sector in that section 11 of the Landlord and Tenant Act 1985 and the Homes (Fitness for Human Habitation) Act 2018 both also apply to social landlords, as do the section 20 consultation requirements. However, there is a further requirement for the social rented sector: the Decent Homes Standard, which reflects the Housing Health and Safety Rating System. The Decent Homes Standard is a minimum standard for rented social housing. At the time of writing it does not apply to the private rented sector, leaseholds, or shared ownership.

A decent home complies with the standard if it:

- Meets the current statutory minimum standard for housing;
- Is in a reasonable state of repair;
- Has reasonably modern facilities and services;
- Provides a reasonable degree of thermal comfort (requiring effective insulation and efficient heating).[4]

In 2021 the Social Housing Decent Homes Standard Review concluded that the Standard was still suitable and effective, and it considered its application to the private rented sector.[5] The latter move did not proceed as the legislation was not passed before the general election in 2024. However, this should still be monitored for future changes, as at the time of writing the Renters' Rights Bill does propose to extend the Decent Homes Standard to the private rented sector.

Some Further Points to Note

This competency has a wide application and there are many elements to it. This chapter is not exhaustive, and it is very important that you consider your role and experience, and the knowledge that underpins this. However, the following may provide a useful list of topics to consider when preparing for assessment:

Building Manuals and Health and Safety Files

This relates closely to the mandatory Health and Safety competency. Surveyors arranging maintenance, repairs, and improvements need access to building records, for example, to arrange suitable servicing and testing, or to ensure that accurate risk assessments can be carried out. This is particularly important when taking on a new instruction.

Buildings constructed after 1994 should have a Health and Safety File (Construction [Design and Management] Regulations 1994, updated in 2007 and 2015), which should include information on:

- Asbestos;
- Coatings;
- Contamination;
- Flammable substances;
- Fragile materials;
- Hazardous substances;
- Other residual hazards;
- Paints.

The Health and Safety File differs from the Operation and Maintenance Manual, although the latter should include safety-related information such as safety certificates and servicing and maintenance requirements.

Contracts and Contractors

The Construction (Design and Management) Regulations 2015 (CDM) which apply to all construction work, place legal duties on your client so you need to be aware of these. You should consider how contractors are selected, 'vetted', approved, and appointed when undertaking maintenance, repairs, and improvements. For example:

- Is the work notifiable under the CDM Regulations?
- Is contractor due diligence done in-house or outsourced?
- Is there an approved contractors list?
- Are references obtained?
- Does the contractor have suitable public liability insurance?

- Have the contractor's health and safety documentation/policies and procedures been checked to confirm that they have the skills, knowledge, and experience to identify, reduce, and manage health and safety risks?
- What contractor selection criteria apply?
- How are contractors' charges benchmarked?
- Has a schedule of rates been agreed?
- What professional/trade body memberships does the contractor have?
- Is the contractor a member of a competent person scheme and able to self-certify Building Regulation compliance? For example:

  - Gas Safe Register;
  - HETAS;
  - NICEIC;
  - FENSA.

- What is the tender/selection process?
- What form of contract will be used, e.g., in-house standard agreements or Joint Contracts Tribunal (JCT) agreements?
- How will contract variations be managed/budgeted for?
- How will contract performance be monitored?
- Will the CDM Regulations 2015 apply to proposed works?

The above list is also relevant to the Maintenance Management and Property Management competencies.

Emergencies

Maintenance may be proactive or reactive and PPM is an extremely useful way of anticipating and budgeting for maintenance, although it can sometimes be challenging for surveyors to obtain client agreement to invest in a PPM schedule. A lack of proper maintenance can increase the likelihood of reactive and emergency repairs being required.

Often the most serious problems happen 'out-of-hours', so emergency and out-of-hours procedures can help minimise damage. Proper provision for emergency cover is therefore a key part of meeting housing needs. Consider how you provide relevant health and safety and access information to a contractor in an emergency, advising of hazards the contractor may encounter when undertaking the work, e.g., asbestos. This should form part of your maintenance procedures.

Related to this, candidates should be aware of insurance aspects, e.g., 'Insured Risks' defined in managed leases, and of the requirements and claims notification procedures if authorised to deal with insurance claims.

Equality Act 2010: Reasonable Adjustments

Landlords may be approached for consent to adjustments, or they may receive requests from tenants to provide reasonable adjustments to a property. You should familiarise yourself with the Equality Act 2010. Landlords and management companies (as the 'controllers') may be obliged to change their policies or to make reasonable physical alterations to a property to enable a disabled tenant to live there. For example, a landlord may have to change taps to a design that the tenant is able to use.

Tenants may self-fund these adjustments, or they may qualify for grants, but in some instances the landlord or management company may need to carry out the work. The Citizens Advice link in the Further Reading and Resources section at the end of this chapter contains very useful information on reasonable adjustments.

This topic is mentioned in this chapter because reasonable adjustments could be considered to be improvements to the property. As this is linked to disability, Equality Act 2010 obligations are also particularly relevant to the mandatory competencies Diversity, Equality and Inclusion, and Inclusive Environments, and the technical competency Legal/Regulatory Compliance. You will find further information on level 1 of these mandatory competencies in the *Mandatory Competencies* book in this *APC Essentials* series.

Funding

Funding could be from a variety of sources, including:

- Grants and government funds, for example, the Boiler Upgrade Scheme;
- Ground rents – if these are collected by residents' management company landlords, ground rents can be a useful source of funds for maintenance, repairs, and improvements; these funds are not subject to the constraints that apply to service charges;
- Landlord's own funds;
- Leaseholder's own funds if the work is their responsibility;
- Loans;

- Reserve and sinking funds (part of service charge funds), if the leases permit;
- Service charges.

Guarantees and Warranties

Funding and budgeting pressures may be alleviated if there is a guarantee (preferably insurance-backed) available or if the work is covered by a new homes warranty such as NHBC or similar cover. These should be checked and procedures for notification of defects followed meticulously to avoid inadvertently invalidating the warranty. Candidates dealing with these should be aware of the key terms, excesses, and exclusions.

Hazardous and Deleterious Materials

This relates closely to the mandatory Health and Safety competency, which is covered in detail in the *Mandatory Competencies* book in this *APC Essentials* series. 'Deleterious materials' is a broad term that covers materials that are hazardous to health, may damage the environment, and/or are liable to failure.

This includes, for example:

- Asbestos;
- Lead;
- Mundic;
- Reinforced Autoclaved Aerated Concrete.

Candidates dealing with housing maintenance, repairs, and improvements need to understand how materials may present a hazard to occupiers, visitors, staff, and contractors, and how to address that hazard when planning and managing works.

Routine Servicing

Maintenance involves routine servicing and testing, which helps to meet housing needs by ensuring equipment is kept in good working order and repairs are anticipated. This includes, for example, testing and servicing of installations, such as:

- Automatic doors;
- Fire alarm systems;

- Fixed electrical wiring;
- Gas installations;
- Lifts;
- Riser systems;
- Smoke vents;
- Water supplies.

Social, Economic, and Political Context

Housing conditions and repair are topics that have – through tragic circumstances – gained political and media awareness and extensive coverage. In particular, in recent years:

- The Grenfell Tower fire – at the time of writing, the final report of the Grenfell Tower Inquiry was expected to be published on 4th September 2024. There is a link to the Grenfell Tower Inquiry website at the end of this chapter.
- Awaab's Law – two-year-old Awaab Ishak died in 2020 from a respiratory condition caused by exposure to mould in his home, despite requests from his parents that the mould be remedied. The Social Housing (Regulation) Act 2023 added to the Landlord and Tenant Act 1985 a new section 10A, which relates to hazards in social housing.

Sustainability

Minimum energy efficiency standards may impact on housing maintenance, repairs, and improvements, for example, if undertaken to gain an improved Energy Performance Certificate rating for rental purposes. When reading up on the Housing Maintenance, Repairs, and Improvements competency, and considering suitable examples for the summary of experience, candidates should bear in mind sustainability implications and relevant laws and RICS publications.

Tenant/Leaseholder Engagement

Tenant/leaseholder engagement can smooth the whole process of planning, funding, and implementing housing maintenance, repairs, and improvements. In some instances, landlords will have a legal obligation to consult, for example, under section 20 of the Landlord and Tenant Act 1985. However, it is advisable for landlords to treat this as a minimum requirement; engagement that follows the spirit of the law can help to promote transparency and trust and is more likely to gain tenants' and leaseholders' support for works.

Engagement can also occur on a national level, for example, with the Social Housing Quality Resident Panel.

RICS Professional Standards and Practice Information

This list of RICS Professional Standards and Practice Information relevant to the Housing Maintenance, Repairs, and Improvements competency is not exhaustive, and it will be subject to change as the RICS updates its publications and processes. However, it should be a helpful indication of the relevant documentation. It is important to check for further standards and information relevant to your role, and for updates to those listed below. Examples (including useful archived publications) are:

- Asbestos, UK 4th edition, 2021;
- Flat roof coverings, 2nd edition, Information Paper, 2011 (archived);
- Health and safety for residential property managers, 1st edition, 2016;
- Mundic problem, 3rd edition, 2015;
- Party wall legislation and procedure, 7th edition, 2019;
- Planned preventative maintenance, 1st edition, 2022;
- Real estate management, 3rd edition, 2016 (archived);
- RICS residential retrofit standard, 1st edition, 2024;
- Service charge, residential management code, 3rd edition, 2016;
- Surveying assets in the built environment, 1st edition, 2017;
- Surveying safely, 2nd edition, 2018.

The following are also worth checking. Although they are less directly relevant than other publications, they do help illustrate the wide impact and context of repairs, maintenance, and improvement issues:

- Real estate agency and brokerage global, 3rd edition, 2016 (archived, but for information, see 5.3 regarding the duty to inform clients of any physical problems with the property when acting for the buyer, and section 7 safety and security,).
- UK Residential real estate agency, 6th edition, 2017. See for example, section 2.1.8 regarding health and safety and personal safety, and 3.6.3.2 'What to consider in property particulars'.

Candidates should refer also to Chapter 10 Property Management and Chapter 11 Building Pathology.

Relevant Laws

This list is not exhaustive, but it indicates the legislation that candidates should be aware of; it is important that all candidates check the law relating to their specific area of practice and keep up to date with changes:

- Building Act 1984;
- Building Regulations 2010;
- Building Safety Act 2022;
- Construction (Design and Management) Regulations 2015;
- Control of Asbestos Regulations 2012;
- Control of Substances Hazardous to Health Regulations 2002;
- Defective Premises Act 1972;
- Deregulation Act 2015;
- Electrical Safety Standards in the Private Rented Sector (England) Regulations 2020;
- Equality Act 2010;
- Fire Safety (England) Regulations 2022;
- Fire Safety Act 2021;
- Gas Safety (Installation & Use) Regulations 1998;
- Health and Safety at Work etc. Act 1974;
- Homes (Fitness for Human Habitation) Act 2018;
- Housing Act 2004;
- Housing Health and Safety Rating System (England) Regulations 2005;
- Landlord and Tenant Act 1985;
- Management of Health and Safety at Work Regulations 1999;
- Occupiers Liability Act 1957
- Occupiers Liability Act 1984
- Regulatory Reform (Fire Safety) Order 2005;
- Social Housing (Regulation) Act 2023;
- The Service Charges (Consultation Requirements) (England) Regulations 2003.

How Can You Demonstrate Level 3?

Your assessors will start at the highest level you have declared, which will be either level 2 or level 3. At level 3 the RICS expects you to present specific examples of reasoned advice that you have provided to a client or your employer in relation to housing maintenance, repairs, and improvements, perhaps considering and explaining the options available, to demonstrate a deeper level of understanding than is needed at level 2. This could cover, for example:

- Obtaining funding;
- Preparing contracts;
- Advising on residents' needs;
- Managing the work programme and/or work in progress;
- Managing payments;
- Dealing with defect liability issues.[6]

Check the pathway guide carefully and think about whether you can provide your own examples to reflect the examples given in the guide. The guide is not exhaustive, and you do not have to provide an example of each bullet-point, but it does provide a useful indication of the type of knowledge and experience that you need to demonstrate.

Examples of the type of level 3 experience that could typically be included in a summary of experience are:

*At (**example**) I was appointed to manage a listed block of flats. The block had a planned preventative maintenance schedule that had not been implemented. The schedule included partial re-roofing due to persistent leaks. The client wanted to minimise the cost and requested replacement of the existing Cotswold stone roof tiles with cement tiles. I advised the client that statutory consultation would be required under S20 Landlord and Tenant Act 1985, as these were major works. I also liaised with the local authority and advised the client that cement tiles were unacceptable due to the building's listed status. The client instructed me to carry out the consultation process and arrange the work using Cotswold stone roof tiles.*

Questions that could be asked about this example include:

- Why did the client want to replace the stone tiles with cement tiles?
- What issues could be associated with using cement tiles in this block?
- Why did you advise that cement tiles would be unacceptable?
- Did you have the roof reinspected to determine whether the condition had worsened?
- What advice would you give if the roof was found to be in a dangerous condition, i.e., tiles falling onto the ground?

- Tell me about Building Regulation approval regarding re-roofing.
- Explain the listed building consent requirements.
- Talk me through the consultation process that you carried out.
- How would this differ if emergency works were required?
- What are major works?
- What advice did you provide in this instruction?
- Talk me through the contract with the appointed contractor.

*At (**example**), as the landlord's managing agent, I was notified by leaseholders of serious damp and mould in three ground floor flats built against a hillside retaining wall. The property was a recently converted former engineering works. The developer had been a company incorporated specifically to convert the property. I first approached one of the company's directors who informed me that the company had no resources and no means to carry out the work. I checked the files and established that there were no damp guarantees, but that NHBC cover was available. I advised the landlord that a claim could potentially be made to the NHBC to rectify the structural defect. I recommended that a surveyor with experience of NHBC claims be appointed to make the claim and to ensure that the damp was rectified to a suitable standard. The landlord agreed so I identified a suitable surveyor and liaised between the landlord, surveyor, and affected leaseholders. The surveyor made the claim, which was accepted by the NHBC, and contractors were appointed to remediate the damp at no cost to the landlord client or the leaseholders.*

Questions on this example could include:

- Explain the management structure of the block.
- What type of damp was diagnosed?
- Talk me through your advice to the client.
- What did you advise regarding liability for the work?
- Why did you recommend that a specialist surveyor be appointed?
- Did the leaseholders have to vacate their flats?
- If so, how did you ensure that their housing needs were met?
- How was the standard of the remediation monitored?
- What NHBC cover is available for structural defects?
- Who arranged the works – the NHBC, the developer, or your client claiming the costs back?
- What would your advice have been if the NHBC had contested or rejected the claim?
- Was the work notifiable under CDM Regulations?

- Was there a need to appoint a principal designer and/or principal contractor?
- What guarantees were received for the remediation?

How Can You Demonstrate Level 2?

Level 2 Housing Maintenance, Repairs, and Improvements is about practical experience of assessing condition, preparing reports, and estimating costs. Typical level 2 questions will start with, 'How have you...', 'Tell me about an example when you...', or 'How did you provide good client care when...'. Remember, all the assessors' questions should be based upon the examples that you provide in your write-up for this competency in your summary of experience – rather than being hypothetical or general.

Examples of the type of level 2 experience that would typically be included in a summary of experience are:

At (**example**) *I was instructed by a landlord to prepare a planned preventative maintenance schedule for a modern block of nine flats. I inspected the grounds, carpark and garage block, and the exterior and interior of the building. I identified several maintenance requirements over a projected three-year period, including external redecoration and re-roofing of the garage block. I prepared my maintenance schedule, applied a condition rating to each item, and a timeframe and budget for each repair.*

Questions on this example could include:

- What repairs were required?
- What were the landlord's repairing obligations?
- Talk me through the condition ratings that you used.
- How did you decide upon the timeframe for repairs?
- How did you decide on the budget allocation?
- What RICS service charge code applied?
- What RICS professional standard applies to PPM?
- Describe how you applied RICS Planned Preventative Maintenance, 1st edition, 2022.
- How did you prioritise the work?
- What documentation did you need to look at?

At (**example**) *I carried out Decent Homes Standard surveys for planned refurbishment by a registered provider. I surveyed the kitchens and bathrooms, heating installations, windows, structure, and exterior.*

I prepared my report identifying compliant and non-compliant properties and the elements requiring repair or replacement to meet the Decent Homes Standard.

Questions on this example could include:

- Describe your role in carrying out the Decent Homes Standard surveys.
- Talk me through how you carried out your surveys?
- Tell me about the Decent Homes Standard.
- When does the Decent Homes Standard apply?
- What compliance issues did you identify?
- What elements typically required repair or replacement?
- How did you report your findings?

How Can You Demonstrate Level 1?

Although the assessors will focus on your highest level, with each competency you may be asked some level 1 questions, focussing on the knowledge behind your practical level 2 (and potentially level 3) examples. The questions on the level 2 and 3 examples above include some level 1 knowledge and understanding.

One way of enhancing your level 1 knowledge and understanding is to explain how you gained your knowledge. This can be through continuing professional development (CPD; formal or informal), through your studies during a degree, and through work experience such as shadowing a colleague. Think about your CPD; does any of your CPD relate to the Housing Maintenance, Repairs, and Improvements competency?

An example level 1 submission could be:

I understand the laws relating to housing maintenance, repairs, and improvements; e.g., I know that landlords must repair the structure, exterior, and installations for heating and services under S11 Landlord and Tenant Act 1985. I also understand that in relation to long residential leases, landlords must comply with their lease repairing covenants, but that service charges can usually be collected to cover reasonable expenditure in accordance with the lease. I have undertaken formal CPD on building defects and through my role I have learnt about maintenance and repairs typically encountered in managed estates, e.g., routine servicing of lifts, and cyclical maintenance such as internal and external redecoration.

The following are examples of level 1 questions:

- Tell me about section 11 of the Landlord and Tenant Act 1985.
- What is a residential landlord's legal repairing obligation?
- What can leaseholders do if they disagree with the cost of repairs?
- What JCT contracts are you aware of?
- What competent person schemes are you aware of for electrical work/gas installations/solid fuel burning installations/windows?
- What legislation relates to works to shared boundary structures?
- Tell me about the Housing Health and Safety Rating System.

Conclusion

Housing Maintenance, Repairs, and Improvements is a competency that reflects a variety of surveying roles such as building surveying, project management, and property management. It therefore works in tandem with competencies such as Health and Safety, Inspection, Building Pathology, Maintenance Management, Landlord and Tenant, and Property Management. The competency requires knowledge and experience of housing needs, building construction and defects, liability for repairs, understanding of the availability and constraints on funding, and the legal framework that surrounds this area. You may find it helpful to refer to Chapter 11 Building Pathology, in particular, and others such as Chapter 10 (Property Management) to further support this competency.

Reference List

1 RICS (2024) *Residential pathway guide* [Online] Available at: https://www.rics.org/join-rics/sector-pathways (Accessed 7 July 2024).
2 RICS (2024) *Residential pathway guide* [Online] Available at: https://www.rics.org/join-rics/sector-pathways (Accessed 7 July 2024).
3 Arden Chambers (2017) *Waaler v Hounslow LBC [2017] EWCA Civ 45* [Online] Available at: https://ardenchambers.com/eflash/waaler-v-hounslow-lbc/ (Accessed 15 July 2024).
4 Department for Communities and Local Government (2006) *A decent home: definition and guidance for implementation* [Online] Available at: https://assets.publishing.service.gov.uk/media/5a7968b740f0b63d72fc5926/138355.pdf (Accessed 24 August 2024).
5 Department for Levelling Up, Housing and Communities, and Ministry of Housing, Communities & Local Government (2021) *Decent homes standard: Review* [Online] Available at: https://www.gov.uk/guidance/decent-homes-standard-review (Accessed 23 July 2024).
6 RICS (2024) *Residential pathway guide* [Online] Available at: https://www.rics.org/join-rics/sector-pathways (Accessed 23 July 2024).

Further Reading and Resources

Candidates with access to isurv will find useful information in the 'Building Maintenance' section.

Arden Chambers (2017) *Waaler v Hounslow LBC [2017] EWCA Civ 45* [Online] Available at: https://ardenchambers.com/eflash/waaler-v-hounslow-lbc/ (Accessed 15 July 2024).

Building Safety Regulator: https://www.hse.gov.uk/building-safety/regulator.htm#.

Christodoulou A (2017) *The health and safety file – a key document for site safety Croner-I* [Online] Available at: https://app.croneri.co.uk/feature-articles/health-and-safety-file-key-document-site-safety (Accessed 24 August 2024).

Citizens Advice (2019) *Getting help with home improvements* [Online] Available at: https://www.citizensadvice.org.uk/housing/improving-your-home/help-with-home-improvements/(Accessed 23 July 2024).

Craig E (2020) *Housing maintenance, repairs and improvements competency* RICS Built Environment Journal 26 April 2020 [Online] Available at: https://www.rics.org/uk/en/journals/built-environment-journal/housing-maintenance-repairs-and-improvements-competency.html (Accessed 4 July 2024).

Department for Levelling Up, Housing and Communities and Ministry of Housing, Communities and Local Government (2019) *Guide for tenants: homes (fitness for human habitation) Act 2018* [Online] Available at: https://www.gov.uk/government/publications/homes-fitness-for-human-habitation-act-2018/guide-for-tenants-homes-fitness-for-human-habitation-act-2018 (Accessed 9 July 2024).

Department for Levelling Up, Housing and Communities and Ministry of Housing, Communities and Local Government (2021) *Guidance decent homes standard: review* [Online] Available at: https://www.gov.uk/guidance/decent-homes-standard-review (Accessed 9 July 2024).

Grenfell Tower Inquiry: https://www.grenfelltowerinquiry.org.uk/.

HASpod (Emma) (2023) *The O&M manual and how it's different to the health and safety file* [Online] Available at: https://www.haspod.com/blog/cdm/the-om-manual-different-to-health-safety-file (Accessed 24 August 2024).

Leasehold Advisory Service: https://www.lease-advice.org.

Lemen J (2022) *Property Elite blog & podcast – hot topic highlight RICS guidance note planned preventative maintenance* [Online] Available at: https://www.property-elite.co.uk/post/hot-topic-highlight-rics-guidance-note-planned-preventative-maintenance-of-commercial-and-resident (Accessed 4 July 2024).

Ministry of Housing, Communities and Local Government, and Department for Levelling Up, Housing and Communities (2006) *Collection: housing health and safety rating system (HHSRS) guidance* [Online] Available at: https://www.gov.uk/government/collections/housing-health-and-safety-rating-system-hhsrs-guidance (Accessed 23 July 2024).

Ministry of Housing, Communities and Local Government, and Department for Levelling Up, Housing and Communities (2006) *Housing health and safety rating system (HHSRS): guidance for landlords and property-related professionals* [Online] Available at: https://www.gov.uk/government/publications/housing-health-and-safety-rating-system-guidance-for-landlords-and-property-related-professionals (Accessed 23 July 2024).

Ministry of Housing, Communities and Local Government, and Department for Levelling Up, Housing and Communities (2023) *Social housing quality resident Panel* [Online] Available at: https://www.gov.uk/guidance/social-housing-quality-resident-panel (Accessed 23 July 2024).

National Housing Maintenance Forum: https://www.nhmf.co.uk/.

RICS (2024) *Hazardous materials* Isurv [Online] Available at: https://www.isurv.com/info/1546/hazardous_materials (Accessed 23 July 2024).

Shelter (no date) *Fitness for habitation in rented homes* [Online] Available at: https://england.shelter.org.uk/professional_resources/legal/housing_conditions/responsibility_for_repairs/fitness_for_habitation_in_rented_homes (Accessed 23 July 2024).

Shelter (no date) *Health and safety standards for rented homes (HHSRS)* [Online] Available at: https://england.shelter.org.uk/housing_advice/repairs/health_and_safety_standards_for_rented_homes_hhsrs (Accessed 23 July 2024).

Shelter (no date) *Local authority duties to deal with poor conditions* [Online] Available at: https://england.shelter.org.uk/professional_resources/legal/housing_conditions/local_authority_duties_to_deal_with_poor_conditions (Accessed 9 July 2024).

Shelter (no date) *Repairs under Section 11* [Online] Available at: https://england.shelter.org.uk/professional_resources/legal/housing_conditions/responsibility_for_repairs/repairs_under_section_11#:~:text=A%20landlord's%20main%20repairing%20obligation,to%20private%20and%20social%20landlords (Accessed 9 July 2024).

13 Legal/Regulatory Compliance

Introduction

Legal/Regulatory Compliance (LRC) is a core technical RICS APC competency that can be selected to level 2 or level 3 for Residential pathway candidates. This means that you do not have to select the competency, but if selected, you will need to write up your summary of experience at both levels 1 and 2, with the option to declare level 3.

The RICS pathway guide sets out the relevant knowledge (level 1), practical application (level 2), and reasoned advice (level 3) for this competency. However, as with all competencies, you do not need to have encountered everything listed, as this will depend on your experience and role.

There is no area of a surveyor's work that is unaffected by LRC in some way, so this competency reflects the fundamental framework that supports and defines the surveyor's role, whatever the specific areas of expertise. This competency should therefore be read in tandem with the mandatory competencies and with all other selected technical competencies.

This chapter will explain what candidates should know in relation to LRC, covering the main requirements of level 1, with guidance on levels 2 and 3.

Should You Select This Competency?

As a core technical competency, you may decide whether to select LRC as one of your competencies. If selected, you can choose whether to take the competency to level 2 or level 3.

The pathway guide is very general. It recognises that LRC is essential for surveyors, and that a residential team is often responsible for ensuring full compliance with all laws and regulations associated with

DOI: 10.1201/9781032705095-13

an asset. The outlines of the levels in the pathway guide are simple and require, in relation to your area of practice:

- Level 1 knowledge and understanding of any LRC requirements;
- Level 2 application of your knowledge to comply with legal/regulatory requirements in specific situations;
- Level 3 evidence of reasoned advice, preparation, and presentation of reports on LRC requirements, for example, liaising with solicitors to provide reasoned advice.[1]

This is a useful and adaptable competency that can be used to support your other competencies. For example:

- If you have selected Leasing and Letting, you could use LRC to demonstrate further knowledge of relevant laws, and to supplement your examples.
- If there is another competency that you have not selected, perhaps because you don't have enough examples to support level 2 or 3, you could consider using the examples that you do have in LRC to help demonstrate breadth of experience.
- If you have selected Valuation to level 3 (and are therefore also seeking Registered Valuer status), you could use LRC to provide further evidence of your valuation knowledge, and your experience of applying the law, for example, when undertaking valuations for taxation purposes, or the impact of non-compliance with Building Regulations on a property's value.
- Selecting LRC can also be helpful if you have depth of knowledge and experience in a particular role but perhaps lack additional technical areas of expertise so are struggling to find another technical competency.

LRC Skills

This section is only brief, as it is recommended that you refer to the relevant chapters for guidance on legal and regulatory requirements for specific competencies. You may also find it helpful to look at the legal and regulatory frameworks for the mandatory competencies, as examples relevant to these competencies could be used to demonstrate LRC. Avoid duplicating examples from other competencies; you will need to think of fresh examples for this competency.

Remember that it is very important when drafting your summary of experience, to focus on relevant laws and regulations. However, this can be broadly interpreted. The competency requires legal compliance, so, for example, interpreting the terms of a lease or contract, or applying case law to inform your approach in a specific situation, could be suitable examples. These could also potentially support other competencies, for instance, when you have instructed solicitors in a landlord or tenant matter, applied for an HMO licence, or complied with minimum energy efficiency standards. Other areas that could be relevant, depending on your experience could include:

- Building Regulations;
- Conservation Areas;
- Contaminated and polluted land;
- Covenants (freehold and leasehold);
- Listed buildings;
- Party walls;
- Permitted development rights;
- Planning laws and planning permission;
- Planning Use Classes;
- Tree Preservation Orders.

As with each competency, the examples in the RICS pathway guide are not prescriptive, so it is not necessary to have experience of each of the bullet-points listed in the guide; rather, these provide guidance on the nature of the professional knowledge and experience expected of a surveyor at the specified level.

In the summary of experience, as with all competencies, it is important to be specific. Avoid making general statements that you 'understand relevant laws'. Instead, state that you are familiar with a particular law or regulation and give an example of something you know about that law, or have applied or advised in practice. Remember that if you say that you understand or are aware of laws and regulations in your summary of experience, ensure that you can answer questions on these!

RICS Professional Standards and Practice Information

The following are suggestions for relevant publications to help you to think around the subject, but as this competency is wide-ranging and will particularly reflect your own experience, it is not prescriptive. It is important to consider the standards and guidance relevant to the mandatory competencies and to your chosen technical competencies. The *Mandatory Competencies* book in this *APC Essentials* series provides useful guidance on those competencies (see details at the end of this chapter). It is important to check for further standards and information relevant to your role, and for updates to those listed below. Examples are:

- Asbestos UK, 4th edition, 2021;
- Countering bribery and corruption, money laundering and terrorist financing, 1st edition, 2019;
- Health and safety for residential property managers, 1st edition, 2016;
- Party wall legislation and procedure, 7th edition, 2019;
- Service charge, residential management code, 3rd edition, 2016;
- UK Residential real estate agency, 6th edition, 2017.

Relevant Laws

As with the publications suggested above, relevant laws will closely reflect the mandatory and chosen technical competencies.

This list is not exhaustive, and it is not prescriptive; there may be laws listed here that you do not encounter in practice, and you may know of others that are not included. However, the list indicates the legislation that you may need to be aware of depending on your area of practice. One of the purposes of listing a wide range of laws here is to encourage you to think around your work and the competencies and recognise the wider legal and regulatory context in which you operate. As mentioned, many of these will overlap with mandatory and other technical competencies and you will need to demonstrate them in these competencies. However, you can also demonstrate them in LRC. Overall, it is very important that you check the law relating to your specialisms and keep up to date with changes:

- Bribery Act 2010;
- Building Regulations 2010;
- Building Safety Act 2022;
- Commonhold and Leasehold Reform Act 2002;
- Companies Act 2006;
- Construction (Design and Management) Regulations 2015;

- Control of Asbestos Regulations 2012;
- Data Protection Act 2018;
- Defective Premises Act 1972;
- Deregulation Act 2015;
- Environmental Protection Act 1990;
- Equality Act 2010;
- Estate Agents Act 1979;
- Fire Safety Act 2021;
- Gas Safety (Installation and Use) Regulations 1998;
- Health and Safety at Work etc. Act 1974;
- Housing Acts 1988, 1996, and 2004;
- Housing and Planning Act 2016;
- Immigration Act 2014;
- Land Registration Act 2002;
- Landlord and Tenant (Covenants) Act 1995;
- Landlord and Tenant Act 1927;
- Landlord and Tenant Act 1985;
- Law of Property (Miscellaneous Provisions) Act 1989;
- Law of Property Act 1925 (regarding, for example, tenure, rights and interests in property, and forfeiture);
- Leasehold and Freehold Reform Act 2024;
- Leasehold Reform, Housing and Urban Development Act 1993;
- Limitation Act 1980;
- Occupiers Liability Acts 1957 and 1984;
- Party Wall etc. Act 1996;
- Street v Mountford [1985] AC 809 (HL);
- Tenant Fees Act 2019;
- Town and Country Planning Act 1990;
- Town and Country Planning (General Permitted Development) (England) Order 2015;
- Town and Country Planning (Use Classes) Order 2015;
- Valuation case law (see Chapter 4 'Valuation').

How Can You Demonstrate Level 3?

Your assessors will start at the highest level you have declared, which will be either level 2 or level 3. At level 3 the RICS expects you to present specific examples of reasoned advice that you have provided to a client or your employer, perhaps liaising with solicitors and considering and explaining the options available, to demonstrate a deeper level of understanding than is needed at level 2.

Examples of the type of level 3 experience that could be included in a summary of experience are:

*At (**example**) my employer had instructed an architectural technician to prepare plans and provide compliance advice for a small extension to a rental house to provide an upstairs bathroom, to enhance its value and market appeal. In accordance with the terms of engagement, my employer had made an initial payment of £500. My employer asked my opinion as the plans had not been received four months later. I reviewed the terms of engagement and made several unsuccessful attempts to contact the technician by telephone and email. I advised my employer that a small claim could be made in the county court to recover the money. My employer asked me to deal with this, so I made the claim online. I also claimed interest, and court fees. The claim was admitted by the technician, and judgement obtained in favour of my employer. I agreed a monthly payment plan and recovered the amount in full.*

Questions on this example could include:

- Tell me about the terms of engagement.
- Was/how was the technician in breach of contract?
- What dispute resolution provisions were there in the terms of engagement?
- What timescale was allowed for provision of the plans?
- Was time of the essence for provision of the plans?
- What is meant by time being of the essence?
- Why had the architectural technician not provided the plans?
- Talk me through the online claims process.
- Why did you advise that a claim be made in the county court?
- What alternative options did you consider?

*At (**example**) I advised on an occupier's status in relation to an apartment owned by my client. My client informed me that there was no written tenancy agreement but that he had agreed informally that his friend could move in for 12 months following a change in the friend's circumstances. I ascertained that the occupier paid a monthly market rent and occupied the whole apartment as his home. I advised that under Street v Mountford, the arrangement may be a tenancy as the requirements for certainty of term and exclusive possession appeared to be met. Payment of rent is no longer an essential characteristic of a tenancy but is very common and can evidence the legal relationship between the landlord and tenant. I confirmed that as the agreement was for 12 months,* *under S54(2) Law of Property Act 1925 it did not need to be in writing. I explained that tenants have more legal rights than licensees and that the arrangement could be an assured shorthold tenancy under the Housing Act 1988. I recommended that my client obtain legal advice, particularly if seeking possession of the apartment.*

Questions on this example could include:

- When is a written tenancy agreement needed?
- When must a tenancy be created by deed?
- Why did you advise that this could be an assured shorthold tenancy?
- What additional legal rights does a tenant have (in comparison to a licensee)?
- Why did you advise that the client seek legal advice?
- How can an assured shorthold tenancy be ended under the Housing Act 1988?

*At (**example**) I attended a managed estate following notification from a resident that he planned to cut down a mature tree that was obstructing the light to his property. I advised the resident that I believed the tree to be located in a communal area, not on the resident's property, and that the tree was likely to be protected by a Tree Preservation Order. I agreed with the resident that the tree would not be removed until its ownership and protected status had been confirmed. I checked the Land Registry filed plan and the arborist's site plan and report and established that the tree was located in the managed communal area and was subject to a Tree Preservation Order. I advised my client and reported to the resident that the tree was on my client's property, and protected, and that consent would be required from my client and the local authority to remove or reduce the tree. I recommended that advice be sought from the arborist regarding removal or reduction before any further decisions were made. I informed the resident that any attempt to cut down or lop the tree would be trespass and that unauthorised cutting down or lopping is an offence, potentially resulting in a fine and a criminal conviction.*

Questions on this example could include:

- Tell me about Tree Preservation Orders.
- How can you avoid a criminal conviction in relation to work to a protected tree/woodland?
- Talk me through how you established the ownership and protected status of the tree.

- What is the maximum fine for an offence?
- Talk me through your reasoned advice to the client.
- How did you ensure legal and regulatory compliance in this example?

How Can You Demonstrate Level 2?

Level 2 LRC is about practical experience of compliance with legal and regulatory requirements in specific situations within your area of practice.[2] Typical level 2 questions will start with, 'How have you…', 'Tell me about an example when you…', or 'Describe how you …'. Remember, as with all competencies, the assessors' questions should be based upon the examples that you provide in your write-up for this competency in your summary of experience.

Examples of the type of level 2 experience that would typically be included in a summary of experience are:

*At (**example**) I was approached by a leaseholder who wanted to make structural and non-structural alterations to their flat. I reported to the leaseholder that they would need to comply with the covenants in the lease, which prohibited structural alterations and required landlord's consent for non-structural alterations. I also reported that further information would be needed and that consent, if granted, would be in a licence for alterations.*

Questions on this example could include:

- Talk me through the proposals.
- What additional information was required?
- Why was a licence for alterations required?
- Was a formal application for consent received? If so, describe your role in ensuring lease compliance.
- What regulations applied to the proposed works?

*At (**example**) I inspected a stone boundary wall at a managed property. A section of the wall had collapsed. I reported that the wall required rebuilding. I checked onsite and on the Land Registry plan and confirmed that the wall was positioned adjoining the boundary in the rear garden. I reported that the Party Wall etc. Act 1996 would apply to repairs.*

- Tell me what you understand about the Party Wall etc. Act 1996.
- Why did you report that the Party Wall Act applied?
- What type of party wall was this?

- Talk me through your review of the Land Registry plan.
- Describe the procedures under the Party Wall etc. Act 1996.

*At **(example)** I arranged annual gas safety tests for my client's residential lettings portfolio. I arranged the checks in advance, giving the tenants two week's written notice. I engaged a Gas Safe Registered engineer to undertake the checks, and I reviewed the safety certificates to ensure that all gas installations had passed and were safe to use. I issued the reports to each tenant within 28 days of the checks. In arranging the safety tests and issuing the certificates, I complied with my firm's management contract and ensured that the landlord complied with the Gas Safety (Installation and Use) Regulations 1998.*

Questions on this example could include:

- Talk me through how you arranged the gas safety checks.
- Describe your role regarding compliance with the gas safety regulations.
- Tell me about the Gas Safety (Installation and Use) Regulations 1998.
- Why did you use a Gas Safe Registered engineer?
- What are a landlord's obligations regarding gas safety?
- Why did you issue the reports to tenants within 28 days?
- Tell me about the Gas Safety (Installation and Use) (Amendment) Regulations 2018.

How Can You Demonstrate Level 1?

Although the assessors will focus on your highest level, you may be asked some level 1 questions, focussing on the knowledge behind your practical level 2 (and potentially level 3) examples. For level 1 questions, look at the examples given in the other competency chapters, think about the RICS publications and laws that apply, and ensure that you have a good understanding of them and are able to answer questions.

An example level 1 LRC summary of experience could include:

I understand the importance of compliance with all laws and regulations affecting my role. For example, I understand that landlords have implied repairing covenants in short-term tenancies under the Landlord and Tenant Act 1985. I am familiar with the Lifting Operations and Lifting Equipment Regulations 1998 (LOLER) and the requirement for periodic thorough examinations of lifts in the communal areas of blocks of flats. I know that Building Regulations help to maintain building standards and that Building Regulation consent may be needed for works. Through my work experience, I understand that competent person schemes enable self-certification of some types of work.

Questions on this example could include:

- Tell me about LOLER.
- What is a periodic thorough examination (of lifts)?
- What does Building Regulation Approved Document B relate to?
- Which Building Regulation Approved Document relates to fire safety/access/charging electric vehicles (etc.)?
- Give me some examples of competent person schemes.
- What are a landlord's implied repairing covenants under the Landlord and Tenant Act 1985?

Some further examples of level 1 LRC questions (depending on your area of practice) could be:

- In what circumstances might a landlord's consent be required?
- Tell me what you understand about occupier's liability.
- What document is used to vary a lease?
- What property transactions require registration under the Land Registration Act 2002?
- Give me some examples of planning use classes.

As mentioned, awareness of 'hot topics' is also required so it is important to keep up to date with changes to the law, news, and developments relevant to the LRC competency.

Conclusion

LRC is a useful competency that gives candidates the scope to show additional knowledge and experience that has not been otherwise demonstrated, or which further supports other mandatory and technical competencies. As all surveying roles operate within, and are affected by, a legal or regulatory framework, it is a versatile competency. It is therefore one that is well worth considering when selecting your technical competencies.

Reference List

1 RICS (2024) *Residential pathway guide* RICS Available at: https://www.rics.org/join-rics/sector-pathways (Accessed 15 July 2024).

2 RICS (2024) *Residential pathway guide* RICS Available at: https://www.rics.org/join-rics/sector-pathways (Accessed 15 July 2024).

Further Reading and Resources

Callister R (2024) *The A-Z of building regulations drawings with building regs checklist* Urbanist Architecture [Online] Available at: https://urbanistarchitecture.co.uk/building-regulations-drawings/ (Accessed 15 May 2024).

Lemen J (2023) *An A-Z of legal and regulatory compliance for APC* RICS Built Environment Journal [Online] Available at: https://ww3.rics.org/uk/en/journals/built-environment-journal/apc-legal-regulatory-compliance-core-building-surveying-competency.html (Accessed 13 May 2024). (This article focuses on the Building Surveying pathway, but it still provides useful information for Residential pathway candidates).

Lemen J (2023) *An A-Z of the building regulations* APC Series Estates Gazette [Online] Available at: https://www.property-elite.co.uk/post/eg-building-regulations (Accessed 15 May 2024).

Lemen J (2024) How to achieve legal and regulatory compliance competency *RICS Built Environment Journal* 11 June 2024 [Online] Available at: https://ww3.rics.org/uk/en/journals/built-environment-journal/apc-legal-regulatory-compliance-competency.html (Accessed 4 July 2024). (This article focuses on the Building Surveying pathway, but it still provides useful information for Residential pathway candidates).

Lemen J (2024) *Mandatory competencies: APC essentials* Abingdon: Routledge.

Ministry of Housing, Communities and Local Government, Department for Levelling Up, Housing and Communities (2014) *Tree preservation orders and trees in conservation areas* [Online] Available at: https://www.gov.uk/guidance/tree-preservation-orders-and-trees-in-conservation-areas#:~:text=The%20law%20on%20Tree%20Preservation,force%20on%206%20April%202012 (Accessed 23 August 2024).

Savills (2024) *Guide to use classes order in England* [Online] Available at: https://www.savills.co.uk/resources-and-tools/guide-to-use-classes-order-in-england.aspx (Accessed 23 August 2024).

Wilcox J, Forsyth J (2022) *Real estate: The Basics* Abingdon: Routledge.

14 Mandatory Competencies as Technical Competencies (& Other Technical Competencies)

Introduction

This chapter covers the remaining competencies, beginning with the mandatory competencies that can also be selected as optional technical competencies, to higher levels than required as mandatory competencies. These competencies are:

- Conflict Avoidance, Management, and Dispute Resolution Procedures;
- Data Management;
- Sustainability.

Data Management and Sustainability, in particular, are rapidly developing aspects of the real estate sector, so it is important to keep up to date with changes. These topics are intrinsic to professional practice and as the RICS reviews its competencies, they may well form an increasingly significant element of future assessment.

The chapter also briefly outlines those other competencies not dealt with individually within separate chapters.

As with all competencies, the RICS pathway guide sets out the relevant knowledge (level 1), practical application (level 2), and reasoned advice (level 3) for these competencies. However, you do not need to have encountered everything listed, but the examples do provide useful guidance on the expectations of the competencies.

Mandatory Competencies

As all candidates need to be familiar with Data Management, Sustainability, and Conflict Avoidance, Management, and Dispute Resolution Procedures to level 1 for the mandatory competencies; they can be good

DOI: 10.1201/9781032705095-14

competencies to select to a higher level as technical competencies. They can be useful for candidates struggling to identify suitable technical competencies and they are likely to be within the experience of most candidates at least to level 2, as they will usually form part of a surveyor's day-to-day role.

If a mandatory competency is selected to a higher level as an optional technical competency, you only need to write the level 1 submission once, as a mandatory competency; it is not necessary to repeat level 1 as a technical competency. This has the effect of increasing the word count available for the summary of experience because level 1 is included within the mandatory competency word limit, while levels 2 and 3 are included within the technical competency word limit.

It is important to note that Sustainability, and Conflict Avoidance, Management, and Dispute Resolution Procedures are alternatives; they cannot both be selected as optional technical competencies although they must both still be covered as level 1 mandatory competencies. Therefore, you must write your level 1 summary of experience on all three of the above competencies and may then decide whether to declare one or two of them as optional technical competencies.

Competency Skills

Candidates should refer to the resources at the end of this chapter and, in particular, to the *Mandatory Competencies* book in this *APC Essentials* series for more details of level 1. It is also worth remembering that Data Management and Sustainability, in particular, are rapidly changing areas, likely to become increasingly significant in the future. For instance, currently all surveyors manage data in some way. However, data and related property technology is becoming increasingly sophisticated. How, for example, might artificial intelligence (AI), smart buildings, smart cities, and data analysis affect the residential sector in the future? You do not need to have a crystal ball to see into the future, but try to keep up to date, and be aware of change, and its implications.

Taking each of the three mandatory competencies in turn:

Conflict Avoidance, Management, and Dispute Resolution Procedures

For level 1, consider sources of conflict, and dispute resolution procedures in relation to your area of practice. Typical residential disputes could include allegations of negligence, breach of contract, and breach of lease. It is important to recognise that this competency is related to the Communication and Negotiation mandatory competency and knowledge of negotiation theories is useful, as is knowledge of key matters such as 'without prejudice' negotiations and Calderbank letters. Level 1 also requires awareness of relevant laws relating to dispute resolution (limitation periods and the Limitation Act 1980), risk management, and options for dispute resolution (i.e., litigation, and alternative dispute resolution or 'ADR' methods, such as mediation).

In the residential sector, important forms of alternative dispute resolution are:

- First-tier Tribunal (Property Chamber) (FTT) – the FTT can decide matters such as:

  - Rent increases for 'fair' or 'market' rates;
  - Leasehold disputes, e.g., service charges;
  - Leasehold enfranchisement;
  - Park homes disputes;
  - Housing Act 2004 improvement notices and prohibition orders;
  - Houses in Multiple Occupation (HMO) licence disputes;
  - Council homes right to buy refusals;
  - Disputes over a change to the land register;
  - Applications to correct or cancel certain documents relating to registered land.[1]

In Wales, these roles are fulfilled by Rent Assessment Committees, Residential Property Tribunals, and Leasehold Valuation Tribunals. There are links to further details at the end of this chapter:

- The Upper Tribunal (Lands Chamber) – this hears appeals from the FTT in England, and from the Residential Property Tribunal and Leasehold Valuation Tribunal in Wales.
- Estate, letting, and managing agents are required to be members of an ombudsman scheme. Ombudsman (or 'redress') schemes are authorised dispute resolution services. Complainants must first follow the agent's complaint-handling procedure but if this does not resolve the matter, the complainant can refer it to the ombudsman who will review the case and make a decision, perhaps requiring a specific action by the agent, or awarding a sum of money. The complainant can decide whether or not to accept the ombudsman's decision, and if not accepted, the complainant can take further action,

e.g., through the courts. There are two authorised ombudsman schemes, and you will find links to each in the Further Reading and Resources section at the end of this chapter.

- The Property Ombudsman;
- Property Redress Scheme.

  Relevant laws are:

- For estate agents: the Estate Agents Act 1979; the Consumers, Estate Agents and Redress Act 2007; and Estate Agents (Redress Scheme) Order 2008;
- For letting and managing agents: the Enterprise and Regulatory Reform Act 2013, and the Redress Schemes for Lettings Agency Work and Property Management Work (Approval and Designation of Schemes) (England) Order 2013.

It is important to remember that this competency, in particular, is also related to the mandatory competency Ethics, Rules of Conduct, and Professionalism. For instance, allegations of negligence or breach of contract could indicate that a surveyor is acting beyond their level of professional competence and/or failed to provide a suitable level of service – an ethical issue. Similarly, RICS-regulated firms must have professional indemnity insurance to protect clients and the firm in the event of a claim.

Example Submissions: Conflict Avoidance, Management, and Dispute Resolution Procedures

Level 3 requires the application of knowledge to provide advice to stakeholders. An example of a level 3 submission could be:

*At (**example**) I advised my landlord client to apply to the First-tier Tribunal (Property Chamber) for a determination under S27A Landlord and Tenant Act 1985 as to whether expenditure on replacement fire doors would be recoverable from the service charges. I prepared and submitted the application to the Tribunal and represented my client at the hearing. The Tribunal held that the expenditure was recoverable, so I issued service charge demands to the leaseholders in accordance with the leases.*

Questions on this example could include:

- Why did you advise your client to apply to the Tribunal?
- Tell me about S27A Landlord and Tenant Act 1985.

- Why were there concerns about recovery of expenditure via service charges?
- What attempts did you make to resolve the matter before applying to the Tribunal?
- Talk me through your submission to the Tribunal.
- Talk me through how you represented your client at the hearing.

Level 2 requires practical experience of conflict avoidance, management, and dispute resolution procedures. The competency can be considered in tandem with Legal/Regulatory Compliance. An example of a level 2 submission could be:

*At (**example**) a leaseholder had failed to pay his ground rent. I checked my firm's records to confirm that the demand had been issued in accordance with the lease and with S166 of the Commonhold and Leasehold Reform Act 2002. I sent the tenant a reminder letter and notified him that interest and costs could become due if he failed to pay on time. I followed this up with a final reminder letter. The leaseholder still failed to pay, so I obtained the Land Registry Register of Title, and noted that the property was mortgaged. I contacted the mortgage lender and notified that there were arrears, and that action may be taken to forfeit the lease. The mortgage lender reminded the leaseholder of the importance of paying ground rent in accordance with his covenants in the lease and the mortgage deed. The leaseholder subsequently paid the arrears without need for legal action.*

Questions on this example could include:

- When was the ground rent due?
- How much notice was given for payment of ground rent?
- Tell me about S166 of the Commonhold and Leasehold Reform Act 2002.
- What did the lease say about interest and costs on arrears?
- How did you check that the demand was issued in accordance with the lease/S166 of the Commonhold and Leasehold Reform Act 2002?
- Tell me about the (final) reminder letter.
- How did you identify that the property was mortgaged?
- What was the significance of the property being mortgaged?
- Tell me about forfeiture.
- What legal action could you take had the leaseholder not paid?

Chapter 9 (Landlord and Tenant) contains a mediation example, which would also be a suitable example for the Conflict Avoidance, Management, and Dispute Resolution Procedures competency.

Data Management

Data management forms an essential element of every surveyor's role, whatever their area of expertise. In every instruction, reliable data will need to be obtained, verified, used, and stored, in accordance with the Data Protection Act 2018 and the UK General Data Protection Regulation (GDPR). Candidates should consider the data sources that they use, and the purposes for which they use data, for example:

* Client record-keeping;
* Internal databases, e.g., of sale prices for market appraisal and valuation purposes;
* External databases, e.g., the Land Registry to confirm ownership, tenure, and encumbrances on the title, Rightmove and other online databases for comparable evidence research;
* Records of inspections, surveys, and valuations etc.

You should also ensure that you are up to date with rapidly changing 'hot topics' such as:

* Data security;
* Social media use and misuse (see RICS 'Use of Social Media: Guidance for RICS Members' Version 2 2024);
* AI and generative AI (such as ChatGPT). There are links to two thought-provoking RICS journal articles on AI at the end of this chapter.

The Information Commissioner's Office (ICO) is an essential source of information on data management, and it is a recommended resource for all candidates whether or not they are selecting this as a technical competency. The link is in the Further Reading and Resources section at the end of this chapter.

Particular areas to focus on are:

The seven principles of data protection:

* Lawfulness, fairness, and transparency;
* Purpose limitation;

- Data minimisation;
- Accuracy;
- Storage limitation;
- Integrity and confidentiality (security);
- Accountability.[2]

Individual data-subject rights:

- The right to be informed;
- Right of access;
- Right to rectification;
- Right to erasure;
- Right to restrict processing;
- Right to data portability;
- Right to object;
- Rights related to automated decision-making including profiling.[3]

You should also understand the difference between data processors and data controllers:

- A data controller decides the purposes and means of processing personal data;
- A data processor processes personal data on behalf of the controller.[4]

Ultimately, the data controller, as the decision-maker, is responsible for compliance with the Data Protection Act 2018 and the UK GDPR.

Example Submissions: Data Management

Level 3 requires reasoned advice on the use and practical application of data and systems, and/or specifying the most appropriate way for your own and/or client organisation to collect, analyse, and apply relevant information and data. Examples could include advising on data storage and filing systems, benchmarking, and advising on the use of a central project database.[5] For instance:

*At (**example**) I recommended and created a database of my firm's sale prices achieved, to support our valuers' comparable evidence research. I anonymised the data and included in the database key information such as postcode, street, number of bedrooms, condition, and price achieved. I provided training sessions for my colleagues on using and uploading to the database, and I also provided them with my* *instruction sheet on its use. My colleagues now input fresh data when a sale completes, and the information is used by my firm's valuers as an additional, verified, and reliable source of comparable evidence.*

Questions on this example could include:

- Tell me about your advice regarding an internal database.
- Why did you recommend the database?
- How did you create the database?
- Talk me through the training that you provided.
- Tell me about the instruction sheet that you prepared.
- How do you ensure client confidentiality is always maintained?
- How do you ensure the reliability of new information uploaded to the database?

Level 2 Data Management requires evidence of practical application of your level 1 knowledge and understanding of the relevance of the data and the uses to which it can be applied. This includes analysis of the data collected.[6] A level 2 example could be:

*At (**example**) I was asked by my supervisor to review and update my firm's database of market appraisal enquiries. I reviewed my firm's records, emailed each enquirer to check whether they still required our services, advised that my firm offers free no-obligation market appraisals, and confirmed that contact details could be removed if this service was no longer of interest. I referred requests for market appraisals to my colleagues to undertake, and deleted personal data for those enquirers who did not wish to proceed, confirming to them that I had done so.*

Questions on this example could include:

- Describe how you reviewed your firm's records.
- How did you use your firm's database of enquiries?
- Why was the review necessary?
- How long had enquirer's details been retained?
- What is your firm's policy on retention of details for enquiries?
- Tell me about your emails to enquirers.
- How did you ensure/confirm deletion of personal data?

Sustainability

Sustainability is an area that is growing in significance and is relevant to all areas of practice. In the residential sector this particularly relates to energy efficiency, which can reflect on market appeal and value. However, you should also think of sustainability in the broader sense, encompassing environmental, social, and economic issues (the triple bottom line). The triple bottom line can also be viewed as the three 'Ps' of 'People, Planet, and Profit'. These need to be balanced locally, nationally, and globally to ensure a sustainable built environment. For instance, a home that has a very low energy efficiency rating may not adequately meet housing needs; it may add to carbon emissions and be economically unsustainable and unaffordable for its occupiers.

This is another broad topic, and you will need to familiarise yourself with key concepts, such as:

- Carbon budgets;
- Carbon net zero;
- Environmental assessment methods such as the Building Research Establishment Environmental Assessment Method (BREEAM);
- Environmental risks (see RICS Environmental Risks and Global Real Estate, 1st edition, 2018);
- Government grants and schemes such as the Boiler Upgrade Scheme and the Green Deal;
- International collaborations, reports, and protocols, such as:

  - The Brundtland Report (Our Common Future);
  - The Kyoto Protocol and the Doha Amendment;
  - The Paris Agreement;
  - The United Nations Sustainable Development Goals.

- Minimum Energy Performance Certificate (EPC) ratings for residential lettings and the exemptions that may apply;
- Retrofitting (see RICS Residential Retrofit Standard UK, 1st edition, 2024);
- The Environmental Protection Act 1990;
- The requirements for an EPC when marketing a property for sale;
- The impact of sustainability on value and marketability (there is a link to an interesting Modus article in the Further Reading and Resources section at the end of this chapter);
- UK minimum energy efficiency standards legislation:

  - The Energy Act 2011;
  - The Energy Efficiency (Private Rented Property) (England and Wales) Regulations 2015;

- The Energy Efficiency (Private Rented Property) (England and Wales) (Amendment) Regulations 2016.
- VPGA 8 of the Global Red Book (2022) (you will also need to refer to the 2024 updated Red Book);
- Whole life carbon assessment (see RICS Whole life carbon assessment for the built environment Global, 2nd edition, 2023, and RICS Whole life carbon assessments – A guide for clients).

You will find further resources at the end of this chapter.

Example Submissions: Sustainability

Level 3 requires evidence of reasoned advice provided to clients and/ or other stakeholders on the policy, law, and best practice of sustainability, including the financial impact of sustainability.[7]

A level 3 example could be:

*At (**example**) I was approached by a prospective first-time investor landlord regarding purchase of a buy-to-let property. I advised that an Energy Performance Certificate would be required with a minimum EPC rating of E, unless an exemption applied. The investor sourced a property with an EPC rating of G. I advised the investor that the EPC rating could impact on the property's market appeal, financial viability, and suitability for purpose. I also explained the exemptions available. I advised the investor to review the potential improvements, costs, and energy cost savings on the EPC and informed her that my firm could advise on the up-to-date cost of bringing the property up to a minimum E rating.*

Questions on this example could include:

- What legislation applies to domestic minimum energy efficiency standards?
- What exemptions apply?
- What was the significance of the EPC G-rating?
- How old was the EPC?
- Talk me through your advice regarding potential improvements/ costs/cost savings.
- What was the potential financial/market impact of the EPC rating?
- Why did you suggest that further advice could be provided?
- What expertise is available within your firm to provide this further advice?

- What proposals were there at the time, relating to higher minimum energy efficiency standards?

Level 2 requires candidates to evidence the application of sustainability in practice. A level 2 example could be:

*At (**example**) I was instructed to market a 1980s house for rental purposes. I obtained the Energy Performance Certificate from the EPC Register and confirmed that the certificate was valid (being two years old) and had an EPC rating of D, which complied with minimum energy efficiency standards for residential lettings.*

Questions on this example could include:

- How did you obtain the EPC?
- Why did you obtain the EPC?
- How long are EPCs valid for?
- What is the minimum energy performance rating for residential lettings?
- How did you use the EPC in your marketing?

Another example could be:

*At (**example**) I identified a small residential development site for my employer. My desktop research established that the local authority had determined the site to be contaminated land due to a spillage of kerosene (domestic heating oil) from an oil tank that had also contaminated the property's water supply. I reported this to my employer and noted that further investigations would be required before proceeding with the acquisition.*

Questions on this example could include:

- Tell me about your desktop research.
- How did you identify that the land was contaminated?
- Tell me about the site.
- Why were further investigations required?
- What further investigations would be required?
- Who is responsible for cleaning up contaminated land?
- What were the potential risks if your employer had proceeded?
- How does the Environmental Protection Act 1990 relate to this example?
- What was the outcome?

Other Technical Competencies

The remaining technical competencies can be very loosely grouped together as:

- Buildings and Maintenance;
- Investment and Development;
- Housing and Policy;
- Finances and Taxation.

Specifically, these are:

Core

- Housing management and policy;
- Housing strategy and provision.

Optional

- Auctioneering;
- Capital taxation;
- Compulsory purchase and compensation;
- Development appraisals;
- Environmental assessments;
- Indirect investment vehicles;
- Investment management (including fund and portfolio management);
- Land use and diversification;
- Local taxation/assessments;
- Maintenance management;
- Planning and development management;
- Procurement and tendering;
- Property finance and funding;
- Risk management;
- Spatial planning policy and infrastructure;
- Strategic real estate consultancy;
- Supplier management.

Further information on each of these is available in the Residential pathway guide, and chapters on related competencies will help you to think of relevant laws, RICS publications, and examples. For instance:

- Auctioneering overlaps with Purchase and Sale, Market Appraisal, Valuation, and Legal/Regulatory Compliance, amongst others;
- Maintenance Management overlaps with Inspection, Building Pathology, and Housing Maintenance, Repairs, and Improvements.

Conclusion

The mandatory competencies selected as technical competencies provide candidates with the opportunity to supplement their knowledge and understanding already demonstrated at level 1 in the mandatory competencies. They can therefore be useful competency choices as most candidates will have practical experience of the application of relevant knowledge and understanding in these areas.

The remaining competencies also provide further opportunities to demonstrate knowledge and experience in a wide range of roles. If your experience reflects these competencies, think about declaring them, using the information contained in this book and the pathway guide to help identify suitable examples for your APC submission.

Reference List

1 HM Courts and Tribunals Service (no date) *First-tier tribunal (Property Chamber)* [Online] Available at: https://www.gov.uk/courts-tribunals/first-tier-tribunal-property-chamber (Accessed 20 July 2024).

2 Information Commissioner's Office (no date) *A guide to the data protection principles* [Online] Available at: https://ico.org.uk/for-organisations/uk-gdpr-guidance-and-resources/data-protection-principles/a-guide-to-the-data-protection-principles/ (Accessed 16 July 2024).

3 Information Commissioner's Office (no date) *A guide to individual rights* [Online] Available at: https://ico.org.uk/for-organisations/uk-gdpr-guidance-and-resources/individual-rights/individual-rights/ (Accessed 16 July 2024).

4 Information Commissioner's Office (no date) *What are 'controllers' and 'processors'?* [Online] Available at: https://ico.org.uk/for-organisations/uk-gdpr-guidance-and-resources/controllers-and-processors/control-lers-and-processors/what-are-controllers-and-processors/ (Accessed 16 July 2024).

5 RICS (2024) *Residential pathway guide* [Online] Available at: https://www.rics.org/join-rics/sector-pathways (Accessed 27 August 2024).

6 RICS (2024) *Residential pathway guide* [Online] Available at: https://www.rics.org/join-rics/sector-pathways (Accessed 27 August 2024).

7 RICS (2024) *Residential pathway guide* [Online] Available at: https://www.rics.org/join-rics/sector-pathways (Accessed 27 August 2024).

Further Reading and Resources

Conflict Avoidance, Management, and Dispute Resolution Procedures

Bristol City Council (2024) *Estate Agency Redress Schemes* [Online] Available at: https://www.bristol.gov.uk/ntselat/estate-agency/estate-agency-redress-schemes#:~:text=What%20are%20the%20approved%20estate,of%20an%20approved%20redress%20scheme (Accessed 27 August 2024).

First-Tier Tribunal (Property Chamber): https://www.gov.uk/courts-tribunals/first-tier-tribunal-property-chamber.

National Trading Standards Estate and Letting Agency Team: https://www.nationaltradingstandards.uk/work-areas/estate-agency-team/#:~:text=The%20National%20Trading%20Standards%20Estate,the%20Tenant%20Fees%20Act%202019.

Ombudsman schemes – Gov.UK, *Registering with a Redress Scheme as a Property Agent* [Online] Available at: https://www.gov.uk/redress-scheme-estate-agencies (Accessed 27 August 2024).

Property Redress Scheme: https://www.theprs.co.uk.

Residential Property Tribunal: https://residentialpropertytribunal.gov.wales.

Shelter (no date) *Council Tenant Right to Buy Process* (see refusals to sell, and valuation disputes) [Online] Available at: https://england.shelter.org.uk/professional_resources/legal/home_ownership/right_to_buy/council_tenant_right_to_buy_process#:~:text=If%20the%20landlord%20refuses%20the,tenant%20receiving%20the%20RTB2%20form (Accessed 27 August 2024).

The Property Ombudsman: https://www.tpos.co.uk/about-us/governance.

Upper Tribunal (Lands Chamber): https://www.gov.uk/courts-tribunals/upper-tribunal-lands-chamber.

Data Management

Information Commissioner's Office: https://ico.org.uk.

McGuinness I (2024) *How Property Sector can Embrace Collaborative AI* RICS Property Journal [Online] Available at: https://ww3.rics.org/uk/en/journals/property-journal/property-sector-collaborative-ai.html (Accessed 24 August 2024).

Navin S (2024) *AI will Support rather than Replace Surveyors* RICS Land Journal [Online] Available at: https://ww3.rics.org/uk/en/journals/land-journal/ai-will-not-replace-surveyors.html (Accessed 24 August 2024).

Sustainability

Building Research Establishment Environmental Assessment Method (BREEAM): https://breeam.com.

Centre for Alternative Technology: https://cat.org.uk.

Clark G (2021) *The planet of cities: Cities can be the engines of the net zero transition* [Online] Available at: https://www.rics.org/news-insights/wbef/ the-planet-of-cities-cities-can-be-the-engines-of-the-net-zero-transition (Accessed 24 August 2024).

Cousins S (2022) *Valuation: green premium vs brown discount* RICS Modus [Online] Available at: https://ww3.rics.org/uk/en/modus/built-environment/ homes-and-communities/home-valuation-green-initiatives-residential.html (Accessed 25 July 2024).

Daas V (2024) *Building materials: the next frontier for decarbonisation* RICS News & Insights [Online] Available at: https://www.rics.org/news-insights/ building-materials-the-next-frontier-for-decarbonisation (Accessed 13 May 2024).

Department for Energy Security and Net Zero, and Department for Business, Energy & Industrial Strategy (no date) *Carbon budgets guidance* [Online] Avaiable at: https://www.gov.uk/guidance/carbon-budgets (Accessed 24 August 2024).

Department for Energy Security and Net Zero, and Department for Business, Energy & Industrial Strategy (2023) *Domestic Private Rented Property: Minimum Energy Efficiency Standard - Landlord Guidance* [Online] Available at: https://www.gov.uk/guidance/domestic-private-rented-property-minimum-energy-efficiency-standard-landlord-guidance (Accessed 27 August 2024).

Gov.uk Selling a Home – Energy Performance Certificates: https://www.gov. uk/selling-a-home/energy-performance-certificates.

Lemen J (2019) *Hot topic highlight – contaminated land* Property Elite Blog [Online] Available at: https://www.property-elite.co.uk/post/hot-topic-highlight-contaminated-land (Accessed 21 July 2024).

Matz S (2022) *Retrofitting for the future: Net zero for existing building stock* [Online] Available at: https://www.rics.org/news-insights/wbef/retrofitting-fo r-the-future-net-zero-for-existing-building-stock (Accessed 24 August 2024).

Passivhaus Trust: https://www.passivhaustrust.org.uk.

RICS (2023) *RICS sustainability report* 2023 [Online] Available at: https://www. rics.org/news-insights/rics-sustainability-report-2023 (Accessed 24 August 2024) (This is not directly related to the residential sector but it covers construction and provides an interesting and up-to-date overview and context).

RICS (2024) *Minimum energy efficiency standard* [Online] Available at: https://www.ricsfirms.com/glossary/minimum-energy-efficiency-standard/ (Accessed 24 August 2024).

RICS (2024) *Whole life carbon assessment (WLCA) for the built environment* [Online] Available at: https://www.rics.org/profession-standards/ rics-standards-and-guidance/sector-standards/construction-standards/ whole-life-carbon-assessment (Accessed 24 August 2024).

United Nations (no date) *What is the Kyoto protocol?* [Online] Available at: https://unfccc.int/kyoto_protocol (Accessed 24 August 2024).

United Nations (no date) *The Paris Agreement* [Online] Available at: https://www.un.org/en/climatechange/paris-agreement (Accessed 24 August 2024).

United Nations (no date) *The 17 goals* (Sustainable Development) [Online] Available at: https://sdgs.un.org/goals (Accessed 24 August 2024).

World Economic Forum (no date) *What does 'net zero' emissions mean And why does it matter?* Video [Online] Available at: https://www.weforum.org/videos/20057-what-does-net-zero-emissions-mean/ (Accessed 24 August 2024).

General Reading

Lemen J (2024) *APC essentials: mandatory competencies* Abingdon: Routledge.

Wilcox J, Forsyth J (2022) *Real estate: the basics* Abingdon: Routledge.

15 Submission Advice

Overview of the APC Assessment

All APC candidates, irrespective of their chosen route, must undergo assessment via a written submission and an online interview. However, the requirements of both elements differ significantly for the senior professional, specialist, and academic assessments, which are considered separately in APC Essentials — Mandatory Competencies.

The written submission element is also slightly different for preliminary review candidates. This is because preliminary review introduces a two-stage written submission process, which will be discussed separately to the final assessment submission.

The online interview is based on the candidate's written submission and lasts for one hour. The final decision as to whether a candidate becomes MRICS is solely based on performance in this interview. There is no separate assessment of the written submission, apart from the requirement for preliminary review candidates to pass this element of their written submission process and for final assessment candidates to meet the minimum RICS requirements, e.g., word count and case study date validity.

Final Assessment Submission (Excluding Senior Professional, Specialist, and Academic Assessments)

All APC candidates, whether undergoing preliminary review or not, will need to submit a written final assessment submission. This applies to candidates on the structured training and straight-to-assessment routes, and candidates who have successfully passed preliminary review. The final assessment submission is, therefore, exactly the same for all of these routes. However, the final assessment submission

DOI: 10.1201/9781032705095-15

is very different in structure and content for the senior professional, specialist, or academic assessments. You will find more information on the senior professional assessment competencies in the *Mandatory Competencies* book in this series.

The written submission will be the product of a substantial period of preparation and not something that can be drafted in a matter of weeks. Rushing the written submission is likely to lead to a poor-quality document, which will not support the candidate through their online interview. Candidates must ensure that they present their submission to the highest written standards, including spelling, grammar, and proofreading. Therefore, the final submitted documents need to be 'client ready' and written formally and professionally.

The APC final assessment submission includes the following elements:

- Diary (structured training candidates only);
- Summary of Experience;
- Case Study;
- Continuing Professional Development (CPD) Record;
- Professionalism Module and Test.

Throughout their written work, candidates should be acutely aware of plagiarism. Under no circumstances should a candidate seek to include work or text written by another candidate or copied from a published source, unless it is correctly and clearly referenced. Any red flags of plagiarism will be identified by RICS using the Turnitin plagiarism detection system, leading to further investigation and potential disciplinary action, including removal from the APC assessment process.

What Does the Structured Training Diary Include and Who Needs to Complete It?

The diary is only required for candidates on the structured training route. Candidates undergoing preliminary review or proceeding straight to assessment do not need to keep a diary.

Structured training candidates should start to record their diary via the RICS Assessment Platform as soon as they enrol on their APC journey. This is because the number of diary days logged counts towards satisfying the minimum 12 or 24 months of structured training requirements. Candidates will also use the diary when compiling their summary of experience, choosing their case study topic, and for discussion of their progress during Counsellor meetings.

Candidates must only log time spent on their technical competencies in their diary. This means that they should not record any activities or time spent on their mandatory competencies, unless these are also selected as technical competencies.

Mandatory competencies will generally be included within a candidate's daily work rather than being their specific focus at any one time. Examples include communicating during the course of an instruction or working within a project team.

Therefore, time spent on the mandatory competencies will not contribute towards a candidate's minimum structured training requirements. However, they must still be recorded in the summary of experience, which is discussed later in this chapter.

Sufficient detail should be included in a candidate's diary, allowing appropriate examples to be identified to meet the requirements of the chosen competencies at levels 2 and 3. The diary does not form part of the candidate's final written submission, although RICS may request it to be submitted separately before a candidate's online interview. Reasons for this include where RICS identifies anything concerning or contentious within a candidate's submission; e.g., the case study topic does not reflect the candidate's declared competencies or the standard of work in their summary of experience.

Therefore, candidates should ensure that their diary is sufficiently relevant and concise, rather than overly detailed and lengthy. It should be written professionally and in a high standard of English.

The following details need to be recorded on the RICS Assessment Platform for each separate diary entry:

- Competency and level relevant to the diary entry;
- Days and start date, logged in a minimum of half-day blocks;
- Title of the activity;
- Diary entry, including a brief description of the activity and relevant competencies. This should be as specific as possible to aid the candidate's memory when they draft their written submission or for discussion with their Counsellor.

Candidates can combine their activities or experience within their diary entries into more substantial blocks of time. This may be sensible given the wide range of activities a candidate will likely undertake within a day or week. This might mean a candidate blocks measurement or inspection activities from various projects or instructions into one diary entry. A candidate may also block together time spent on one larger project into one entry to avoid repetition. How candidates split their entries will be directed by their competency choices, as some are much broader topic areas than others. Valuation, for example, is typically wider in scope than Measurement.

What Is the Summary of Experience?

The summary of experience focusses on the candidate's competencies. This includes the mandatory competencies relevant to all candidates, as well as the technical competencies specific to a candidate's chosen pathway. The RICS provides a case study template to download on the RICS Assessment Platform, which should be followed rather than the candidate using their own format or structure.

The technical competencies are split into core technical competencies, i.e., a requirement for the specific pathway, and optional technical competencies, i.e., where the candidate can select competencies that best suit their role, knowledge, and experience. The chosen competencies will either have a stated achievement level, i.e., Inspection, Measurement, and Valuation to at least level 2, or candidates may have a choice of the level attained, e.g., optional technical competencies.

The word counts for the summary of experience are absolute: 1,500 for the mandatory competencies and 4,000 for the technical (core and optional) competencies. There is no leeway to exceed these; a candidate's submission can be rejected outright by RICS for exceeding the word limit.

The word count for each section (i.e., mandatory and technical competencies) can be allocated as the candidate wishes between each competency. Generally, assigning a higher word count to level 3 statements is advisable to ensure that sufficient experience and detail can be included.

The summary of experience requires candidates to write a summary of their knowledge at level 1 and experience at levels 2 and 3 for each level of each chosen competency. Unlike AssocRICS, this includes Ethics, Rules of Conduct, and Professionalism. Candidates should ensure that they refer directly to the pathway guide and competency descriptors when preparing their summary of experience, as this is what they will be assessed against by their final interview panel.

If a competency is selected to level 3, then candidates must write a statement for each of levels 1, 2, and 3. For level 2, a statement must be provided for levels 1 and 2. At level 1, only a level 1 statement is required. At levels 2 and 3, it is advisable to use subheadings or other appropriate formatting (e.g., bold – see the examples in the competency chapters) to highlight examples, aiding the candidate and assessment panel in the final assessment interview by signposting specific examples.

At level 1, candidates must explain what they know or have learnt about a competency. This may link to CPD activities or academic learning, e.g., university modules. Given the limited word count, a bullet-point list of knowledge could be used to reflect the competency descriptor, although a carbon copy of this is not allowable and would constitute plagiarism.

Candidates should ensure that the knowledge they declare is relevant to their experience, as the assessment panel can question anything included in the written submission. Candidates should ensure in level 1 that they demonstrate current knowledge of legislation and RICS guidance, together with any relevant hot topics.

At level 2, candidates should include two to three practical examples of their work-based experience. This will discuss how they acted or carried out relevant tasks. The range of relevant activities or tasks for a specific competency should be related to the pathway guide and competency descriptor, although these are not exhaustive lists.

Candidates should seek to be as specific and refined as possible in their examples. This could be by stating a specific instruction, property, or client, to help focus their final interview questioning. Candidates should avoid using vague or broad examples as this can make it harder to demonstrate the required level in the final assessment interview. If a project or instruction is very broad, then candidates could focus on a specific aspect of their involvement or advice that clearly meets the requirements of the relevant competency. For example, measurement of a property that the candidate subsequently values, or inspection of a site that a candidate subsequently advises on the planning and development potential.

At level 3, candidates should again include two to three practical examples of their work-based experience. These examples should relate to where the candidate has given reasoned advice to a client (or to their employer or another stakeholder). Again, candidates should use very specific examples, which clearly demonstrate their integral role in a project or instruction.

Candidates should ensure that they write any examples using the first person, using I, me, and my. This ensures that the assessment panel knows that the work is that of the candidate rather than that of a colleague, friend, or superior. This also provides the assessment panel with the perception that the candidate has given professional advice and handled instructions competently from start to finish, with minimal supervision.

What Is the Case Study?

The case study provides an in-depth discussion of a specific project or projects with which a candidate has been involved and provided reasoned advice. Candidates should ideally focus only on one project, which helps to keep the detail refined and the project easy to understand by the assessment panel. The choice of project or instruction may include work outside of the candidate's geographical assessment region. However, in the final assessment interview, candidates should be aware of the legislation and guidance relating to both the geographical regions of the case study project and assessment location.

The choice of project should reflect the candidate's chosen pathway and competencies. However, the case study does not need to include aspects of every competency, which is unlikely to be realistically achievable. The competencies demonstrated should consist of level 3 aspects, clearly showing reasoned advice being given to a client.

The candidate must have been involved in the case study project or instruction within the last two years from the submission date. If a project is out of date, this is a point for referral, and a candidate will not be permitted to proceed to the online interview stage. Some projects, e.g., a construction project or a site disposal, may extend for more than two years. However, the candidate's primary involvement must have occurred during the two-year validity period. Including a clear timeline to demonstrate the candidate's involvement in their case study project is helpful. This can also help to demonstrate a candidate's visual communication skills.

The candidate should have played a key role in the case study project. For some instructions, this will include running, managing, and leading the project from start to finish. For larger, more complex projects, a candidate may not have been running the project independently but will have played a key role in giving reasoned advice to the client.

Some candidates may have been involved in only one aspect of a project, been involved after the commencement of a project, or have finished their involvement before the project was completed. This is acceptable, provided the candidate can demonstrate their reasoned advice in the stated level 3 competencies. If a project has not been completed when a candidate writes their case study, they may wish to discuss the prognosis within the case study and provide an update in their final interview presentation.

The case study choice does not need to be the most complex, high value or large project or instruction that the candidate has been involved with. Given the limited word count, using a highly complex case study that the assessment panel does not understand clearly or fully can be challenging and counterproductive. This can lead to misunderstandings and confused questioning as the candidate's role and advice have not been made clear in the context of the limited word count and written case study structure. The best case studies are often simple but succeed in setting out a clear and logical story of the candidate's involvement and reasoned advice.

Within their project or instruction choice, candidates should identify and discuss two or three key issues, involving challenges they encountered and needed to overcome during the instruction. This will demonstrate the candidate's problem-solving and analytical skills, leading to the provision of reasoned advice and recommendations to the client. If a candidate is unable to identify at least two key issues, the project or instruction is unlikely to be a suitable case study topic.

Example case study key issues for a secured lending valuation instruction could include:

- Key issue 1 – Assessment of Market Rent;
- Key issue 2 – Assessment of Market Value, including choice of yield;
- Key issue 3 – Advice on secured lending to the client.

Example case study key issues for a level 3 Building Survey could include:

- Key issue 1 – Defect 1 – wet rot;
- Key issue 2 – Defect 2 – condensation;
- Key issue 3 – Remedial advice to the client.

The word count for the case study is 3,000 words, which is again absolute with no leeway. This includes everything between the end of the contents page and the start of the appendices. Candidates can be referred before being invited to interview by RICS for exceeding the word count. As such, it should be treated as a strict client requirement. Candidates should avoid using the appendices to include additional detail that could not be fitted within the main body of the case study. This does not demonstrate adherence to a client's strict requirements and will not be viewed favourably by the assessment panel.

Rather than using footnotes, candidates should include core references to legislation or RICS guidance within the main body of the case study. This prevents the case study becoming overcomplicated and untidy.

The RICS provides a case study template to download on the RICS Assessment Platform, which should be followed rather than the candidate using their own format or structure. The following sections should be included:

1 Introduction – summary of the project, candidate's role, responsibilities, key stakeholders, and timeline.
2 My Approach – this should discuss two to three key issues relating to the project and the challenges that the candidate overcame. Some candidates may only use one key issue, but this should be avoided as the level of detail and advice will likely be limited. Trying to include more than three key issues is likely to lead to insufficient detail and analysis, given the relatively limited overall word count. The candidate should explain the issue, options considered, and the solution, advice, and recommendations given. This requires analysis of the advantages and disadvantages of each option considered or the specific considerations in giving reasoned advice to the client.
3 My Achievements – the candidate should discuss their key achievements, potentially using subheadings for each competency demonstrated. This provides helpful structure and relates the actions and advice to the candidate's competency choices. The candidate should also discuss the outcome of the instruction and their overall achievements in terms of the level-3 reasoned advice they gave to their client.
4 Conclusion – the candidate should reflect on and critically analyse their involvement in their case study project, including lessons learnt and how they will improve their performance in the future. This section requires just as much thought as the preceding ones and demonstrates a candidate's commitment to their professional

development. It is also advisable to discuss the candidate's professionalism and demonstration of ethics within the case study project, as this is a crucial aspect of being a Chartered Surveyor.

5   Appendices – The candidate should include an initial Appendix A to list the mandatory and technical competencies demonstrated within the case study. The other appendices should consist only of relevant illustrations, photographs, or plans, which should be referenced within the main body of the case study. Excessive or irrelevant appendices should not be included.

Confidentiality is a crucial ethical issue for candidates to consider. Candidates must have the express consent of their employer and client to disclose sensitive or confidential details within their submission. Suppose that this is not provided by one or more parties. In that case, specific details should be redacted, e.g., use Project X instead of the address, or secured lending client instead of the lender's identity. Anything litigious should also be redacted to ensure that identifiable details, such as the client's name, address, or sensitive financial information, are not disclosed. Candidates can be referred for not dealing with confidentiality appropriately, as it relates to a candidate's ethics and professionalism. RICS also confirms that anything in the candidate's submission will not be disclosed further than the assessment panel.

What Does the CPD Record Include?

APC candidates must record at least 48 hours of CPD for every 12-month period. Candidates requiring 24 months of structured training must record 24 months of CPD, with the minimum requirement recorded for each 12-month period. Candidates who need to record 12 months of structured training must record 12 months of CPD, with the minimum requirement recorded for this period.

All other candidates need to record their last 12 months of CPD activities. For preliminary review candidates, 12 months of CPD is required before both the preliminary review submission and the final assessment submission. The latter should be updated to reflect the relevant 12-month period.

Candidates do not need to submit CPD records for a period in excess of this; i.e., there is no requirement to submit CPD for a period longer than the required 12 or 24 months. Submitting an extended CPD record could lead to additional questioning that a candidate could otherwise avoid. Where this relates to historic CPD, the detail and outcomes may be difficult to remember or less relevant to the candidate's current role and experience.

A candidate would be better served by including relevant CPD for the required period and in sufficient depth and detail. In particular, candidates should never forget that their assessment panel can question anything they write in their final assessment submission, including their CPD record.

RICS calculates the CPD requirement on a rolling basis from the candidate's submission date. For example, suppose a candidate submitted in February 2025. In that case, their CPD must be undertaken in the 12 or 24 months, as appropriate, before this, i.e., from February 2023 or 2024 to February 2025. The CPD requirements do not relate to the CPD recording requirements for qualified Members, which are lower. This is a common source of confusion for APC candidates.

All CPD logged by APC candidates should relate clearly to the chosen technical and mandatory competencies relevant to the candidate's scope of work, role, and responsibilities. Ideally, a candidate will undertake various types of CPD to maximise their learning opportunities. Candidates should also plan their CPD and ensure that they reflect on what they have learnt afterwards, demonstrating their analytical and evaluative skills.

At least 50% of the minimum 48 hours' CPD must be formal. This requires a structured approach with clear learning objectives. Examples of formal CPD include structured seminars, professional courses (which do not have to be run by RICS), and structured self-managed learning and online events where there is a clear learning outcome.[1]

CPD is logged by candidates via the RICS Assessment Platform, including the following key details:

- Description of the activity – for example, 'Webinar – JCT Contracts' or 'Self-managed learning on the Red Book';
- Activity status – future or completed;
- Start date;
- Time – hours and minutes allocated to the CPD activity;
- Activity type – formal or informal and method, e.g., webinar, conference, private study, or mentoring;
- Learning outcomes – reflection on what was learnt during the CPD activity. This should be written in the first person and past tense, e.g., 'I learnt about the different procurement methods and how

they can be applied in my role', or 'I learnt about the new RICS Professional Standard and the core principles which I can apply in the workplace'.

Candidates must provide sufficient detail in their CPD record to allow the assessment panel to understand how the activity relates to a candidate's competencies, roles, and experience. If poorly written or incomplete, it may constitute grounds for referral. The same applies if insufficient hours have been undertaken or activities are informal rather than formal, meaning the minimum requirements are not met. Candidates should also proofread their CPD record carefully and ensure that the detail provided is accurate, relevant, and concise.

What Is the Professionalism Module?

Candidates must also complete the online RICS Professionalism Module and Test (accessed via the RICS Assessment Platform) within 12 months of applying for final assessment. The module is also a helpful revision tool that candidates should consider using to prepare for their final assessment interview. Ethics is the only area for an automatic failure at the interview stage; candidates should appreciate the importance and content of this module.

What Is the Preliminary Review Submission?

Candidates who do not have an RICS-accredited degree, i.e., a non-cognate degree, will need to undergo the additional preliminary review submission stage.

This means that a candidate prepares their written preliminary review submission and submits this for a written review by RICS, before submitting their final assessment submission roughly four to six months later, or longer, if preferred.

The candidate's final assessment and preliminary review submissions do not differ in structure or format. It is simply a 'pre-check' process carried out by RICS for candidates without an RICS-accredited degree, which provides confidence that minimum standards of writing, structure, and quality are being met.

The purpose of preliminary review is to determine whether a candidate's submission, in terms of content, quality, and professionalism, is of the standard RICS requires. Essentially, this allows the candidate's assessment panel to effectively prepare for and conduct the final assessment interview.[2]

The preliminary review assessment panel will consider the following:

- Whether holistically the candidate's submission is of the required standard;
- Whether basic RICS requirements are met, including word count, professionalism, written English, structure, and sufficient examples at levels 2 and 3;
- Whether content requirements are met, such as including relevant detail and evidence relating to a candidate's chosen competencies in their summary of experience and case study. This requires the candidate to reflect on the requirements of the pathway guide and competency descriptions within their written submission.

The results for preliminary review candidates typically take around eight weeks to be issued on the last working day of the month. Substantial feedback will be provided within the feedback report whether or not the outcome is a pass or a referral.

If the submission is acceptable, the candidate may submit their final assessment in a future submission window. Candidates and their Counsellors should closely scrutinise the feedback report to ensure they make relevant improvements in the final submission.

Candidates may also wish to update their experience, examples, and CPD activities to reflect new work undertaken following their preliminary review result being received. It is worth remembering that the preliminary review feedback is the subjective view of the specific panel at the time; sometimes it is impossible to make every single amendment particularly given the opinions or advice of a candidate's Counsellor or employer.

Candidates must also ensure that their case study remains valid (i.e., within a two-year window) when they come forward for final assessment. For example, this may not be the case if the preliminary review stage was passed more than six months prior. In this case, the candidate may need to write a new case study, considering the general feedback provided at preliminary review. If a candidate does change their case study topic or examples included in their summary of experience, they do not need to submit for preliminary review again.

If the submission is not acceptable, the candidate will receive a feedback report and will need to resubmit for preliminary review before submitting for final assessment. Again, candidates and their Counsellors should review the report together and ensure improvements are made before the candidate resubmits for re-assessment at a future preliminary review window.

A successful preliminary review outcome is not a guarantee of success at the candidate's final assessment interview. This is because the decision to become MRICS is solely based on the candidate's final interview.

Conclusion

Candidates should be able to apply what they have learnt in this book's preceding chapters when writing their final submission. The next chapter will explain how this will be taken one step further during the final assessment interview.

This chapter is based on Lemen J (2024) *Mandatory Competencies: APC Essentials Chapter 14* Abingdon: Routledge.

Reference List

1 RICS (no date) *Annex A: examples of types of formal and informal CPD activity* [Online] Available at: https://www.rics.org/content/dam/ricsglobal/documents/standards/cpd-annex-a-160518-mb.pdf (Accessed 12 August 2024).
2 RICS (2024) *Assessment of professional competence candidate guide* [Online] Available at: https://www.rics.org/content/dam/ricsglobal/documents/join-rics/APC-Candidate-guide_final_February-2024.pdf (Accessed 11 March 2025).

Further Reading and Resources

Lemen J (2024) *Mandatory competencies: APC essentials* Abingdon: Routledge.
RICS *Sector Pathways* [Online] Available at: https://www.rics.org/join-rics/sector-pathways (Accessed 27 August 2024).

16 Interview Advice

What Is the Final Assessment Interview?

After candidates submit their final assessment via the RICS Assessment Platform, they will be notified by email of their final assessment interview date with a minimum of two weeks' notice beforehand. All interviews are online, and at the time of writing, RICS plans no further assessments to take place face-to-face.

If a candidate submits their final assessment documents but subsequently wishes to defer until the next sitting, they can do so by emailing RICS. No charge is payable if the deferral is notified within 14 days of submitting. However, a charge will apply thereafter. Candidates may defer for a variety of reasons, e.g., extenuating circumstances that affect their availability or if they feel that they are not ready to be assessed.

The assessment panel will consider the following during the candidate's final assessment interview:

- The candidate's communication skills both through a ten-minute presentation on their case study and responses to the assessors' questioning on their final assessment submission;
- How well the candidate can verbalise and explain their advice and actions discussed within their written submission, demonstrating the stated competency levels;
- Whether the candidate understands the role and responsibilities of a Chartered Surveyor, including advising clients diligently and acting ethically and professionally;
- Whether the candidate can act independently and unsupervised, i.e., that they are a safe pair of hands. This is particularly relevant because after qualifying as MRICS, a candidate could, in theory,

DOI: 10.1201/9781032705095-16

set up in practice as a sole trader. The assessment panel must be confident that any successful candidates in their APC would be competent to do this ethically and professionally.

The assessors will assess the candidate's written submission, although this will be considered holistically within the interview context. Unless there is an evidence deficiency or issue regarding word count or basic requirements of the written submission (e.g., Continuing Professional Development [CPD] hours), a candidate will not be referred on their written submission alone. Any substantial issues, such as the word count being exceeded, should be picked up by RICS after the candidate submits via the RICS Assessment Platform, and the candidate would then not be permitted to proceed to the final interview stage.

Candidates will be assessed by a panel of two or three Chartered Surveyors: one chairperson and either one or two assessors. All will be trained APC assessors, or chairs, and experienced in providing final assessment interviews. To ensure that the interview is tailored to the candidate's experience, two of the panel members will be from the same pathway as the candidate. Some pathways also have specialist areas and at least one panel member will be experienced in this area.

Assessors are trained to give every candidate a fair interview process and to treat all candidates with respect and dignity. The interview process should encourage and facilitate all candidates to succeed if they meet the required levels of competence. The online assessment process means that an even more diverse range of assessors is available to participate in the assessment process, which is likely to give candidates a much more positive, fair, and transparent interview experience.

Candidates should be made to feel at ease by their panel, who should be positive and provide candidates with an environment in which they can excel. Ways they may do this include:

- Asking open questions, one at a time, to avoid being confusing or overly elaborate;
- Being flexible in their questioning approach and following up on a candidate's answers with further questions if appropriate;
- Supporting a candidate and encouraging them if they are nervous or stressed.

However, panels will not give candidates any indication of how they are doing during the interview or whether they have passed or been referred.

Therefore, the best indication of a correct answer is sometimes the panel moving onto another competency or question. If an assessor is pursuing the same line of questioning or driving at a specific point, this may indicate that the candidate's answers need further thought or clarity. At this point, asking for clarification, or returning to the question at the end of the interview may be sensible.

A staff facilitator may also be present during the interview to assist the candidate and assessment panel with any technical issues. An auditor may also be present to observe the assessment panel's performance, not the candidate's. They are simply there to assess whether the panel is undertaking the assessment in accordance with RICS standards. They do not take any part in the panel's decision-making on your performance.

The assessment panel should have no perceived or actual conflicts of interest in assessing the candidate fairly and transparently. This could be either personal, e.g., a candidate and assessor having met at a CPD event or being familiar in a professional context, or prejudicial, e.g., where an assessor may benefit from the candidate's success. A personal conflict may not present an issue if both parties are happy to proceed. However, a prejudicial conflict should be declared and the assessor removed from the panel. If a candidate becomes aware of a conflict of interest on the day, they should make their chairperson aware. The matter will be dealt with either by a two-person panel proceeding or the interview being rescheduled with a non-conflicted panel.

Candidates should have made RICS aware of any access arrangements (formerly known as special considerations) or extenuating circumstances during the submission process. RICS may request supporting medical evidence to enable relevant, reasonable adjustments to be made. Suppose a candidate feels the panel may benefit from knowing how specific issues affect them. In that case, they may wish to prepare a written statement to read out to the panel during the initial welcome at the start of the interview.

The interview lasts 60 minutes and is conducted online using Microsoft Teams. Candidates should ensure that they test the system beforehand and have a good quality video camera and microphone. There is no excuse for hardware or systems not working on the day.

Candidates can prepare effectively for the interview by:

- Choosing a quiet interview location, where disturbances are kept to a minimum. This may mean asking others to keep quiet or to leave the location for the duration of the interview. If a candidate's home environment is too noisy, they may prefer to sit their interview in an office or external meeting room;

- Having good quality Wi-Fi or tethering to 5G or 4G if not available. This should be tested beforehand, and if weak, a candidate should reconsider their choice of location or ask other users to switch their devices off during the interview;
- Having good lighting and a background that is neutral and clear. Candidates could sit near natural light or have a lamp beside or behind them. They should avoid sitting in front of a window which can be blinding to the camera;
- Ensuring their interview environment is comfortable, including a supportive chair, adequate height desk, notepad, pen, and a glass of water. Candidates may also choose to use a second screen, such as a tablet or monitor, for their presentation notes only;
- Using headphones or a separate microphone to ensure good quality audio;
- Avoiding using a smartphone which can be too small to allow an effective interface during the interview;
- Closing any applications not being used to minimise the risk of technical issues, as well as putting any devices on silent or do not disturb;
- Ensuring their camera is at eye height to keep a natural connection with the assessment panel;
- Wearing smart, professional clothing appropriate for a client meeting or job interview. Ideally this should be simple and plain to avoid being distracting on camera;
- Ensuring that any devices are connected to a power source rather than relying on battery power which is quickly drained.

A candidate is not permitted to record their interview. Any attempt to do so may lead to disciplinary action and immediate termination of the interview.

The 60-minute time limit is strict and will be managed closely by the chairperson. In the event of technical difficulties, up to ten minutes can be added to the end of the interview. If interruptions total more than ten minutes, the chairperson will terminate the interview, which will be rescheduled.

A candidate's interview may also be extended if any special considerations or extenuating circumstances dictate that additional time should be given to allow the candidate to respond fully to questions asked. In this case, the candidate will not be asked more questions than they would otherwise be in a standard 60-minute interview. Instead, it is the amount of time they are given to listen, comprehend, and respond to questions that may be extended.

Candidates should join their interview video link five to ten minutes beforehand. They will then be permitted access from the virtual lobby when their assessment panel is ready.

The interview will be structured as follows:

- Initial welcome by the chairperson before the 60-minute time limit starts. This will include the candidate being asked to complete a 360-degree view of their surroundings to ensure that no outside assistance is being provided. The chairperson is free to ask for this to be repeated at any time during the interview. The chairperson will then explain the interview structure and ask whether the candidate is fit, well, and ready to proceed;
- Ten-minute presentation by the candidate, focussing on their case study;
- Ten minutes of questioning by the assessors on the candidate's case study;
- Thirty minutes of questioning and discussion by the assessors on the candidate's summary of experience, CPD, Rules of Conduct, and professional practice;
- Ten minutes questioning by the chairperson on any outstanding competencies and ethics. This will include the chairperson's closing comments and the opportunity for the candidate to have the last word. This may consist of returning to any questions the candidate was unable to answer earlier on or to make any additional comments, which can be noted down on a piece of paper during the interview.

The candidate's case study presentation could focus on one or more of the key issues. However, it should not simply repeat verbatim what a candidate has written. The presentation could be made interesting by delving deeper into one of the key issues, looking at progress of the project since the case study was written or discussing further the candidate's analysis of the options and advice given to the client. The main aim of the presentation is to demonstrate strong communication and presentation skills to the panel. Therefore, the presentation does not need to be complicated, nor does it necessarily need to introduce anything new to the panel.

A visual aid can support the presentation. This can be screen shared with the panel.

The best visual aids are generally simple and used only to support key points within the presentation. This could be a simple PowerPoint presentation or a series of PDF slides. Avoiding animation or overly complex slides is advised.

Using a flipchart or visual aid held up to the camera is not recommended, as this is likely to be hard to read by the assessment panel. Visual aids should be professionally presented, with a clear title and large, easy-to-read text or graphics. Given the reliance on IT technology to screen share, candidates should be prepared not to use a visual aid in the event of technical difficulties.

Candidates can use cue cards or brief notes for their presentation. During the rest of the interview, they cannot use any notes or have a copy submission to hand.

The timing of the case study presentation is key, and candidates will be asked to stop if they exceed this by more than 10 to 15 seconds. Equally, being substantially below this will be a negative consideration in the context of the assessors' overall decision. Candidates should practice their presentation frequently to ensure that they are fluent in giving it and can accurately meet the timing requirement. A stopwatch, clock, or timer can be used, providing that it is not overly distracting to the candidate and their assessment panel.

Given that the interview is conducted online, candidates must best use both verbal and non-verbal communication. Candidates should aim to speak clearly and concisely, taking time to understand and listen to questions before answering. They should also be aware of avoiding too much movement or gesticulation, which can be distracting on camera. Positive body language will help to portray a confident candidate and practising this on camera beforehand with a friend, family member, or colleague can be helpful. Candidates should always try to look directly into the camera and maintain good eye contact with their assessment panel.

The interview is based on the candidate's written submission. The assessment panel can question anything included in the candidate's case study, summary of experience, and CPD record. Therefore, candidates may wish to limit references to complex caselaw, for example, in their written submission, unless they are confident to discuss these in their interview. Candidates should also be aware that they will be assessed concerning the legislation and guidance relating to the geographic region of their final assessment. If experience is declared from other countries, candidates must know the legislative and regulatory requirements for each jurisdiction.

Candidates may also be asked about current hot topics regarding industry or market issues, providing they are relevant to the candidate's area of practice. This means that having a good level of market awareness is essential, which can be obtained through reading trade press and a good quality newspaper, listening to relevant podcasts, and watching CPD videos.

Assessors are trained to begin questioning at the highest level declared, with supporting level 1 knowledge-based questions potentially being asked in order to explore the justification for the advice or actions of the candidate. Candidates should ensure they are familiar with any examples in levels 2 and 3, as these should form the basis of their answers. Candidates will not be asked questions on competencies they have not selected or at levels beyond those declared; i.e., they will not be expected to give reasoned advice (level 3) if they have declared a competency only to level 2 (acting or doing).

Questions posed by the panel should not be hypothetical, and they should encourage the candidate to answer based on their experience. If possible, all competencies will be questioned by the assessment panel, with ethics questions included within the main body of the interview. The chairperson will also ask additional ethics questions in the final ten minutes. Candidates should be aware that elements of their mandatory competencies may be assessed within their technical competency questioning. A candidate's communication skills will also be evaluated during their case study presentation and response style to the panel's questions.

Assessors are trained to signpost candidates to the competency area being questioned. Candidates should ask for clarification if they are unsure of the question or area of focus being sought by the assessor. Candidates should also ensure they listen carefully to the questions they are being asked, take a deep breath before answering, and then seek to give only the response the assessors require.

As mentioned in the Introduction, this book provides example questions, but it does not provide the answers. You should think about how you would respond to the questions, and answer concisely and precisely, in your own words, in the first person "I", and reflecting your own experience of what you actually know/did/advised etc. For example, a suitable answer to the Property Management competency question 'Why did you recommend purchase of modern freehold houses?' could be: 'I recommended this to minimise potential mainte-nance costs compared to those associated with period properties, and because the landlord would have more control over maintenance and management of a freehold house compared to a leasehold flat. I was also aware – from my local knowledge and experience – that this type of house appeals to the market and usually offers a good return on investment.' A typical follow-up question might then relate to returns on investment, and yields. Therefore, when you answer a question, try to think about where your answer might lead the assessors and avoid introducing a topic about which you are not confident.

The overall assessment decision is holistic; one wrong answer (unless related to ethics) will not constitute a referral. This means that poor per-formance in one competency may be balanced out by good performance elsewhere. However, an inability to demonstrate several competencies to the required level will likely constitute a referral, particularly if these are the competencies declared by the candidate at level 3. Candidates are not expected to be experts in every area of their professional prac-tice. The assessors are, therefore, seeking to confirm that the candidate has met the minimum required levels of competence declared.

Candidates should also be mindful that acting ethically is at the heart of being a Chartered Surveyor. Ethics, Rules of Conduct, and Professionalism is the only competency where a wrong or unethical answer will constitute an automatic referral.

The assessment is not designed to be an exam. It is an assessment of professional competence, and there will be questions that a candidate cannot answer. This requires a toolbox of potential responses to be practised by candidates. For example, some questions may relate to experience or knowledge outside the candidate's core scope of com-petence or practice. For these questions, the candidate can state this and identify where they would seek specialist advice, input, or support from. This shows that the candidate can take responsibility and is a safe pair of hands when dealing with clients.

It is important to remember that further questions may arise as you answer, as assessors may want to explore an aspect of your reply. If you mention an additional point that is not written in your summary of experience, be prepared to be questioned further on the point.

Candidates may also encounter questions they simply cannot answer due to the pressure of the interview process. In these situations, referring or signposting the assessors to suitable RICS guidance or documents is helpful. When under pressure, candidates should avoid explaining everything they know about a topic or issue to the assessors. This does not show diligence or a considered approach to advising clients. Instead, a candidate would be better placed to return to the question later or use some of the aforementioned tools and tactics.

The assessment panel will decide on the final result immediately after the interview. In the case of a three-person panel, the assessors will make a decision and if a split decision is reached, the chairperson will make the final decision. The same applies for a two-person panel, where the chair and assessor will make their own decisions, although the chairperson again has the final say.

What Other Assessment Routes Are There?

This chapter has focused on the 'normal' route to assessment. However, there are three other assessment routes:

- Senior Professional Assessment – this requires candidates to demonstrate additional qualities (or indicators) of leadership, managing people and managing resources;
- Specialist Assessment – specialist candidates need advanced responsibilities in a specialist or niche area of work;
- Academic Assessment – this is appropriate for academic professionals, e.g., lecturers or researchers.

The submission and interview requirements differ for these three assessment routes, although candidates must still satisfy mandatory and technical Residential pathway competencies. Candidates considering these routes to MRICS qualification will find detailed information on each one in the relevant Candidate Guide and in the *Mandatory Competencies* book in this series (see Further Reading and Resources section at the end of this chapter).

How Do Candidates Receive Their Results?

Candidates will receive notification of their assessment result within five working days of their final assessment interview via the RICS Assessment Platform and shortly after via email.

For senior professional, specialist, and academic candidates, the result may take longer, generally seven days for senior professionals and specialists and 21 days for academics.

After qualifying, candidates will be added to the RICS Global Members Directory within 24 hours, a public announcement will be placed on the RICS website a few days later, and an Award Pack will be issued by post six to eight weeks later. Candidates must also pay an upgrade fee to reflect their MRICS qualification status. Concessions may apply to certain professionals, and RICS can advise on eligibility, for example, academics working in academia rather than in a surveying role.

Conclusion

After reading this chapter, candidates should feel confident in applying what they have learnt throughout this book to their final assessment interview.

This chapter is based on Lemen J (2024) *Mandatory Competencies: APC Essentials Chapter 15* Abingdon: Routledge.

Further Reading and Resources

Lemen J (2023) *RICS APC lifeline – top ten revision tips* Property Elite Blog & Podcast [Online] Available at: https://www.property-elite.co.uk/post/rics-apc-lifeline-top-10-revision-tips (Accessed 21 July 2024).

Lemen J (2024) *Mandatory competencies: APC essentials* Abingdon: Routledge.

Property Elite Free Resources: https://www.property-elite.co.uk/free-resources.

RICS (2024) *Senior professionals, specialists and academics* [Online] Available at: https://www.rics.org/join-rics/rics-member-grades/chartered-member-mrics/senior-specialist-academic-assessment (Accessed 13 August 2024).

Saint R, Parkes M (2024) *Dealing with nerves* Property Elite Video Blog [Online] Available at: https://www.property-elite.co.uk/post/dealing-with-nerves?utm_campaign=f72b2cba-132e-4714-870c-f436098ead7c&utm_source=so&utm_medium=mail&cid=6a4f1eba-d2c0-4655-91d9-c9ded5770fe9 (Accessed 13 August 2024).

Saint R, Parkes M (2024) *What will my APC interview be like?* Property Elite Video Blog [Online] Available at: https://www.property-elite.co.uk/post/video-blog-what-will-my-rics-apc-interview-be-like?utm_campaign=3a02e463-3e79-4598-8eb6-eba48afb6ebe&utm_source=so&utm_medium=mail&cid=cfbaf86c-b870-471f-96cd-b3a6a56db828 (Accessed 12 August 2024).

Index

For Product Safety Concerns and Information please contact our EU
representative GPSR@taylorandfrancis.com
Taylor & Francis Verlag GmbH, Kaufingerstraße 24, 80331 München, Germany

www.ingramcontent.com/pod-product-compliance
Lightning Source LLC
Chambersburg PA
CBHW061144220326
41599CB00025B/4352